E 3 -
gav

18134.

Mugging
as a social problem

Mugging
as a social problem

Dr Michael Pratt

Routledge and Kegan Paul
London, Boston and Henley

First published in 1980
by Routledge & Kegan Paul Ltd
39 Store Street, London WC1E 7DD,
9 Park Street, Boston, Mass. 02108, USA and
Broadway House, Newtown Road,
Henley-on-Thames, Oxon RG9 1EN
Set in Press Roman by
Hope Services
Abingdon, Oxon
and printed in Great Britain by
Redwood Burn Ltd
Trowbridge and Esher

British Library Cataloguing in Publication Data

Pratt, Michael
Mugging.
1. Mugging – Great Britain
I. Title
364.1'55   HV6665.G7   80 40857
ISBN 0 7100 0564 4

Contents

Figures

Tables

Preface

The idea of embarking upon a detailed study of mugging in the Metropolitan Police District developed out of my own interest in the subject — an interest generated, no doubt, by my position as Principal within the Criminal Investigation Department of the Metropolitan Police — coupled with the realisation that very little academic research into this, or even related topics, had previously been carried out.

I would like to record my grateful thanks to Dr Susanne MacGregor Wood of Birkbeck College, University of London, for her help and encouragement; to Miss Pat Plank, and other members of the Metropolitan Police Commissioner's Reference Library, for their ungrudging assistance; to those many authors who, unknown to them, have provided such a wealth of relevant material; and, most of all, to my wife Joan, who, for thirteen of sixteen happily married years, has, with admirable good humour, put up with a husband engaged on time-consuming, part-time study.

Finally it must be stressed that, although this study was carried out with the full approval of the Assistant Commissioner (Crime), all comment and opinion, as well as all errors and omissions, are of course mine.

M. J. Pratt
Birkbeck College

Acknowledgments

The author and publishers would like to thank the following: Curtis Brown Ltd, for permission to reproduce the diagram on p. 160 from *Law and Order News*; the *Daily Mail*, London, for permission to reproduce the article on p. 58; Hutchinson Publishing Group Ltd, for permission to reproduce material from p. 79 of *Resistance Through Rituals: Youth Subcultures in Post-War Britain*, edited by S. Hall and T. Jefferson, Hutchinson, 1976; the *Sun*, for permission to reproduce the headline on p. 46 from the *Sun* of 13 February 1976; the *Sunday Mirror*, for permission to reproduce the headline on p. 46; and *The Times*, for permission to reproduce the article on p. 55. The cartoons on pp. 119 and 121 are reproduced by permission of *Punch*.

[1] General introduction

Background

> by discovering how much crime is committed, and by showing how
> and why it is committed, criminologists can help to show what
> policy goals are reasonable; and if given certain aims, they can try
> to discover by research the best means of accomplishing them.[1]

This statement would seem to provide a good starting-point for any
investigation of a particular category of crime since it correctly suggests
that, before anything can be done by members of the executive, the
legislature or the judiciary, the exact nature and extent of the offence
in question must first be established. This is precisely the aim of this
book which deals with mugging in the Metropolitan Police District.

The definition and history of the word 'mugging' will be discussed
in some detail in a later chapter, and it is sufficient at this stage to point
out that, while robbery consists of theft accompanied by some form of
violence, however slight, 'mugging'[2] 'embraces the situation in which
the offenders made a sudden attack and robbed a citizen in the street
or other place to which the public have access'.[3]

The essence of the problem has been well summarised by Professor
F. H. McClintock:[4]

> Youths robbing ordinary citizens, especially at night time, are
> causing growing concern in London and other northern European
> capitals. Often these are vicious attacks, resulting in considerable
> injury to the victim and with little financial gain to the perpetrators.
> Solitary citizens returning home late from public houses, restaurants
> and private parties are easy prey for this kind of robber. Outbreaks
> of such crimes have occurred simultaneously on the Metro in Paris
> and the Underground in London. Direct preventative measures are
> difficult to adopt. The more that some citizens take to taxis or

private cars under these conditions, the more vulnerable become the other citizens who walk or use public service transport.

As to the 'Metropolitan Police District', this covers an area slightly bigger than that governed by the Greater London Council. It can be seen from Figure 1.1 that it comprises all the London boroughs plus, in the north and south-west, eight other local councils. Later in this study the precise relationship between the twenty-five districts into which the Metropolitan Police District is divided and the various local council areas will be of some importance, and the opportunity is therefore taken here to list these in full:

Police District	Local Authority
A	City of Westminster (part)
B	LB Kensington and Chelsea
C	City of Westminster (part)
D	City of Westminster (part)
E	LB Camden
F	LB Hammersmith
G	LB Hackney
H	LB Tower Hamlets
J	LB Redbridge, LB Waltham Forest, Epping Forest (UD)
K	LB Barking, LB Havering, LB Newham
L	LB Lambeth
M	LB Southwark
N	LB Islington
P	LB Bromley, LB Lewisham
Q	LB Brent, LB Harrow
R	LB Bexley, LB Greenwich
S	LB Barnet, Hartsmere (UD)
T	LB Hounslow, LB Richmond-on-Thames, Spelthorne (UD)
V	LB Kingston upon Thames, LB Merton, Elmbridge (UD)
W	LB Wandsworth
X	LB Ealing, LB Hillingdon
Y	LB Enfield, LB Haringey, Broxbourne (UD), Welwyn Hatfield (UD)

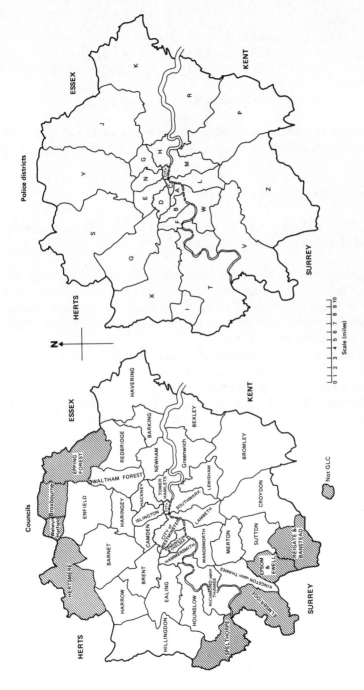

Figure 1.1 The Metropolitan Police District: local councils and Police Districts

Police	
District	*Local Authority*
Z	LB Croydon, LB Sutton, Epsom and Ewell (UD), Reigate and Banstead (UD)

(plus Thames and Airport districts)

In total the Metropolitan Police District covers an area of some 787 square miles and has a population of over seven and a half million.

Reasons for carrying out the study

McClintock has put forward the following reasons why people should be interested in criminal violence as such:[5]

1   Because there is a strong feeling that this type of behaviour has been getting worse and, as a result, members of the general public wish to be better informed and to receive answers to the question whether there has really been an increase and, if so, what is its extent and nature and why has it occurred.
2   Because of the concern of those who have an immediate practical share in prevention and control − namely the police, the judiciary, the administrators and the correctional training personnel.
3   Because the academic thirst for investigation stimulates research into the phenomenon, and attempts to explain it either in terms of theoretical explanations or on the basis of the existentialist experience of the offenders and the victims in the context of the social, ideological and cultural setting in which it occurs.
4   Because of the inherent fascination of the subject − a fascination which appears to be lacking in property crimes. The curiosity may be merely morbid or may perhaps spring from primary disposition or instinct because aggression in one form or another is elemental in each of us as human beings.

Naturally all of these points also have considerable relevance when it comes to any discussion of robbery or mugging, but the precise reasons for choosing these particular subjects for detailed study may be listed as follows:

(a) because robbery in general and mugging in particular are, by any standards, 'serious' crimes in the eyes both of the general public and of those who enforce the law;

(b) because, as far as could be ascertained, surprisingly little research had previously been carried out in this field;

(c) because it was felt muggings are highly likely to be reported to police (thus minimising the effect of the 'dark figure' (see chapter 4 for a discussion of the 'dark figure'));

(d) because robberies and muggings are types of crime which have recently experienced numerical increases even greater than those in respect both of most other categories, and of indictable crime in general;

(e) because the raw data required for such a detailed study, normally difficult to obtain, was readily available to the author.

Each of these factors had an important bearing on the undertaking of this study and will therefore be analysed in more detail in the following paragraphs.

(a) *Robbery and mugging as serious crimes*

John Conklin, in his book *Robbery and the Criminal Justice System* (1972), believes that robbery is the 'bell-wether' crime in America today: it is felt that, in this country too, few people would dispute the basic statement made in 1970 by the then head of the Metropolitan Police Criminal Investigation Department that 'after murder and rape I consider robbery to be the next most serious offence'.[6]

Just why this should be what one must call the 'general feeling' is not difficult to analyse. Not only is there the obvious reason that robbery is a crime of violence against the person, but there is the additional and crucial element of it being a crime almost always committed by a stranger. As Conklin (1972: 29) puts it:

> Robbery, by definition, combines violence and theft, is almost always committed by the predatory stranger and is thus distinguishable from such other crimes of violence as homicide, rape and assault where the victims and the perpetrators in most cases are known to each other.

If theft, violence, and perpetration by a stranger is a telling combination in most cases of robbery, it is particularly so in the case of mugging, since there appears to be a strong fear of being attacked 'out of the blue' whilst going about one's ordinary everyday business. Perhaps this is because one would presumably be automatically on one's guard and almost *expect* trouble if carrying a large amount of cash from, say, a betting shop to the bank: but, when it is simply a case of an ordinary person, walking along an ordinary street, carrying only an ordinary amount of personal effects and cash, then the thought of a sudden attack by a complete stranger seems to fill everyone with dread. The following examples, taken direct from police reports, provide some evidence that such fears are by no means wholly imaginary:

Typical examples:

By four coloured men who pushed victim against wall, threatened him, and stole wallet from his pocket.

By woman accosting victim whilst male companion caught him from behind, pinned him to the ground and removed cash from pockets.

By four coloured youths who threatened victim with violence and thereby induced him to hand over his wallet and cash.

The victim was stopped by a white man and a coloured man: the latter produced a knife, put it against the victim's throat, threatened him and stole from his top pocket.

More serious examples:

By three coloured youths stopping him in the street, assaulting him, rendering him unconscious, and causing injuries requiring thirty-six stitches (amount stolen just £1.30).

. . . slashed victim across face with knife, causing wounds requiring twenty-one stitches.

Suspect placed hand over victim's mouth, threw her to the ground, struck her head repeatedly on the ground, and stole bag.

By two men stopping victim in street, one asked him for a light, the other one struck him on the head with an instrument. One of the men then stabbed him in the stomach, then both went through his pockets and stole cash (20p).

There was another reason for concentrating on mugging rather than on robbery in general. As we shall see, in purely numerical terms relatively few robberies are committed compared, say, to burglary or fraud and forgery: nevertheless, robbery is a category of crime which embraces a whole host of possible offences ranging from the theft of 5p (accompanied by a punch on the nose) from one 10-year-old child by another, to an armed bank robbery involving £100,000 or more, serious injury, and occasionally even deaths.

In such circumstances it is clearly unrealistic to look at one overall total for robbery in general, and could be positively misleading if comparisons of any kind are to be attempted. To quote a somewhat trivial example, an increase from, say, 200 robberies to 300 in one year would scarcely merit panic measures if the former total included 50 organised and armed attacks on banks, security firms, betting shops and the like, while the latter was made up almost exclusively of 'inter-child' thefts involving only very small amounts of money and only a modicum of violence.[7] And obviously the reverse applies. As Conklin (1972: 48) asks:

> Can one analyse the motives, modi operandi or career patterns of robbers if they include as a class the burglar surprised in his act of theft, the professional bank robber, the youthful mugger, a juvenile gang robbing drunks, the taxi holdup man, the playground tough forcibly taking money from his schoolmates, etc.?

While, as the present writer pointed out in 1972:[8]

> it may be felt that there is at least some merit in a suggestion put forward in 1971 that it would possibly be more realistic to effect a further breakdown, viz. those offences of a serious nature or where the circumstances fully merit the classification, and those that are borderline or merely technically fit the requirements of Robbery and are possibly more worthy of 'theft' or 'theft and assault' classifications.

That is to say, 'Robbery' is too diffuse a category, while 'Mugging' can be sufficiently well defined to enable meaningful study and comparisons to be made.

(b) *Previous research*

Accepting for the moment that the very seriousness of robbery is, in itself, reason enough for detailed study, it seems remarkable that so little research into the subject seems to have been carried out. Certainly there are a number of American publications such as that by John Conklin referred to above, and (at least on the basis of the title) the even more appropriate *The Mugging* by Morton M. Hunt: but, although these are no doubt of considerable worth in methodological and even penological terms, and also contain a great deal of useful background material, they appear to add little to any precise knowledge of the topic in hand. Their journalistic style is very readable, but they tell us surprisingly little about such matters as 'who commits robbery?', 'who is most likely to be the victim of a robbery?', or 'what time of the day or day of the week are robberies most likely to occur?'.

As far as this country is concerned, it is certainly true that writers and commentators of many kinds have been concerned with robbery and its effects for a long time. For example, Mrs M. D. George in her *London Life in the XVIIIth Century* observes that at the beginning of that century 'the forces of disorder and crime had the upper hand in London' (p. 16), and quotes the following statement made by the City Marshall in 1718:

Now it is the general complaint of the taverns, the coffee-houses, the shop-keepers and others, that their customers are afraid when it is dark to come to their houses and shops for fear that their hats and wigs should be snitched from their heads or their swords taken from their sides, or that they might be blinded, knocked down, cut or stabbed. (pp. 10–11)

Some thirty years later Henry Fielding, the pioneer Bow Street magistrate, wrote his famous and oft-quoted work, *An Enquiry into the Causes of the Late Increase of Robbers*, in which he pointed out that:

The innocent are put in Terror, affronted and alarmed with Threats and Execrations, endangered with loaded pistols, beat with Bludgeons and hacked with Cutlasses, of which the Loss of Health, of Limbs, and often of Life, is the Consequence; and all this without any Respect to Age, or Dignity, or Sex . . . (pp. 2–3).

Street Robberies are generally committed in the dark, the Persons
on whom they are committed are often in Chairs and Coaches, and if
on Foot, the Attack is usually begun by knocking the party down,
and for the Time depriving him of his senses. (p. 45)

Or again, in 1775 Jonas Hanway wrote:

I sup with my friend; I cannot return to my home, not even in my
chariot, without danger of a pistol being clapped to my breast. I
build an elegant villa, ten or twenty miles distant from the capital:
I am obliged to provide an armed force to convey me thither, lest
I should be attacked on the road with fire and ball. (p. 224)

There is much similar evidence, described by other authors, whose
works have been excellently reviewed and analysed by J. J. Tobias in
his *Crime and Industrial Society in the Nineteenth Century*. However,
although again of considerable intrinsic interest, such accounts need
concern us no further here since they are more in the nature of personal
impressionistic views, and by no stretch of the imagination could they
be put under the heading of research studies.

This also applies to the vast majority of somewhat later 'historical'
works composed in similar vein. Even so, it is felt that specific mention
should be made of Henry Mayhew's gigantic survey of conditions
among the London proletariat, *London Labour and the London Poor*,
particularly the fourth volume entitled 'Those That Will Not Work'.
Though still highly subjective and descriptive, and in no sense 'scientific',
many passages contained therein give such a good insight into life in
London a hundred years or so ago that it might even be possible to con-
struct some sort of framework on the basis of which comparisons with
the situation today may be made. For example:

low coarse ruffians who follow in the wake of prostitutes, or garotte
drunken men in the midnight street, or strike them down by brutal
violence with a life-preserver or bludgeon. These felonies are generally
committed in secluded spots and by-streets, or in the suburbs of
the metropolis. Many robberies are committed on the highway by
snatching with violence from the person. These are generally done in
the dusk, and rarely during the day. When committed early in the
evening, they are done in secluded places, intersected with lanes and
alleys, where the thieves have a good opportunity to escape, such as
in the Borough, Spitalfields, Shoreditch, Whitechapel, Drury Lane,

Westminster and similar localities. These are often done by one person, at other times by two or more in company, and generally by young men from nineteen years and upwards. (p. 234)

As to method:

A ruffian walks up and throws his arm around the neck of a person who has a watch, or whom he had noticed carrying money on his person. One man holds him tightly by the neck, and generally attacks from behind, or from the side. The garotter tries to get his arm under his chin, and presses it back, while with the other hand he holds his neck firmly behind. He does it so violently the man is almost strangled and is unable to cry out. He holds him in this position perhaps for a minute or two, while his companions, one or more, rifle his pockets of his watch and money. (pp. 237-8)

Of more recent work, H. Silcock's unpublished paper on 'The Increase in Crimes of Theft 1938-47' was found to contain little in the way of meaningful analysis — especially of robbery as such — while papers sponsored by the Centre for Contemporary Cultural Studies, at the University of Birmingham, though providing a far more fruitful potential source of information, were found to contain few quantifiable facts and figures of the type which it had been hoped might form a useful basis of comparison for this study.

Even in the apparently very appropriately titled paper (also unpublished) 'Down These Mean Streets . . . the Meaning of Mugging' by T. Jefferson and J. Clarke the approach is entirely one of descriptive as opposed to analytical sociology, with arguments and conclusions being based (apparently) on a review of well-publicised events, and with statistical trends assumed rather than discovered. For example:

During the period we are concerned with, the late 1960s and early 1970s, we believe that 'muggings' *did* increase, and that West Indian youths from 'deprived' inner ring areas were significantly over-represented in the statistics. (p. 1)

An excellent hypothesis, one might conclude, but unfortunately, it is used as a statement on which further arguments are built without any attempt being made to discover, or even quote, relevant statistics. Such an approach, though again of some interest as an aid to developing one's own arguments concerning such matters as race and social background, has very little relevance to the aim of at least the first part of this study[9] which is a detailed analysis of mugging offences as, and when, they were committed.

A number of authors have, of course, made what one might call a passing reference to robbery (though hardly ever, it would seem, to mugging) in general assessments of crime as a whole. One such example is Sellin and Wolfgang's *The Measurement of Delinquency*. In fact, their results have not been used in any sort of direct comparative sense mainly because the sample they used was extremely small (only twenty-seven cases); related to juveniles only; and to arrested persons only; but despite their limited base a number of interesting findings emerged and these will therefore be referred to again (as will some of the other studies mentioned, such as Mayhew's) at the appropriate juncture. However, after prolonged research, it has now been concluded that only one author comes near to adopting the approach advocated and used in this study, and that is Professor F. H. McClintock, both in his *Crimes of Violence* (written with others) and, more particularly, in his *Robbery in London* (written with Mrs E. Gibson).

Both of these publications have, of course, rightly attained an enviable reputation, and in the field of criminology they certainly rate as 'essential reading'. In fact, the obvious plan of comparing my own results with those of Professor McClintock has been adopted and will be discussed at some length below.[10] But, despite the standing and, especially in the case of *Robbery in London*, the relevance of McClintock and Gibson's work, and despite the usefulness of comparisons eventually made with his findings, there are a number of reasons why this current study is in no way a duplication of effort. The three most important of these should be pointed out at this stage.

(i) The McClintock and Gibson study was published in 1961, and relates, in the main, to robberies which occurred in London in 1950 and 1957. The very latest figures quoted are the provisional totals for 1960 and, as we shall eventually see, the really dramatic increases in this category of crime have taken place since that time. It therefore follows that, if nothing else, the present study should help to update some of the findings of eighteen or more years ago.

(ii) *Robbery in London* consists of about 120 pages of analysis into the various aspects of the phenomenon in question. Three-quarters of this total deals with matters which, although of the utmost importance and relevance, would be quite beyond the scope of one individual's resources. Such topics as 'Penal Records and Previous History of Violence' and

'Subsequent Conduct' have simply not been dealt with here, one result of which is that only about thirty pages of the book cover similar ground to the present study. When it is further considered that these thirty pages cover *all* robbery and not just mugging, then perhaps it can be appreciated that the chance of a major duplication is slight.

(iii) Even in that relatively small part of McClintock's study which does deal specifically with mugging, the statistics he uses have largely been derived from 'official' sources in respect of the year as a whole, whereas this author has concentrated mainly on an actual, randomly chosen and precise sample.[11]

(c) *Unreported and unrecorded crime*

Some types of crime are more likely than others to be reported to, or to be recorded by, the police. For example, one might argue that most murders find their way into the crime statistics, whereas the observed (let alone the unobserved) theft of a packet of sweets by a 10-year-old child is much less likely to do so. Hence the 'dark figure' of crime can be of variable size: it is a problem with which all criminological researchers are obliged to live, but its exact nature and the extent to which it must be taken into account depends a great deal on the type of crime being studied. As Sellin and Wolfgang (1964: 30) put it:

> All the researchers mentioned were aware of the fact that in different crimes there exist differences in the likelihood of their being reported to public authorities and differences in the ease with which they can be detected. They understood that these differences depended on public attitudes towards criminal conduct in its various manifestations and on the degree to which the public authorities themselves were active in the enforcement of the law.

In other words, if a study of a particular category of crime is based broadly on 'crimes known to police', then, it might reasonably be argued, the greater the probability of such a crime being reported, the more meaningful any results obtained or conclusions drawn are likely to be. Thus, in terms of offences finally appearing in police records it would be rather pointless to spend much time on a study of shoplifting, which is a category of crime known to go unreported in a very large proportion of cases,[12] and far more useful to study theft of a motor vehicle which is a class of crime which almost invariably comes to the notice of police.[13]

As to this study, it was felt from the beginning (and in chapter 4 it will be shown that, despite possible alternative interpretations, such a feeling was substantially correct) that, due to its very nature, mugging is far more likely to be reported to police than most other categories of crime. This, then, was one reason why this type of robbery was considered to be such a suitable subject for research.

(d) *The statistics*

Given that, whatever the category of crime under discussion, there will be *some* offences which do not survive the reporting and recording stages, but also arguing that in the case of robbery, and even more so in the case of mugging, the effect of this is relatively minimal, one can make out a case for a detailed study of such crimes purely on the grounds of a demonstrable statistical increase. This aspect will be covered fully in chapter 4 but, to anticipate some of the results contained therein, it can be shown not only that robbery has increased by some 2,500 per cent since the end of the Second World War, but also that the annual robbery total of 671 which caused McClintock, and many others, such concern only some eighteen years ago, has now risen to well over 6,000. In the more specific category of mugging, moreover, the rate of increase has been even more marked.

But if justification for detailed study is to be sought on the basis of robbery having become increasingly prevalent, then particular attention must be paid to the last few years. In fact, this research was contemplated and begun long before the figures for 1975, 1974, or even 1973 had become available. The increase over the twenty years up to and including 1972 had seemed quite dramatic enough to justify a closer investigation of the problem, but then, as may be seen from Table 1.1, although in 1973 and 1974 there was something of a lull in what is otherwise a remarkable upward trend, this was more than compensated for by what took place in 1975 and thereafter. The figures show, in fact, that robberies in London have more than doubled in just three years.

In view of the fact that, as discussed above, robbery and mugging are considered by 'expert' and 'layman' alike to be 'serious crimes', the demand from all sides that 'something should be done about it' comes as no real surprise. The real point, however, is that no meaningful decision can be made, no action can be taken, and no remedy can be administered, until at least a certain amount of detailed information

Table 1.1 *Robbery in the Metropolitan Police District 1967-77*

1967 – 2,012
1968 – 1,910
1969 – 2,236
1970 – 2,369
1971 – 2,727
1972 – 3,167
1973 – 2,680
1974 – 3,156
1975 – 4,452
1976 – 5,522
1977 – 6,826

(Source: G. 10 Branch, Metropolitan Police Office, Annual Abstracts of Crime Statistics)

and knowledge has been gained: which is precisely the object of this book.[14]

(e) *Availability of material*

One of the main reasons for deciding to carry out research into mugging in the Metropolitan Police District was the purely practical one of personally working at New Scotland Yard, and therefore being in an ideal position to obtain easy and unrestricted access to the raw data, notably the police Crime Report Sheets (Form 478). It should be explained at this point that, following the commission of a crime (which normally comes to the notice of police by way of a complaint to that effect by a member of the public), a Crime Report Sheet is opened on which a whole series of relevant data is entered. In this connection, four points are worthy of note:

(i) The recording and classification of a crime as reported is very largely a local, that is to say a District, responsibility.

(ii) The original assessment or classification of the crime committed is almost always retained for evermore.[15]

(iii) The Crime Report Sheet is not the only record of a crime having been committed. Any one crime can easily (and, particularly when an arrest has been made, usually does) attract a whole host of dockets, reports, statements and the like.

(iv) The Crime Report Sheet itself is primarily designed as a means of supplying the Metropolitan Police central statistical department[16] with a record of all indictable, and certain non-indictable, crime which has been reported and which has been 'accepted' at a local level.[17]

The central statistical department is guided primarily by a statutory requirement to supply the Home Office annually with certain data and the Crime Report Sheets are processed accordingly. The main emphasis is, as one might imagine, on indictable crime, which has to be broken down into a whole series of Home Office classes; but perhaps the most important factor which emerges from all of this is that whatever the breakdown, whatever the refinements, the final result, these days with the help of a computer, must inevitably be simply a list of figures or an assortment of statistical tables. It is just not practicable to break down every aspect of a crime into its component parts in readiness for computer programming. A really close analysis, as was the aim of the first part of this study, can only be achieved by detailed research of the actual Forms 478 themselves (on which the descriptive detail can often be particularly revealing), backed up if necessary by a reference back to source documents.

None, or at least very little, of this type of information is restricted if used in an anonymous sense, and has indeed been made use of before:[18] but there can be little doubt that when it comes to detailed follow-up investigations, a considerable advantage attaches to being actually involved at the scene of these operations.

Summary

For the above reasons it was felt that a significant and original contribution to existing knowledge relating to the problem of mugging in the Metropolitan Police District could be made. It should be pointed out, however, that this study was frankly exploratory from the outset, and that the main intention was never to test, let alone accept or reject, precise hypotheses. This by no means renders it invalid, for as Hood and Sparks (1970: 11) tell us:

A great deal of effort is often expended on the critical analysis of a theory before someone remembers to check whether the behaviour the theory is explaining actually exists! There is obviously a need to study thoroughly the phenomenon of crime before embarking on explanations of its varying incidence and the patterns of criminal behaviour.

or, as Hunt (1975: 13) points out:

> A major reason for our apathy and for the inadequacy of our actions
> concerning crime and the criminal justice system is the depth of our
> ignorance. The average middle-class citizen has had very little per-
> sonal experience of the police, criminal courts, city jails, trials, or
> prisons. Very few of us know what muggers are like as human
> beings, how and where muggings are most likely to occur, what
> effects they have upon the people who experience them directly
> or even indirectly . . .

The main aim of the remainder of part 1 will therefore be to describe exactly what is meant by the word 'mugging', and then to carry
out a detailed analysis of a random sample of such offences in the
Metropolitan Police District against a background of the general crime
statistics: while in part 2 account will be taken of a number of relevant
criminological and sociological factors, in the hope that answers can be
suggested to questions such as: 'What are the main features associated
with mugging?', 'To what extent does reality measure up to subjective
opinion?', 'What changes have taken place over time?', 'Which of the
existing sociological theories provide adequate explanation?', 'In which
areas would further research be an advantage?', 'What suggestions or
recommendations can be made?'. To this end, the study has been divided
into the following chapters:

Part I

Chapter 2 Some definitions

A precise definition of 'theft', 'robbery' and 'mugging' with particular
reference to the principal Acts concerned with larceny and related
offences.

Chapter 3 The attitudes of society

A discussion of those factors (especially the mass media) affecting the
public conception of robbery and sentencing policy.

Chapter 4 Statistics in theory and in practice

A further discussion of the 'dark figure' of crime, together with an analysis of recent statistics relating to mugging, robbery and indictable crime as a whole.

Chapter 5 A study of mugging in London during the 1970s

A detailed study of a random sample of more than 1,000 muggings which occurred within the Metropolitan Police District during certain months of the years 1972, 1973 and 1974. Also an analysis and an assessment of the results obtained with particular reference to comparisons made with other similar studies.

Part II

Chapter 6 Theories of deviance

A review and an evaluation of some of the apparently more relevant sociological theories, especially those relating to social ecology, or pointing to the relationship between delinquency and deprivation.

Chapter 7 Race

An appraisal of the effects of immigration, racial discrimination, historical and other factors on the incidence of mugging.

Chapter 8 Conclusions and recommendations

A final assessment of the facts brought to light in part 1, against a background of the theories reviewed in part 2, together with suggestions relating to practical measures which ought to be taken and future policies which ought to be adopted.

In addition, there are a number of matters which will be touched upon during the course of the main study but which, although considered well worthy of inclusion, might best be presented in isolation. These have therefore been included in Appendix form as follows:

Appendix I

Sections dealing with robbery in the principal Acts concerned with larceny and related offences.

Appendix 2

Robbery

A table of crimes known, arrests, and methods of dealing with convicted offenders, 1832-1976.

Appendix 3

Detailed tables of results for each category, and for each of the eight months included in the sample.

It would be very convenient if it could be guaranteed from the outset that the result of all the effort expended on a study such as this would ultimately be the production of meaningful conclusions. Whether or not this actually proves to be the case, it is sincerely hoped that the store of information contained herein does indeed make a distinct and original contribution to current knowledge about a type of crime which, justifiably or not, is causing increasing concern in the western world.

Part I

[2] Some definitions

Introduction

This book deals with a category of crime commonly termed 'mugging': it is an obvious first step therefore to try to describe exactly what is meant by such a term. This is not easily done, since mugging is just one particular form of robbery — which is itself just one particular form of theft. Consequently it is necessary to begin with a brief review of the law relating to theft and then progress, step by step, to a statement of the definition of mugging employed in this study. Such a process, it is hoped, will prove both enlightening and interesting.

(It should be said that due to the nature of the material being reviewed in this chapter there is no preferable alternative to the 'note' format which has, in places, been used. Also, although not quotations in the usual sense of the word, all court cases cited have, in the interests of clarity, been indented from the main body of the text.)

Theft, robbery and the law

Until 1968 the English law relating to theft developed gradually, over several centuries, and in an extremely haphazard and piecemeal fashion. The old law of stealing was contained in the *Larceny Act of 1861*,[1] followed by the *Larceny Act of 1916*.[2] Both these Acts were intended, in effect, to reproduce the common law, but one of the main results of this was the creation of a great number of different crimes, separately defined to prescribe an enhanced punishment for a single circumstance of aggravation: there were, for example, many types of stealing with greater or lesser penalties according to the nature of the property stolen, the place where it was stolen, and the relationship between the thief and the owner. Thus, the fact that the object of the larceny was a will, title-deed, or mailbag was a sufficient aggravation to raise the maximum penalty to penal servitude for life, while other circumstances which could attract enhanced punishment were larceny of cattle, of goods in the process of manufacture, from a ship, by a clerk or servant, or by a tenant or lodger. On the other hand, lesser punishments were provided if, for example, the larceny was of ore from a mine, or of a dog.

It was against such a confused background that the Criminal Law Revision Committee[3] was asked on 18 March 1959 by the then Home Secretary, Mr R. A. Butler:

> to consider, with a view to providing a simpler and more effective system of law, what alterations in the criminal law are desirable with reference to larceny and kindred offences and to such other acts involving fraud and dishonesty as, in the opinion of the committee, could conveniently be dealt with in legislation giving effect to the committee's recommendations on the law of larceny.

After reviewing the background to the whole subject, the committee under the chairmanship of Frederick Sellers decided that, in order to provide the 'simpler and more effective law' called for by the terms of reference, it would be necessary to make far-reaching changes. They decided, moreover, that such changes could not satisfactorily be made by amendments to the existing law, but that completely new legislation was required. In fact, the law relating to most of the various larceny offences proved on examination to be so defective that it was necessary to go back to first principles, to consider what were the essential elements of the offence, and to reconstruct the law relating to it accordingly. This took a great deal of time and it was 5 April 1966 before the committee's Eighth Report, entitled *Theft and Related Offences*, was completed. This contained a draft of a Bill to 'revise the law of England and Wales as to theft and similar or associated offences, and for purposes connected therewith', which Draft was ultimately adopted, following only minor amendment, as the *1968 Theft Act*.

Section 1(1) of this Act states:

> A person is guilty of theft if he dishonestly appropriates property belonging to another with the intention of permanently depriving the other of it; and 'thief' and 'steal' shall be construed accordingly.

In essence, the crime of robbery consists of stealing as so defined, *plus* the use, or the threat of the use, of force. Thus there can be no robbery where there is no theft.[4]

In Appendix 1 are outlined those Sections of the three relevant Acts which deal specifically with robbery. One particular feature that is immediately apparent is the relative simplicity of the 1968 Act when compared with its predecessors, theft now being seen as a wilful act regardless of extenuating circumstances. Under the Acts of 1861 and 1916, for instance, there were five specific offences covered by the general term 'robbery with violence', or — to use a term preferred by McClintock and Gibson (1961: 122), and later adopted by the Criminal Law Revision Committee — 'aggravated robbery', as follows:

(i) Robbery by a person armed with any offensive weapon or instrument, or
(ii) Assault with intent to rob by a person armed with any offensive weapon or instrument, or
(iii) Robbery by any person in company with one other person or more, or
(iv) Assault with intent to rob by any person in company with one other person or more, or
(v) Robbery accompanied by any personal violence used either at the time of the robbery or immediately before or immediately after it.

Under such provisions, while the slightest personal violence could be enough to attract the penalty of life imprisonment, to rob a person by threatening to kill him on the spot would only be simple robbery. Moreover, under headings (i) to (iv) above, either robbery or assault with intent to rob might be regarded as 'aggravated robbery' even though no actual violence had been used, while an assault with intent to rob by a single unarmed offender would not come under heading (v), and technically would therefore *not* be 'robbery with violence' even if a victim had in fact been violently attacked.

Such a state of affairs was clearly unsatisfactory, and in accordance with the overall policy of the Criminal Law Revision Committee the law has now been simplified by the omission of any special provision for aggravating features, the avoidance of any unnecessary distinction between different types of robbery, and the resultant 'standardisation' of maximum penalties.

Robbery is now defined by Section 8(1) of the *1968 Theft Act* which states that:

A person is guilty of robbery if he steals, and immediately before or at the time of doing so, and in order to do so, he uses force on any person or puts or seeks to put any person in fear of being there and then subjected to force.

In English law this is in fact the first statutory definition of robbery since, even under the 1916 Larceny Act, whenever a problem arose on a question of interpretation, scope or applicability, those persons dealing with the case in question had recourse to the common law, assuming that the Act was intended to preserve it even in those many instances where the wording of the Act was somewhat difficult to reconcile with this view.

Under the 1968 Act in only a very limited number of instances is it now necessary, or desirable, to resort to earlier case-law.[5] However, apart from the fact that it would simply not be possible to dispense with previous case-law altogether (if only because a great deal of the law of property is still to be found in decided cases), many of the old cases retain their importance as illustrations of actual situations which have caused difficulties in the past. It is mainly for this reason that a number of such cases have been included in the following more detailed explanation of those various elements contained in the statutory definition.[6]

('Steals')

To establish the offence of theft, the prosecution are required to prove only the four elements of (i) dishonesty; (ii) appropriation; (iii) property belonging to another; and (iv) intention permanently to deprive.

For simple theft, and therefore for robbery, appropriation of the property is sufficient whether it has been taken away or not. Thus, in *R* v *Lapier* (1784):

> while a lady was stepping into her carriage, the accused snatched at her diamond ear-ring and separated it from her ear by tearing her ear entirely through — but there was no proof of the ear-ring ever having been seen in his hand, and upon the lady's arrival home it was found amongst the curls of her hair.

It was held by all the judges that there was a sufficient taking from the person to constitute robbery as the ear-ring was in the possession of the prisoner separate from the lady's person, though but for a moment, and though he could not retain it, but probably lost it again in the same instant.

And in *R* v *Peat* (1781):

> the accused took a purse of money from a gentleman and then returned it to him immediately, saying 'If you value your life you will please take it back and give me the contents of it', but was arrested before the gentleman had time to give him the contents of the purse.

The Court held that there had been sufficient taking to complete the offence even though the possession had continued for only an instant.

Robbery, when once actually completed by taking the property of another, cannot be purged by any subsequent re-delivery. Thus, if A requires B to deliver over his purse and he delivers it accordingly, whereupon A, finding it contains only 10p, gives it back, this is still robbery.

It is of no importance under what pretext the robber obtains the money or property. For example, in the very old case where an old man, with sword drawn, asked alms of a man who gave it to him 'through mistrust and apprehension of violence', it was as much robbery as if he had demanded money in the ordinary way.

('immediately before or at the time of doing so')

The force or threat of the use of force must be immediately before or at the time of stealing and be for the purpose of stealing. Force used after a theft is complete would not now amount to robbery (as was the case under the 1861 and 1916 Acts), though difficulties may arise in deciding precisely when a theft is in fact complete, as in *R* v *Harman* (1620):

> a thief clandestinely stole a purse, and, on its being discovered in his possession, 'threatened the loser with violence if she should dare speak of it', and then rode away.

This was not, and would not now be, robbery since the threats were not used in order to steal, and were only made after the theft was complete.

Similarly, as may be seen from the comments of the Criminal Law

Revision Committee, force used to make good a get-away after committing a theft does not seem naturally to constitute a robbery.[7] Thus, in *Archbold*[8] is cited the hypothetical case of two thieves who gain entrance to a warehouse and pick up a carton of goods. While still in the warehouse but on their way out they are confronted by the nightwatchman who is assaulted by one of the thieves in order that his companion might escape with the carton. In such a case it would seem wrong to bring in a conviction of robbery as the force was used *after* the theft was complete. Of course, if the nightwatchman is able to gain control of the carton while struggling with the thieves and the struggle ends with the thieves wrenching the carton from the nightwatchman's control before escaping, then a charge of robbery would seem to be appropriate since the wrenching of the carton from the nightwatchman's control could be held to constitute a second and new appropriation and a new act of theft, accomplished by force.

('in order to do so')

The force must be threatened in order to steal. For example, in *R* v *Blackham* (1787):

> the accused assaulted a woman with intent to rape her, and she,
> without any demand from him, offered him money. This he took
> and put into his pocket — but continued to treat the woman
> with violence, in order to effect his original purpose, until he was
> interrupted.

In 1787 this was held to be robbery by a considerable majority on the grounds that the woman, as a result of the violence and the terror occasioned by the prisoner's behaviour, and to redeem her chastity, offered the money which it was clear she would not have given voluntarily; and that the prisoner, by taking it, derived an advantage to himself from his felonious conduct even though his original intention was to commit rape. Under the 1968 Act this would *not* now be robbery since the force was not used in order to steal.

('uses force')

To constitute robbery force must be used. A classic exposition of this principle came in *R* v *Shendley* (1970). The complainant said that the accused had attacked him, taken some of his property, and forced him to sign receipts purporting to show that the property had in fact been purchased. The judge directed the jury:

> if you come to the conclusion that the violence was unconnected
> with the stealing, but you were satisfied there was a stealing it
> does not mean that is an acquittal because it would be open
> to you to find [him] guilty of robbery, that is robbery without
> violence.

However, it was held by the Court of Criminal Appeal that the directions were wrong — *there is no such thing as robbery without violence.*[9]

It might be noted at this point that in the 1968 Act the term 'force' has been preferred to 'violence' which was used in both the 1861 and 1916 Acts to designate an aggravated form of robbery. Although the difference between the two words is somewhat elusive it is probable that 'force' is a slightly wider term: thus it might be argued that simply to hold a person down is not violent but it certainly involves the use of force against the person. Force denotes the exercise of any physical power against another, whereas violence seems to signify a dynamic exercise of strength as by striking a blow.

The force must be used in order to prevent or overcome resistance and not merely to gain possession.[10] In *R* v *Gnosil* (1824) the precedent was set that:

> the mere act of taking being forcible will not make this offence
> highway robbery; to constitute the crime of highway robbery the
> force used must be either before or at the time of the taking, and
> must be of such a nature as to show that it was intended to over-
> power the party robbed, and prevent his resisting, and not merely
> to get possession of the property stolen; thus, if a man walking
> after a woman in the street, were by violence to pull her shawl from
> her shoulders, though he might use considerable violence, it would
> not be highway robbery, because the violence was not for the pur-
> pose of overpowering the party robbed, but only to get possession
> of the property.

However, as we have seen in the case of *R* v *Lapier*, any force which actually causes bodily harm is sufficient.

If a man knocks down another, stealing his property while he is insensible on the ground, that is, of course, robbery: but the force need not necessarily amount to physical touching, as where a revolver or shotgun is discharged in a bank or post office in order to intimidate the cashiers and as a result an amount of money is handed over.

The force used need only be minimal, and if there is the slightest degree of resistance and the thief persists — and is successful in appropriating the object of his attention — he will be guilty of robbery. A number of old cases illustrate this principle, including:

> *R* v *Mason* (1820). The victim's watch was fastened to a steel chain which was around his neck — the seal and chain hanging from his fob. The accused laid hold of the seal and chain and attempted to pull the watch from the fob, but the steel chain still secured it: then with two jerks he broke the steel chain and made off with the watch.

The judges were unanimous that this was a robbery as the prisoner did not get the watch at once but had to overcome the resistance made by the steel chain, and used actual physical force for that purpose.

> *R* v *Moore* (1784). A lady was wearing a diamond pin with a cork-screw stalk twisted in her hair, which was 'close frizzed and strongly crêped'. The accused snatched out the pin, tearing away some of the lady's hair at the same time.

It was held that the violence used was sufficient to constitute robbery.

> *R* v *Davies* (1712). The prisoner snatched at a sword hanging at a gentleman's side hoping not to attract his attention. However, the gentleman saw him, instantly grabbed hold of the scabbard, and a struggle ensued in which the accused got possession of the sword and carried it away.

The court held that this was robbery.[11]

Naturally, any force or threat of force must be in some sense unexpected and there must be no question of consent or collusion. This is well illustrated by *R* v *Macro and Others* (1969). The accused pleaded guilty to robbing a postmaster but said that the latter had persuaded him to commit the offence. The postmaster had, in fact, informed on them to the police with the object of claiming a reward, so that he was aware that a raid was to take place at his post office and a police officer was on hand to protect him. An original conviction of four years' imprisonment was quashed on the grounds that it might well have been that the postmaster's will was not overcome either by force or fear.[12]

Finally, where threats are used they must amount to threats of *then and there* subjecting the victim or some other person to force (though a less immediate threat might well, of course, constitute blackmail).

('on any person')

The force, or threat of force, must be directed specifically towards the person. In *R* v *Simons* (1773):

> the accused, who was a ringleader in a series of riots, came with about seventy companions to the house of the prosecutor and said that 'they would have from him the same as they had from his neighbours, namely, a guinea, or else they would tear his mow of corn, and level his house. He gave them a crown to appease them; when the prisoner swore that he would have five shillings more, which the prosecutor, being terrified, gave him.'

In 1773 it was held that this was robbery; under the 1968 Act this would not now be so because the threat of force was directed towards property and not towards the person.

Clearly the force may be directed towards a person who is not actually the victim of the theft if such force is used in order to effect the theft. Hence, if a person threatens a woman with violence in order to persuade her husband, who is present, to hand over his wallet or some other property, then this would most certainly be robbery. Indeed, this 'common-sense interpretation' was widened in *Smith* v *Desmond* (1965), where the accused overpowered a nightwatchman and a maintenance engineer in a bakery, and then broke into a cash office some distance away and there stole from a safe. The House of Lords, reversing the decision of the Court of Criminal Appeal, who had ruled that the theft had to be from the person or in the presence of the victim, held that Desmond was guilty of robbery since it was sufficient if force or the threat of force was used on a person who had the property to be stolen in his immediate personal care and protection.

Finally, in summary of many of the foregoing points, the comments of the Criminal Law Revision Committee itself, in presenting the Draft Bill, are of interest:

the definition requires that the force be used or threatened for the purpose of the theft: but it seems sufficient to limit this to force used or threatened immediately before or at the time of the stealing. It will not be necessary that the person on whom the force is used or who is threatened should be the person from whom the property is stolen. If, for example, the only force used at the time of the Aylesbury train robbery in 1963 had been on a signalman, this would under the Bill have been sufficient. But the force will have to have been used for the purpose of stealing; force used only to get away after committing a theft does not seem naturally to be regarded as robbery (though it could be charged as a separate offence in addition to the stealing). We should not regard mere snatching of property, such as a handbag, from an unresisting owner as using force for the purpose of the definition, though it might be so if the owner resisted. In the case of robbery by putting in fear the draft requires the fear to be that of being then and there subjected to force. This seems to us to correspond to what should be the essence of the offence.

Mugging

Robbery, then, is simply one particular type of theft: similarly mugging is simply one particular type of robbery. There is, however, one crucial difference: whereas robbery is legally defined as theft involving an element of violence, mugging has no legal meaning at all and has entered the vocabulary of crime statistics purely as a result of popular usage. A person can be charged with theft, he can be charged with robbery, but he certainly cannot be charged with mugging.

Dealing first with the word itself, in the *Daily Mail* of 16 April 1973 we are told that:

> the term 'mugger' was used in this country at the beginning of the nineteenth century to mean a blow to the face. Later, the usage broadened to a 'swindler', especially one who operates in the street, a strangler, a garrotter. At the turn of the century the word was being used in America, but it fell out of currency in both countries until its revival in the US a few years ago. Last summer it suddenly returned to Britain.

Extensive research into the history of the word has shown this précis of the situation to be substantially correct: however, one surprising fact which has emerged is that, despite its usage in this country a hundred years or so ago, and again in the past decade, a reference to the word 'mug', or 'mugging', or 'mugger', involving the concept of 'attack', 'robbery', or the like, is not to be found in any modern 'standard' English dictionary, even one published as recently as 1977. Indeed, only one appropriate entry of any sort could be found, in the *New English Dictionary* of 1908:

> **mug-hunter** 1887, J. W. Horsley, 'Jottings from Jail' 95 – 'An old mug-hunter, one, that is to say, of the wretched horde who haunt the street at midnight to rob drunken men.'

A study of the 'standard' American dictionaries proved, as perhaps one might expect, somewhat more successful. For example, in *Webster's Third New International Dictionary* (1959):

> **mug** one of a criminal element: Punk, Thug ('that hooey about what good guys the mugs are at heart' – John Byron)
> **mugger** (probably from 'mug' – to punch in the face) one who attacks usually from behind with intent to rob,

while it is interesting to note that in the same dictionary under:

> **mug/mugged/muggings/mugs** to assault someone especially by garrotting with intent to rob,

the only references and derivations quoted are themselves from the mass media – 'supported themselves by mugging' (*Saturday Evening Post*), 'was mugged from behind and forced into a hallway' (*New York Times*).[13]

A somewhat more comprehensive definition is given in *Webster's New World Dictionary* (1966):

> **mug** to assault a person from behind by strangling him with an arm thrown around his neck, especially with intent to rob him,

and one in simpler and more concise terms in *Webster's New Collegiate Dictionary* (1973):

> **mugger** one who attacks with intent to rob,

but the general gist of the meaning is clearly the same and is, indeed, confirmed by almost all the other American dictionaries.

Turning to what might be termed historical references the most fruitful source proved to be dictionaries of slang, not, as might be expected, Eric Partridge's *A Dictionary of Slang and Unconventional English*[14] which offered only:

mug a punch or blow to or on the mug or face,

but rather *A Dictionary of the Underworld*[15] by the same author:

mug 1. Garrotting. November 26th, 1862. Session Papers (case: Roberts), police witness, 'I apprehended Roberts . . . he said, "you want me for putting the mug on do you? I will put the b----y mug on you". Mug is slang used by thieves; it means garrotting', also Henry Leverage ('Dictionary of the Underworld' in *Flynn's*, early 1925) – a neck hold. 2. A rough, a thief, a thievish rogue.

The second meaning, the author suggests, probably comes by antiphrasis from the meaning 'dupe'. It is also the meaning quoted in Barrère and Leland's *A Dictionary of Slang, Jargon and Cant*; while this possible connection between 'mug' as used in the (supposedly) modern sense of 'something of an idiot', or 'an easy catch', and the notion of robbery, is well illustrated by the following quotation from Henry Mayhew's *London Labour and the London Poor*:

The woman looks out for a 'mug', that is a drunken fellow, or a stupid, foolish sort of fellow. She then stops him in the street, talks to him, and pays particular attention to his jewellery, watch, and everything of that sort, of which she attempts to rob him. If he offers any resistance, or makes a noise, one of her bullies comes up, and either knocks him down by a blow under the ear, or exclaims, 'What are you talking to my wife for?' and that is how the thing is done, sir. [a member of the Metropolitan Police explaining the art of 'picking up']

But clearly the most pervading theme of all the various definitions quoted above is that of garrotting.[16] The garrotte was once a Spanish method of capital punishment by strangulation (and in a modified form still is) but over the years the word 'garrotting' came to mean something like 'highway robbery performed by throttling', or 'throttle in order to rob'. Thus Mayhew (1862: 237–8) tells us:

Highway robberies are also effected by garotting . . . . The garotter tries to get his arm under [the victim's] chin, and presses it back, while with the other hand he holds his neck firmly behind. He does it so violently the man is almost strangled and is unable to cry out . . . . Should the person struggle and resist he is pressed so severely by the neck that he may be driven insensible. When the robbery is effected they run off. In general they seize a man when off his guard, and it may be some time before he recovers his presence of mind.

Recent usage of the word 'mugging' seems to suggest that there is no longer a 'requirement' for strangulation, still less for garrotting as such: any unexpected attack on an individual carried out with the intention of robbery is today often talked of as a mugging. The situation is very adequately explained by Hunt (1975: 30) in the following way:

A decade or so ago, 'mugging', like its synonym, 'yoking', was informally used by police to signify an increasingly common crime committed chiefly by youths who were not professional criminals: namely, an unarmed assault from behind, in which the attacker locks a forearm around the victim's neck and throttles him while demanding his money or having a confederate empty his pockets. Police departments and the FBI (in its *Uniform Crime Reports*) assign reported muggings to the category 'strong-arm robbery' — that is, robbery in which physical force, but no weapon, has been employed — a genre also including face-to-face attacks with the fists, running knock-downs, stompings, and others.

But as the term 'mugging' became increasingly popular with the public, it lost its specialized meaning and came to refer to almost any form of strong-arm robbery and, more than that, to robberies in which the victim is threatened with — and even wounded by — a knife, club, or other simple weapon; beyond this, moreover, it is even occasionally employed to refer to robberies in which a gun is used; and, finally, it is sometimes applied to robberies which result in injuries serious enough to bring about the victim's death.

But while the term has lost something by becoming so diffuse, it has apparently filled a need, becoming the useful generic label for robberies with varied techniques but a single underlying behavioural style — one characterized by desperation, recklessness, impulsivity, a lack of criminal professionalism, and, especially, the use of physical contact often involving violence far in excess of what is needed to obtain the victim's money.

It is important to remember, however, that since the word has no legal meaning and since, even if it were possible to carry out a survey of public opinion, no two people would be likely to define the offence in exactly the same way, any study of mugging must, of necessity, begin by stating its terms of reference very precisely.

Definitions and the present study

The published statistics give no true indication of the seriousness of the crimes actually recorded. Using the hypothetical case of a domestic brawl in which a husband hits his wife over the head with a hammer, Nigel Walker shows convincingly in his *Crime and Punishment in Britain*[17] just how inadequate are the descriptive terms used in the *Criminal Statistics, England and Wales*, published annually by the Home Office. The offence could be classified as an attempted murder if it could be proved that the husband said before hitting his wife, 'I am going to kill you.' If he said nothing, or no one heard what he said, then his crime might be recorded as one of felonious wounding. If the blow merely rendered her unconscious, the offence might be recorded as malicious wounding; if she dodged it, it might even be treated as a non-indictable assault.

Moreover, as far as the published statistics for robbery are concerned, no attempt at all is made to distinguish between any of the various 'grades' or 'types' of offence, however trivial or however serious.[18] The disadvantage of such a simplistic system is pointed out by Conklin (1972: 17):

> The substantive criminal law offers a codification of various components of criminal acts and the relative seriousness with which different offences should be regarded. But the categorical definitions legislated in the criminal code may provide only a rough and often misleading classification for advancing our understanding of the origins of criminal acts and effective means of crime control. The criminal code provides a useful starting point for enquiry into different types of crime problem, but the search for understanding and control quickly leaves such categorisations behind.

While the difficulty of using the 'official' statistics for research purposes is further stressed by McClintock in his unpublished paper on 'Criminal violence in industrial society' (1974) when he tells us that:

Most of the systems of official criminal statistics are broadly based upon legal classifications of offences. To a large extent therefore they carry information on a formal legal level and give little indication as to the factual content of the criminal acts in relation to the social context in which they occurred.

It was for this very reason that in his major enquiry into *Robbery in London* (1961) he evolved the following classification, broken down into five groups, and based entirely upon the circumstances in which the victim was attacked:

Group I
Robbery of persons who, as part of their employment, were in charge of money or goods:
(a) in transit,
(b) carried during every-day employment
(c) in shops, banks, etc. during working hours,
(d) in factories, offices and other premises during working hours,
(e) on business premises following illegal entry.

Group II
Robbery in the open following sudden attack:
(a) male victim (wallets, etc.),
(b) female victim (handbags, etc.),
(c) child victim, under 14 years

Group III
Robbery on private premises:
(a) by offenders who knocked and forcibly entered on the door being opened,
(b) by housebreakers subsequently disturbed by a member of the household.

Group IV
Robbery after preliminary association of short duration between victim and offender (mainly for heterosexual or homosexual purposes):
(a) of victim decoyed by prostitute,
(b) of prostitute by client or by person waylaying her for her takings,
(c) of victim in street or open space following preliminary association,
(d) of victim in vicinity of public house after drinking with offender,
(e) after going home together.

Group V
Robbery in cases of previous association of some duration between victim and offender, e.g. friends, lovers, workmates.

As pointed out by McClintock himself (1961: 15) there are several advantages in such a classification. It is sufficiently objective to be applied in any police area; it can include all crimes recorded by police, and not only those in which the offender has been apprehended; and it indicates the vulnerability of different classes of person to attack. Its main disadvantage is that

> it does not distinguish the degree of premeditation; offences committed on the spur of the moment are grouped with those which have been carefully planned. But this element in a crime will always be difficult to assess: it was found that even when the offender was caught, the amount of planning which had preceded the attack could not easily be ascertained.

Not everyone would agree with this last point: for example, Conklin (1972) makes use of a typology based on offenders rather than offences — his argument being that robberies that are similar in appearance are sometimes committed by quite different types of offenders, and that 'drawing conclusions about the nature of the offender from data about the robbery can be misleading'. Conklin's main headings are:

(i)   The Professional Robber
(ii) The Opportunist Robber
(iii) The Addict Robber
(iv) The Alcoholic Robber.[19]

But clearly the main, and critical, disadvantage of Conklin's 'system' is that, in order to be classified under one of the above headings, the robber must first be caught and, as we will discover later, about three out of every five reported robberies are never cleared up. If 60 per cent (or more) of all robberies recorded by police have to be excluded from any overall analysis, this would seem to invalidate entirely any results obtained, particularly when one takes into account differences in the likelihood of detection between, let us say, the 'alcoholic robber' and the 'professional robber'. (By their very nature this must surely be the case. In his intoxicated state the 'alcoholic robber' must normally represent a very easy 'pick-up' for police.)

The groups suggested by McClintock may possibly be open to one or two minor criticisms but in general they provide a very useful means of classifying a type of crime which can include such a variety of offences that a single overall total is practically meaningless.[20] In any event, since the publication of the *Robbery in London* the Metropolitan Police have made use of the headings suggested therein for the classification of all robbery offences: thus it is possible to obtain far more precise information from the robbery statistics for London than it is from those for the rest of England and Wales.

At the same time, the adoption of McClintock's system has led to rather a strange situation as far as mugging is concerned. When this word came into general usage in this country in 1972, it soon became apparent that appropriate statistics would be required for this 'new' type of crime and, of the five groups listed above, the one approximating most closely to what it was felt, both subjectively and as a result of studying the available evidence, would normally be thought of as mugging, seemed to be Group II. Issued statistics for mugging refer, therefore, to this heading — it being a case of having tried to adapt an existing set of figures to what it was *thought* was required.

It is clear that this does not misrepresent the true situation to any great extent; nevertheless, it is important to remember that there are some offences which a member of the general public may well think of as muggings, but which are not included as such in the statistics because they happen to fulfil the requirements of another of McClintock's categories, that is to say either Group I ('Robbery of persons who, as part of their employment, were in charge of money or goods') which would include cases such as robbery in the street of a betting shop employee as he set out for the bank with the day's takings; or Group IV ('Robbery after preliminary association of short duration between victim and offender') which would include such cases as the robbery of a youth in a park after a homosexual advance.

Worthy of mention, too, are those offences which may not be included as muggings simply because of their location. The term 'in the open' may be subject to a great number of interpretations and possibly something like 'areas to which the public have access' would be preferable, though then there would be the difficulty of distinguishing between, say, a museum and a bank. In fact, whatever yardstick is used to separate out muggings from other forms of robbery, it is inevitable that certain anomalies will arise and, after much consideration, it was decided for the purposes of the present study to make no attempt to reclassify in accordance with the view supposedly held by the public.[21]

Thus, very much in line with McClintock's classification, 'mugging' is taken to mean:

Robbery in the open following sudden attack (of private property only, and *not* following even a brief association).

[3] The attitudes of society

Introduction

Having stated the main reasons for undertaking this study and having defined its subject-matter in both legal and 'everyday' terms, this chapter now pays some attention firstly to the public idea of robbery, secondly to the way in which this is influenced by the mass media and, finally, to the reaction of society as reflected in its adopted sentencing policy.

Public conception of robbery

> Mugging — robbery with varying degrees of violence — is not the commonest or the most dreadful of American crimes Yet it is almost certainly the crime that American city-dwellers most fear, and the one that is most destructive of civilized urban life and of faith in the integrity and viability of society. It is a crime that concerns us in Britain too, since its shadow already falls across our society. [1]

A number of studies have been carried out by social scientists with the essential objective of establishing how important looms the crime of robbery in people's minds. Though not confined to robbery, one of the most important, certainly the most detailed, contributions in this field is the analysis carried out in the early 1960s by Sellin and Wolfgang, who tried to establish what is generally termed an 'index of crime', the aim of which is to take some account of the greater seriousness of certain offences.[2] As a major part of their research, Sellin and Wolfgang asked two samples,[3] one of Pennsylvanian police officers and one of university students, to rate 141 carefully prepared accounts of different crimes. Twenty of these related to some form of robbery, as follows:[4]

8   The offender robs a person of $1,000 at gunpoint. The victim is shot and requires hospitalisation.

9   The offender robs a victim of $1,000 at gunpoint. The victim is wounded and requires treatment by a physician but no further treatment is needed.

10   The offender robs a victim of $1,000 at gunpoint. No physical harm occurs.

11   The offender, armed with a blunt instrument, robs a victim of $1,000. The victim is wounded and requires hospitalisation.

12   The offender, with a blunt instrument, robs a person of $1,000. The victim is wounded and requires treatment by a physician but no further treatment is needed.

13   The offender, armed with a blunt instrument, takes $1,000 from a person. No physical harm is done.

14   The offender, using physical force, robs a person of $1,000. The victim is hurt and requires hospitalisation.

15   The offender robs a person of $1,000 by physical force. The victim is hurt and requires treatment by a physician but no further treatment is required.

16   The offender, using physical force, robs a victim of $1,000. No physical harm is inflicted.

17   The offender threatens to harm a victim if he does not give . money to the offender. The victim hands over $1,000 but is not harmed.

18   The offender robs a victim of $5 at gunpoint. The victim is shot and requires hospitalisation.

19   The offender robs a person of $5 at gunpoint. The victim is wounded and requires medical treatment but no further treatment is required.

20   The offender robs a person of $5 at gunpoint. No physical harm occurs.

21   The offender, with a blunt instrument, robs a person of $5. The victim is wounded and requires hospitalisation.

22   A victim is robbed of $5 by an offender with a blunt instrument. The victim requires treatment by a physician but no further treatment is needed.

23   The offender, armed with a blunt instrument, robs a victim of $5. No physical harm is inflicted.

24   The offender, using physical force, takes $5 from a victim. The victim is hurt and requires hospitalisation.

25   The offender, using physical force, robs a person of $5. The

victim is hurt and requires treatment by a physician but no further treatment is required.

26 The offender takes $5 from a person by force but inflicts no personal harm.

27 The offender threatens to harm a victim if he does not give money to the offender.

Now, clearly, these hypothetical cases can be grouped in the sense that the first ten relate to the robbery of $1,000 and the last ten to the robbery of only $5; while each of these two main groupings includes one entry for each of the following combinations:

Gun	Serious injury	8 and 18
	Slight injury	9 and 19
	No injury	10 and 20
Blunt instrument	Serious injury	11 and 21
	Slight injury	12 and 22
	No injury	13 and 23
Physical force	Serious injury	14 and 24
	Slight injury	15 and 25
	No injury	16 and 26
Threat only	No injury	17 and 27.

As far as the sample of police officers[5] was concerned, what Sellin and Wolfgang call the 'Mean Raw Category Scales Scores' were as follows:

8	10.64	18	10.18
9	9.73	19	8.64
10	9.36	20	9.09
11	9.64	21	10.18
12	8.54	22	9.40
13	8.36	23	8.82
14	10.09	24	9.18
15	9.36	25	9.27
16	8.09	26	9.09
17	8.54	27	6.73

It should be stressed that such ratings have no true quantitative value and are meaningful only in a comparative sense.[6] It can be seen from the above table that, although robberies involving guns are given the highest ratings, there is no great difference between any of the possible combinations (apart, perhaps, from no. 27). Since Sellin and Wolfgang also show that the age of the offender has very little effect on the ratings,[7] the overall conclusion must be that the type, the stolen value, the degree of injury, the age of the offender, and the weapon used are all relatively unimportant considerations in any general assessment of the seriousness of robbery.[8]

The question therefore becomes one of establishing, not how detailed changes affect the rating of robbery, but rather how this rating compares with that of the *other* 121 offence descriptions. In fact only three of these have a rating of ten or more, namely:

1	The offender stabs a person to death	10.86
2	The offender robs a person at gunpoint. The victim struggles and is shot to death	10.91
3	The offender forcibly rapes a woman. Her neck is broken and she dies	10.93

The following are examples of offences which, although surely serious, received a lower rating than that for many types of robbery:

4	The offender kills a person by reckless driving of an automobile	9.73
5	The offender forces a female to submit to sexual intercourse. The offender inflicts physical injury by beating her with his fists	7.00
30	The offender wounds a person with a gun. The victim lives but requires hospitalisation	9.09
33	The offender wounds a person with a knife. The victim lives but requires hospitalisation	8.54

Finally, in order to give some impression of the scope and scale of the ratings, the following offences are included purely for comparison purposes:

43	The offender breaks into a department store, forces open a cash register, and steals $5	5.00
75	The offender picks a person's pocket of $5	4.36
86	The offender embezzles $5 from his employer	2.50
117	The offender is intoxicated in public	1.60

These comparative differences are also reflected in the ratings of the sample of students: it can therefore be seen that, although their findings have here been used in a way rather different from that originally envisaged, Sellin and Wolfgang's research provides some interesting evidence to suggest that robbery rates very highly on any 'scale of seriousness'.

In much the same vein L. Lenke, an assistant at the Institute of Criminal Science at the University of Stockholm, has quoted the results of 'ranking order' surveys carried out in France, Sweden and Finland which again (despite the inadequacies of the sampling frame) give some idea of the concern with which people view the activities of the robber (1974: 81) (see Table 3.1).

Table 3.1 *Ranking order of certain categories of crime**

| | France | Sweden | Finland | |
			Public	Judges
Robbery	1	3	1	1
Burglary	2	4	–	–
Rape	3	2	–	–
Embezzlement	4	–	3	2
Causing death by negligence	5	1	–	–
Abortion	6	–	2	3
Theft	7	–	4	4
Wounding	8	–	5	5

*France. Students of law and of literature asked to rank in order of suitable punishment. Sweden. Attitudes of students towards crime and punishment. Finland. 2,023 members of the public, 143 judges in ranking of 'punitive demands'. Source: Lenke (1974: 81).

In the same article Lenke also quotes opinion polls carried out in a number of different countries, all of which appear not only to confirm the high level of concern with crimes of violence in general but also to emphasise that this level is rising. For example, in 1968 a Gallup Poll was carried out in England which included the question 'Do you regard any of these [questions from a list] as raising very serious social problems in Britain today?'. The list included such headings as 'immigrants', 'bad housing', and 'juvenile delinquency'. 'Crimes of violence' was placed second with 78 per cent, and only 'drug taking' received more votes (83 per cent). In 1971 the exercise was repeated with much the same results. In a Swedish poll the question was asked 'Should our

Police authorities be able to do more to protect citizens against crimes of violence?'. Positive responses increased from 45 per cent in 1955 to 72 per cent in 1970. (The same poll also asked if people 'hesitate to go out on the streets when it is dark because they feel unsafe', and this was in fact the case for 23 per cent in 1970.) In an American poll in 1968, 43 per cent said that 'they stayed off the streets at nights because of their fear of crime. (In 1963 the figure had been 31 per cent.)

The way in which public opinion can be influenced by a sort of 'collective obsession' with violent attacks in the street is further illustrated by a study carried out in Sweden in 1972[9] when a random sample of 1,200 persons was asked 'How many persons do you think were attacked and killed on the streets of Stockholm last year?', and 'How many pedestrians do you think were killed in Stockholm during the same period?'. Their answers can be grouped in the following way:

Estimated number of persons killed	From violent attacks	From traffic (pedestrians)
0	0	0
1–5	6	1
6–10	15	4
11–20	20	12
21–50	23	25
51–100	15	23
101–200	10	18
201–500	5	9
500+	1	3
No Answer	5	5

It can be seen that no less than 16% (about one million Swedes if generalised) believed that more than 100 persons were killed in 'attacks' in Stockholm in that year. In fact the right answer is '0' in the case of violent street attacks (and in the range '21-50' in the case of pedestrians killed in traffic accidents). Furthermore, although persons with low education and income tended to give higher estimates of the violence, a further small sample of judges and police officers[10] also considerably overestimated the risk of violence and underestimated the risk of traffic.

This rather strange phenomenon is explained by Hunt (1975: 41-2) in the following way:

Thus muggings, in addition to their other dismaying and alarming characteristics, seem all but uncontrollable by the police and the courts. Victims of muggers – and virtually all who fear they might someday become victims – feel helpless, unprotected, and without any means of redress . . . . It is for such reasons that robberies, and muggings in particular, have so powerfully corrosive an effect upon American life, for, over and above everything else they do to us, they cause a loss of faith in our society, and a pervasive and demoralizing fear. Other things which might be expected to cause far greater fear do not, and have no such demoralizing effect. Automobiles, to take but one example, killed 56,400 Americans and injured two million in 1969 – roughly 20 times as many deaths, and 25 times as many injuries, as were caused by muggers. Yet in comparison to our fear of muggers, our fear of automobiles is almost non-existent. This does not mean that we are fools, but that we far better tolerate the thought that an accident may harm us than that another human being – a total stranger to whom we have done no wrong – may suddenly and viciously attack us.

Whether or not such an explanation is accepted, it is still interesting – and perhaps just a little surprising – to note how unrealistically and illogically large in people's minds looms the spectre of violence – especially violence perpetrated, apparently at random, by a stranger in the street.

The mass media

The media love the crime statistics because they tend to go for 'hard' facts and there is no fact so hard as a number, unless it is the percentage difference between two numbers.[11]

Certainly violent crime, of which mugging is something of a classic example, is a very 'newsworthy' subject and in recent years it has come as no great surprise to encounter headlines such as 'The Violent Truth of Life in London' (*Daily Mail*), 'Violence on South London Streets' (*The Times*). 'In the Footsteps of Fear' (*Sunday Telegraph*), or 'Violent City Where Fear is Just a Fact of Life' (*Evening News*). Indeed, in the more 'popular' press what appears to be an insatiable need to attract attention results in what surely must be considered wild claims, such as, 'At night when you are lying in bed you often hear screams from people who are being attacked' (from an *Evening News* article written in 1975), or 'Four times each day the thud of cosh on innocent skull'

'FLOG THE GIRL THUGS'
MP wants female muggers whipped

From the Sun, *of February 13, 1976.*

MAULED BY THE MUGGERS
MP's midnight terror in a quiet street

From the Sunday Mirror, *10 August 1975.*

(from an article in the *Sun* written in 1972 following the issue of a booklet by the present author on the subject of robbery in the Metropolitan Police District)[12] — or even in headlines such as those reproduced above.[13]

The intention of this section is not to analyse in great detail the influence of the press or the interaction between crime, the media and the public, but since one of the ultimate objectives of this study *is* to put mugging into some sort of sociological perspective and since, as Stuart Hall (1975) tells us:

The British 'mugger' was a bit like a self-fulfilling prophesy, if you like. This does not mean that the media made 'mugging' up, but it does mean that the press play an active role in constructing the events they are later to report.

it seemed highly appropriate that some consideration should be given to the effect of the media, and more particularly the press, on the problem in hand.

The 'mass media' (or mass communications) is defined by Janowitz (1968: 42) as:

> the institutions and techniques by which specialised groups employ technological devices (press, radio, films, etc.) to disseminate symbolic content to large, heterogeneous, and widely dispersed audiences.

This being so, the mass media must be associated very closely with modern industrial society — indeed many writers (such as Daniel Bell (1961) in his *End of Ideology*, and C. Wright Mills (1956) in his *The Power Elite*) have pointed to, and criticised, the role the mass media play in creating what they see as a 'mass society' unable to think for themselves. But the first problem to resolve is whether the mass media is a cause or an effect in the development of such a society. One's answer to this question depends to a very large extent on which 'model' is considered the more acceptable, that is to say either the 'Mass Manipulative' model, which suggests that the public are passive absorbers of a set of messages which cannot but influence their behaviour and values, or the 'Commercial' model, which is more cautious about the question of effects, adherents of this position stressing that the public is neither so dumb nor so passive.

This is an issue on which sociologists are by no means unanimous. At the one extreme we have the neo-Marxist view, as expressed for example by Marcuse (1964: 11) in his *One-Dimensional Man*, that the mass media

> comprise an instrument for maintaining a form of totalitarianism which does not rely on terror, but works through the creation and manipulation of 'false needs' — for entertainment, relaxation, information and personal consumption.

These needs are said to be superimposed on the individual by vested interests and their existence serves to uphold prescribed attitudes and habits: they also serve to assimilate potentially opposed classes into a state of uncritical acceptance of the *status quo*. And yet, in direct conflict with this viewpoint, many empirical studies of the mass media have concluded that individuals are unaffected, at least as far as their direct actions are concerned, by what they see on television, what they hear on the radio, or what they read in the newspaper.[14]

But even here there is conflicting evidence. For example, in 1975 in a book entitled *Mass Media, Violence and Society*, Dennis Howitt and Guy Cumberbatch took as their central theme the fact that 'the Mass Media do not have any significant effect on the level of violence in society' and yet, in 1977, some well-publicised research by W. Belson of the North East London Polytechnic suggested that long hours watching television can make some boys more violent in real life.[15] The dispute is never likely to be adequately resolved. There seems to be no satisfactory way of establishing with any certainty whether vicarious violence satisfies (by catharsis),[16] or stimulates individual urges.[17] Certainly it is well beyond the scope of this study to suggest the degree to which the propensity to mug is influenced by violence portrayed in the media. However, there are other aspects of the 'power of the press', in particular the effect of what might be called 'attitude reinforcement'.

As we have seen, many of the remarks contained in the press simply cannot be taken at their face value, but they still tend to reinforce the opinion of the general public that there *is* a lot of violence in London and that it *is* something that they have every justification to be worried about. They see, in fact, no reason whatsoever to doubt the truthfulness or the sincerity of such passages as:

> what most alarms us and most gravely damages our faith in our society is the ever present threat of some sudden, unpredictable, savage assault upon our own body by a strange — a faceless, name-less, fleet-footed figure who leaps from the shadows, strikes at us with his fist, an iron pipe, or a switchblade knife, and then vanishes into an alley with our wallet or purse, leaving us broken and bleeding on the sidewalk. (Hunt, 1975: 11)

It is with reference to such statements that Leslie Wilkins, in putting forward his theory of 'deviance amplification', argues[18] that there is a noticeable tendency to dramatise the seriousness and extensiveness of crime and suggests that the press uses the considerable power at its disposal to keep alive, direct, and to some extent exaggerate, the problem as it is purveyed to the public.[19] Or, as McClintock tells us:[20]

it is quite clear that the selection of items for the news is very un-representative of the different kinds of violence that occur. For example, serious violent incidents in the domestic situation are given little news space, whereas robbery with violence or violence connected with spectator sport or public demonstrations of an aggressive nature, have very full coverage.

This phenomenon is extremely well illustrated by Stanley Cohen's study of the 'Mods' and 'Rockers' at seaside resorts during Bank Holiday weekends in the mid 1960s.[21] Phrases such as 'riot', 'orgy of destruction', 'battle', 'attack', 'siege', 'beat up the town' and 'screaming mob' used by reporters left an image of a besieged town from which holidaymakers were fleeing to escape a marauding mob, when in fact, even allowing for perhaps a little counter-bias on the part of Cohen himself, there was little beyond stone-throwing, one or two broken windows and some baiting of police officers. In McClintock's words:[22]

> Events can be over-dramatised as well as substantially distorted by the selective processes of the media. As a result of these processes the public — through the media — may merely move from being *uninformed* to being *ill-informed* whereas, of course, what is required is that they should be reasonably *well-informed.*

Or, as Jock Young (1971: 36-7) puts it:

> The media play on the normative concerns of the public and by thrusting certain moral directives into the universe of discourse, can create social problems suddenly and dramatically.

Specifically as far as mugging is concerned, there was an excellent example of just such a development in April 1976, when, at an obscure meeting of serving police officers, Mr Enoch Powell (somewhat predictably) made a comment to the effect that mugging was racially biased. Due *entirely* to the press coverage it received, this immediately became a national issue involving lengthy discussion, debate, 'questions in the House', letters to the Editor, and statements by community leaders.[23]

In summary, although it can be argued that the media do not appear to have much of a direct influence on the amount of crime actually committed, there can be little doubt that, when it comes to a specific category such as mugging, the indirect effect can be substantial if only because the more it is brought to the attention of the public the more it is likely to be reported, and, indeed, the more police may feel they should do something about it by way of such measures as paying special attention or forming special squads.

To this extent, then, mugging has indeed been a self-fulfilling prophecy.[24] And, as Cohen (1973: 59) tells us:

> Unlike the case of natural disasters where the absence of predictions can be disastrous, with social phenomena such as deviance, it is the presence of predictions that can be 'disastrous'.

or, as Stuart Hall (1975) puts it in a passage which sums up this section as a whole:

> The image is already familiar — the 'mugger' is callous, violent; he attacks the weak and vulnerable, robs for kicks rather than gain. Naturally, certain features which fall outside this image don't get reported. Now, the general public is sensitised to 'mugging' via this image, and they then express fears about 'mugging' — perhaps in letters to the press. Judges who are deciding on a sentence refer to this 'public anxiety'. The sentences get longer. This, in itself, is newsworthy; it becomes a news story, and it refocuses public attention. This is an amplification spiral, and the media don't stand outside this spiral. They form part of it.

The reference to judges taking heed of public opinion is of particular interest, and is an aspect of the debate to which we now turn.

Sentencing policy

Changes over time in possible sentences for convicted robbers have been outlined in chapter 2. Figure 3.1 now illustrates in more detail the measures available for dealing with offenders from 1800 to date, while the maximum penalties available for persons convicted of robbery, as specified by each of the principal Acts dealing with larceny and related offences are shown in Table 3.2.

It can be argued that this gives a broad idea of the changing attitude of society towards robbery and robbers, if only in the sense that the move from, for example, the death penalty and flogging could possibly be interpreted as an indication of a general 'softening' of approach.

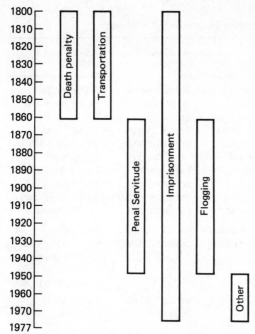

Figure 3.1 Robbery: measures available for dealing with convicted offenders, 1800 to 1977

More realistically, the picture which emerges probably reflects a process of gradual refinement and simplification influenced to a considerable degree by specific occurrences such as the end of the transportation system in 1857; and, in any event, a far more meaningful approach would be to analyse not *possible* but *actual* sentences.

As part of the present study an analysis has therefore been undertaken of the disposal of all persons arrested for robbery in each year from 1832 to 1976 – for the Metropolitan Police District between 1832 and 1931, and for England and Wales as a whole from 1932 onwards.[25] (Since, as far as can be ascertained, this is information which is not available elsewhere, at least in such a convenient form, and which could well be of use to other researchers, especially in the field of penology, the results, which may be summarised as follows, are attached in full in Appendix 2.)

In the earliest available record for the year 1832, just eleven men and one woman were brought before a London court for the offence of robbery as then defined: three of the men and the woman were acquitted but, of the eight men found guilty, six were executed and

Table 3.2 *Maximum penalties for convicted robbers*

Act	Robbery	Attempted robbery	Robbery with violence
Larceny Act 1861, Sec. 40–3	3–14 years penal servitude or up to 2 years in prison with or without hard labour and with or without solitary confinement	3 years penal servitude or up to 2 years in prison with or without hard labour and with or without solitary confinement	3 years–life penal servitude or up to 2 years in prison with or without hard labour and with or without solitary confinement
Larceny Act 1916 Sec. 23	up to 14 years penal servitude	up to 5 years penal servitude	up to life penal servitude plus (if male) liable to be once privately whipped
(*Criminal Justices Act 1948*)	up to 14 years in prison	up to 5 years in prison	up to life in prison
Theft Act 1968, Sec. 8	up to life in prison	up to life in prison	up to life in prison

two were sentenced to be transported for life. By 1852 the level of punishment had reduced considerably for, of the twenty-six men and nine women found guilty of robbery, eleven were sentenced to transportation (for varying periods, though all less than for life), while twenty-four were imprisoned for periods of less than two years. Thereafter, various methods of disposal have come into or out of 'fashion', though it should be noted that 'there has during the present century been no substantial difference in the conditions under which sentences of penal servitude and sentences of imprisonment are served',[26] and also that there has been a considerable fragmentation of methods of disposal since the passing of the 1948 Criminal Justices Act.[27]

Since it is notoriously difficult to interpret tables of statistics, the percentages relating to each main method have been calculated and are illustrated in Figure 3.2, the main aim here being, 'instantaneously' as it were, to give at least some idea of changes in attitude towards robbers brought to trial. It can be seen in particular that the level of acquittals has been much lower in recent years than in the past.[28] Though apparently of little significance, it is felt that this fact is actually of the

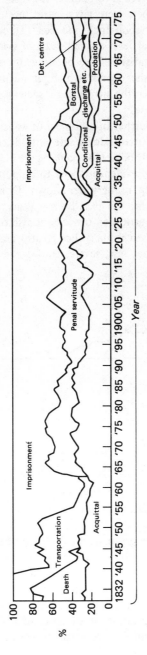

(Breakdown for each year represents the percentage distribution of each method)

Figure 3.2 Robbery: persons brought to trial — methods of disposal

utmost importance since it tends to counter the main argument of the hard-liners — that, if robbers were given more severe sentences, this form of crime would correspondingly reduce.[29] Directly contrary to this theory we now have at least a small shred of evidence to suggest that, while the robbery statistics have been making such a dramatic advance, the attitude of the courts (which, it might reasonably be argued, is likely to reflect the attitude of society in general), has become more, not less, severe.

This can be illustrated further in a number of ways. For example, if the flogging statistics are plotted side by side with the robbery statistics for the appropriate years (1863-1948) (*vide* Figure 3.3), then it can be seen that there is very little evidence indeed to support the contention that 'when flogging went up, robbery went down'. Or again, taking just the imprisonment figures for the past twenty years, there is further evidence to suggest that attitudes towards convicted robbers have, during the very period when robbery has greatly increased, recently tended to become more, not less, severe. During the period 1955 to

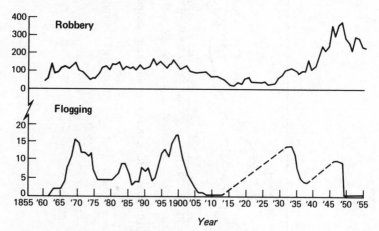

Figure 3.3 Robbery and flogging, 1855-1955

1974 inclusive, the average prison sentence for robbery was as illustrated in Table 3.3. Clearly, the change over time has not been great but the point is that (notably on the basis of the 5-year averages) the movement has been *upwards*.[30] It is also of interest to note that this does not reflect a general trend in respect of crime as a whole. Taking, for example, terms of imprisonment of more than five years,[31] the proportion of the overall total represented by convicted robbers has

Table 3.3 *Average prison sentence for convicted robbers, 1955–74*

Year	Average	5-yr average
1955	2.16	
1956	2.37	
1957	1.98	2.17
1958	2.30	
1959	2.06	
1960	2.29	
1961	2.42	
1962	2.46	2.46
1963	2.46	
1964	2.68	
1965	2.62	
1966	2.87	
1967	2.76	2.77
1968	2.89	
1969	2.73	
1970	2.61	
1971	2.81	
1972	2.87	2.88
1973	3.03	
1974	3.06	

gone up from under 10 per cent in the 1950s to well over 20 per cent in the 1970s.[32]

Lastly, a specific study was carried out in an attempt to assess the effect which very heavy and extremely well-publicised sentences, passed on three young boys convicted of mugging, had on the subsequent number of crimes of this type occurring in the London area.[33] The offence, the trial, and the announcement on 20 March 1973 of a sentence of twenty years' detention, took place in the Birmingham area,[34] but received such wide publicity (see, for example, the reports from the London editions of two national papers) that it had always been felt that it must have had a marked effect on the subsequent decline in this type of offence in the Metropolitan Police District.

Judge sentences three Birmingham boys for 'serious and horrible' offences

Mugger aged 16 given 20 years' detention

From Arthur Osman
Birmingham, March 19 1973
A boy aged 16, described by Mr Justice Croom-Johnson at Birmingham Crown Court today as 'clearly the ringleader in a series of serious

and horrible offences', was ordered to be detained for 20 years. Two
companions, both aged 15, who had been involved with him, were
ordered to be detained for 10 years each.

The boy, Paul Storey, of The Grove, Villa Road, Handsworth,
Birmingham, had pleaded guilty to attempting to murder Mr Robert
Keegan, aged 31 and robbing him of five cigarettes, a bunch of keys,
and 30p. The two other boys, Mustafa Fuat, of Terrace Road, and
James Joseph Duignan, of Churchill Road, both Handsworth,
pleaded guilty to wounding Mr Keegan with intent to do him grie-
vous bodily harm. Duignan also admitted stealing five boxes of
chocolates from a local shop.

Later today it was learnt that the case had been put in the judge's
list for hearing on Wednesday, when it is expected the three accused
will again appear before him.

Earlier, the judge said to Paul Storey: 'It is quite impossible for
me to do other than order you to be detained in such a place on
such conditions as the Secretary of State may direct. I fix the period
at 20 years.'

Mr Patrick Bennett, QC, for the prosecution, said that Mr Keegan
was on his way home on the evening of November 5 last. He had had
a fair amount to drink, was singing, and was in a somewhat happy
frame of mind. He added: 'Then he had the misfortune to encounter
these three young persons.'

The three accosted him, asked him for a cigarette, and while his
attention was distracted knocked him to the ground. They dragged
him to some waste ground, where he was robbed.

Mr Bennett continued: 'It did not stop there. They used more
violence on Mr Keegan, and Storey used a brick in the attack, while
the other two used their feet.'

The boys went away but came back and attacked Mr Keegan
again. He suffered head injuries and there might be permanent
behaviour changes and some loss of mental capacity because of
them.

Later Paul Storey and James Duignan called an ambulance and
went to a police station, where they told a pack of lies about having
found Mr Keegan lying injured. The matter weighed on the con-
science of James Duignan and Mustafa Fuat and after what they told
the police Paul Storey was arrested.

Mr Bennett said that Storey said they agreed to 'roll' Mr Keegan
and that it all started as 'a bit of fun'.

Mr Phillip Cox, QC, on Paul Storey's behalf, said the boy had a very disturbed family background, with a history of some violence being used in the home. He added: 'Perhaps one is driven to the conclusion that this sort of background can affect the human mind so as to lead to otherwise completely unexplainable behaviour.' Paul Storey had a previous conviction, having been fined for committing a disorderly act last May.

James Duignan, it was stated, had absconded from an approved school at the time of the offences. On his behalf Mr J. Field Evans said he did nothing to prevent the attack going on because he had been afraid to interfere. He very much regretted what had been done.

Mr Richard Tucker, QC, on behalf of Mustafa Fuat, said the whole affair had got out of hand and it scared him. As they left the scene Mustafa Fuat had placed a small pillow which was near by under Mr Keegan's head.

Lord Colville, Minister of State at the Home Office, told the House of Lords last November that though it was 'no part of the Government to advise the courts on sentences they pass, it may well have been widely noticed that the judges have recently been taking a very severe view of violent crime and have visited upon muggers some very severe penalties.'

Earlier this year Mr Carr, Home Secretary, told the Commons that mugging had increased in urban areas in the past two years, notably London and Liverpool. It was now being contained, partly because of special police patrols in high-risk areas.

Lord Hailsham of St Marylebone, Lord Chancellor, speaking last month about the 'appalling' rise in indictable crime, said one of the human rights was the right not to be mugged. He said: 'Every time someone is robbed with violence, that person is being deprived of his human rights.'

Muggings rose by one-third in the Metropolitan Police area last year, and were 129 per cent up on 1968.

Under the Children and Young Persons Act, 1933, the boys will be detained 'in such a place and under such conditions as the Home Secretary may direct'.

They are likely to be taken to the borstal allocation centre at Wormwood Scrubs prison before being transferred to a young prisoner's centre.

This is likely to be at Aylesbury, Buckinghamshire, the former women's prison. They will be segregated from adult male prisoners. They can be kept there until they are between 18 and 20, after which they can be reclassified and transferred to a prison.

Paul Storey's mother, Mrs Ethel Sanders, said last night that she was 'very, very shocked' at the sentence. She blamed the environment in Handsworth for the fact that he had got into trouble.

She added: 'I think it is a terrible thing. I do not know what can be done now.

'He used to be a very good boy. He went to work as a labourer when he left school, but he had been unemployed and had got into the habit of staying in bed in the morning and mixing with other youths.'

Mrs Saunders said that she had been separated for some time from Paul Storey's father, a West Indian.

Our Legal Correspondent writes: A young person (under the age of 17) tried on indictment for an offence which, if it were committed by an adult, would be punishable by imprisonment for 14 years or more, can be sentenced by the court to detention under the direction of the Home Secretary for a specified term. Attempted murder is such an offence.

The term of 20 years is, however, extremely high for an offence which did not result in death. It is believed to be the longest period of detention ordered for a juvenile for an offence other than murder. (*The Times*, 19 March 1973)

Three young muggers attack man – then controversy breaks over judge's sentence for a 16 year old

Storm as boy gets 20 years

Daily Mail Reporters

A row broke out last night over a 20-year sentence passed yesterday on a boy mugger of 16.

Two 15-year-old boys were sentenced to ten years.

POLICE welcomed it – 'If this doesn't frighten them, nothing will.'

SOCIAL ORGANISATIONS in general were appalled, and talked about 'the growing hysteria over mugging.'

SOME MPS with violence problems in their areas expressed satisfaction that the muggers were at last being tackled with deterrent sentences.

THE JUDGE who passed the sentence at Birmingham Crown Court, Mr Justice Croom-Johnson, said: 'This was a very serious and horrible case.'

He ordered Paul Storey, a half-West Indian, to be detained for 20 years. Storey was said to have led the two 15-year-olds – one a Turkish-Cypriot, the other Irish – in an attack on a home-going Bonfire Night reveller.

'We are at war . . !'

The victim was battered with a brick wielded by Storey and robbed of 30 pence.

The legal officer of the National Council for Civil Liberties, Mr Larry Grant, said: 'This is incredible.

'If we send 16-year-old boys to jail for 20 years, we will end up with 50-year sentences. What good have life and 99-year sentences achieved in America?'

And Mr Tom Sargeant, secretary of Justice, the all-party lawyers' organisation, said that the sentences were excessive when compared with those given to worse offenders.

But Mr Edward Taylor, Tory MP for Glasgow Cathcart, said that stiffer penalties were the only way to crack down on violent crimes.

He said: 'We must have sentences of this sort to strike real fear into the young thugs and criminals.

Tory MP Mr Sydney Chapman, who sits for the area where the mugging happened – Handsworth, Birmingham, – said: 'We are at war with this sort of crime in Handsworth. The only way we can cope is to stamp it out ruthlessly before it gets an even firmer hold.'

Mr Rex Ambler, a Birmingham community relations leader, said he thought the sentences 'severe.' He pointed out that many youths in Handsworth were frustrated and resentful at society's apparent lack of concern for them.

The muggers' victim was 31-year-old building labourer Mr Robert Keegan, of Carpenters Road, Birmingham.

After the attack he was unconscious for ten days and has still not returned to his £35-a-week work.

A relative said: 'His mind is inclined to ramble, and he is nothing like the man he was.'

Scales of Justice

TWO CASES reported today vividly emphasise the difficulty faced by judges when called on to award sentences for crimes so horrible in themselves as to make any degree of severity seem lenient. At Birmingham, a 16-year-old boy was given 20 years for an assault which was held to constitute attempted murder, and his two 15-year-old companions, who were involved in the same affray, each got 10 years. Already, these sentences have been denounced as far exceeding the normal punishment for such offences. Many will feel, however, that this is a criticism of the norm and that recent statistics of violent crime make a stiffening of sentencing policy urgently necessary.

Would it have been more merciful and just as effective to give the ringleader (who is convicted of having attempted actual murder) an indeterminate life sentence? Such sentences are most appropriate to crimes which may be supposed to have arisen from some mental abnormality, or to cases in which the alternative sentence would be so harsh as to be inhumane. But 20 years, two thirds of which could be served on parole, is not in principle a morally indefensible sentence for a dangerous 16-year-old.

It was on grounds of mercy that the Court of Criminal Appeal yesterday refused to convert an indeterminate life sentence on a man who had committed rape five times into a determinate sentence. The doctors say that the 'precise cause' of this man's trouble has not yet been diagnosed. Can they diagnose sheer moral failure to control lust? (*Daily Mail*, 20 March 1973)

In the *Metropolitan Police Crime Statistics Summary for 1973* it was stated that

the big drop [in muggings] occurred in April and it seems possible that the severe and well publicised sentences imposed in Birmingham earlier in the year could have had some deterrent effect.

Indeed, Figure 3.4, which gives the monthly total of muggings in the Metropolitan Police District from November 1972 to August 1973, shows quite clearly that a completely new pattern *did* begin to emerge as from April 1973: a clear indication, one might think, of the theories of those advocating heavier punishments. Figure 3.5 is, however, of considerable interest. On the day immediately following the Birmingham announcement there was indeed not a single recorded mugging in London (though even this is not quite as improbable as one might imagine), but, if we compare the twenty days after the announcement with the twenty days before, we find a reduction of only three cases — from 76 to 73 — while it was during the *next* twenty days that there occurred the really substantial further reduction of 23 cases. What this appears to indicate is that, apart from the unlikely possibility of a delayed effect, the Birmingham case had little or no impact on the situation in London.

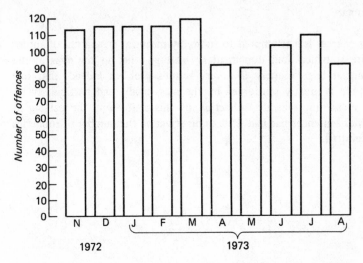

Figure 3.4 Mugging in the MPD: monthly totals, November 1972 to August 1973

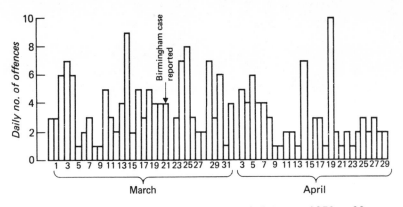

Figure 3.5 Mugging in the MPD: daily totals, 28 February 1973 to 29 April 1973

Although it would be interesting — and more convincing — to extend this line of enquiry to the country as a whole, or to Birmingham in isolation, the real point is that this case provides still further evidence to suggest that there is in fact *no inverse relationship between sentences passed and robberies committed.*

Summary

This chapter has attempted to show, by means of an analysis of appropriate statistical and documentary material, that in the eyes of the public at large robbery is a very serious problem indeed; that this attitude is greatly reinforced by the mass media and particularly by the press; but that the reflection of this attitude in the passing of heavier sentences has had little or no effect on the number of robberies committed.

[4] Statistics in theory and in practice

Introduction

It is most certainly not the intention that this study should amount to
little more than an endless succession of facts, figures and statistical
tables. Nevertheless, the aim of Part 1 is unashamedly descriptive, not
only because it is felt that mugging should be placed in its correct perspective rather than be thought of entirely in isolation, but more
especially because, before any reasoned comment can be made, it is
necessary to quantify the extent of the problem in both absolute and
comparative terms.[1]

Here the use of statistics is inevitable[2] — even though there is no
denying that certain difficulties are involved. As Cicourel (1964: 4)
tells us:

> because of their dependence for stability on the actor's perception
> and the interpretation of them, the measurement of the stated and
> formal features of everyday life, and, especially, the unstated condi-
> tions of everyday life, are sufficiently indeterminate to raise serious
> questions about the measurement systems now in use.

This theme will be expanded upon later in the chapter, but when it
comes to any form of crime statistics it is the mettle of the 'dark figure'
which must first be grasped. A discussion of this problem is included
here, but more important is the brief review of the general statistics
relating to robbery and mugging in the Metropolitan Police District.
These, it is considered, form an essential background to the more
detailed study described in full in chapter 5.

The 'dark figure' of crime

As soon as one enters the realms of crime statistics, one encounters the problem of the 'dark figure' of crime, which, in very simple terms, may be defined as those offences not *reported* to police, plus those offences not *recorded* by police[3] – in other words, those crimes which actually take place but which, for a great variety of reasons, never appear in the published statistics. Research into any aspect of crime must inevitably confront this problem and hence it is a subject which has been discussed at great length and analysed to the nth degree, indeed it is with some justification that it is included as the very first of Hood and Sparks's *Key Issues in Criminology*.

The problem has been formally expounded by Paul Wiles in 'Criminal Statistics and Sociological Explanations of Crime' in the following terms:

> Our understanding of precisely why offences are not reported is at present rudimentary, but the existence of a dark figure has one crucial implication for the explanatory use of criminal statistics. It is possible that the variation in the reporting of offences could account at least partly for fluctuations in the recorded rates for offences. If this is so, then variations in the official rates demand a different kind of explanation. While no one can prove that, for example, the increase in recorded crime is due to changes in reporting behaviour, such a hypothesis is not completely unrealistic. Conversely, the implication for the interpretation of changes in the crime rate is that their real significance cannot be understood unless the extent to which they emanate from changes in reporting behaviour is known. (p. 184)

This may be illustrated as in Figure 4.1.

The exact level of the dark figure has always been the subject of some dispute:[4] for one thing, as will be expanded upon later, it must vary considerably in accordance with the category of crime under discussion.[5] In general terms, though, there seems no reason to dispute the findings of a study, carried out by Richard Sparks and others (1978), which show that indictable crime is *over eleven times greater* than the police statistics suggest. Clearly, evidence of this type must be borne in mind and, where possible, taken into account at all times, but even more important than the actual level is an appreciation of the factors mainly involved.

These can best be thought of in terms of the relationship between the individual and society. A full discussion of the more far-reaching sociological aspects involved may be found in Part 2, but here an ex-

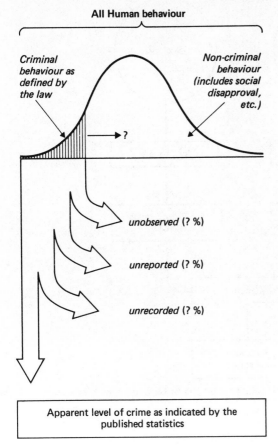

Figure 4.1 Human behaviour and its relationship to the apparent level of crime as indicated by the published statistics

planation will be attempted in terms of the simple 'model' in Figure 4.2 (the lettering of which refers to the subsequent notes).

Individuals

(a) The offender. Obviously an individual who has transgressed the law in any way is hardly likely to bring this fact to notice. In some cases this may be because of a genuine belief that, on the occasion in question, the law did not apply to him; in others, as with white-collar or

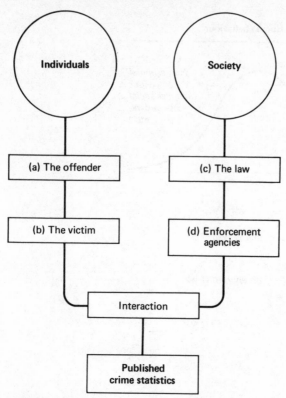

Figure 4.2 Individuals, society, and the published crime statistics: a simple model

business crime, he may feel that since everyone else 'bends the rules' his own actions were fully justified; more frequently still, he may have been involved in a 'victimless' crime where the offence was unlikely to have affected or even come to the notice of anyone other than himself.[6] But whatever the circumstances, and whatever the self-justification, it is self-evident that if the reporting of crime was left to the offender alone, then the dark figure would be very near to 100 per cent – thus resulting in an apparent crime rate of zero.

(b) The victim. There are a great many occasions on which a victim, too, will be unlikely to report an offence. This may be for a number of reasons as indicated, for example, by the following list which is based on a typology devised by Nigel Walker (1965), and for which, in each case, a typical example is included in parentheses:

because all those involved may fail to realise that an offence has been committed (assaults and indecencies by children at play);

because all those involved may be willing participants (certain sexual offences);

because even an unwilling victim may not wish to involve the offender in the supposed consequences of prosecution (shoplifting);

because the victim himself may be antagonistic towards the law in general or the police (minor assaults in 'slum' areas);

because the victim may regard the offence as too trivial to be worth the trouble of reporting (minor theft);

because the victim may be so pessimistic about the chances of the offender being apprehended that he does not bother to report the offence (theft in the street);

because the victim may simply be too embarrassed (indecent exposure);

because the victim may be intimidated by the offender's threats of violence or blackmail (theft by a prostitute).

Society

(c) The law. The law itself must have a crucial influence on the published crime statistics since it is the law which, in virtually all societies, originally defines certain acts as criminal. For, as Durkheim (1958: 11) puts it:[7]

> there is no such thing as a 'natural crime': there are no acts which are always crimes in themselves irrespective of cultural definitions. Crime comprises those classes of behaviour which, if committed in certain social contexts and ways, are defined as crimes by the laws or customs of the society.

This may be manifested in one of two ways. Firstly, the boundary between the law and mere discouragement by social disapproval is drawn at a slightly different point in different penal systems. This is well illustrated by Wilkins' idea of a normal curve (developed, of course, from the Durkheimian notion of crime as a normal phenomenon, and used in an adapted form in Figure 4.1), covering the whole range of human behaviour, from 'saints' to 'sinners', with an infinity of possible 'cut-off points' to separate out those actions which are, from those which are not, legally acceptable. Secondly, the situation quite frequently arises whereby, in any given society, a particular action may at one time be considered 'criminal', and yet at another time may be perfectly acceptable. Homosexual acts between consenting adults represent one recent case in point in this country, while, in America, Prohibition provides an excellent example of the way in which the written law may be manipulated so as to define crimes into or out of existence.[8]

(d) Enforcement Agencies. As Wiles (1971: 182) tells us, 'what we are examining when we analyse "crimes known to the Police" is merely a selection of all the behaviour which would be defined as criminal if it were reported'. There are a number of ways, too, in which the police themselves can have a marked influence on the apparent crime rate. Some of these may be categorised as follows:

(i) in the general sense that it may be presumed the very existence of a police force is likely to be a limiting factor to the amount of crime actually committed;

(ii) at the 'point of contact' between the policeman on the beat and a member of the public, the attitudes adopted by, and the interaction between, the two 'sides' must frequently affect the way in which the situation subsequently develops (this, of course, being 'police discretion' in the most normally accepted sense);[9]

(iii) in certain well-defined instances it may be expedient for a police force as a whole to turn a 'blind eye' towards a particular category of crime, either because it is well known that the law is about to 'catch up with' public opinion (as just a few years ago in cases of attempted suicides), or simply because political expediency has led to some form of 'decree from above';[10]

(iv) similarly, it can often happen that a given police force tends to concentrate on the detection of certain types of crime, one aspect of which may well be the setting up of a specialist squad — to deal, for example, with drug offences or with fraud — which in turn may lead, especially in the case of victimless crime, to the discovery of offences which would otherwise remain forever unreported;[11]

(v) perhaps most important of all, there are a great many pressures, both within and outside the police service, which will affect the actual recording of the data as collected, particularly as between one category of crime and another, and particularly at Sub-Divisional or at Divisional level.[12]

All of the above factors have a bearing on which, and how many, offences eventually appear in the published crime statistics. What we must do now is to go on to look at these statistics themselves.

The crime statistics

The well-known and oft-quoted adage tells us that there are 'lies, damned lies, and statistics' — nevertheless there is no denying that these same statistics play an increasingly important role in nearly every phase of human endeavour, and frequently form an essential concomitant to a true understanding of any situation. Demographic data is perhaps the best example here. If we wish to know the number of births or deaths, the number of marriages or divorces in respect of a given period of time or of a given area, then the published data will provide us with an almost precise indication of what is required, since (in this country at least) the recording of such information is both universal and obligatory. Alternatively we may, as in the computation of the cost of living, make use of an index, a compilation of fluctuations in a sample of items taken from the whole — the relationship to the whole being known, and the index serving as a convenient short-cut to an accurate approximation of the overall variation.

Statistics relating to crime do not, unfortunately, come under either of these headings. As we have seen, no one is likely to suggest that the published crime statistics indicate in any way the 'true' amount of crime (however defined) that has occurred — neither can the indicated rate be thought of as a sample, since the whole cannot be specified. Even so, I would argue that there is no need to go anything like as far as Barbara Wootton (1959: 25) when she tells us:

That we should reject the official statistics as evidence of criminal trends is a hard doctrine, because it means that we must be content to confess ourselves quite ignorant as to whether our population is becoming more, or less, addicted to crime. Nevertheless, such ignorance has to be admitted.

Certainly English criminology, with its tradition of pragmatic empiricism, has always tended to regard criminal statistics as social facts *par excellence*. Even for sociologists such as the American Thorstein Sellin — whose strongly-held view is that criminology should be based not on the criminal law which, he argues, has grown up almost haphazardly, but on 'conduct norms' — it is the published statistics[13] which, almost of necessity, must constitute the normal starting-point for any broadly-based criminological research or discussion.

There is another important consideration. As pointed out in chapter 1, one of the reasons for selecting a particular kind of robbery for detailed study was precisely because it was felt that this was a category of crime which was reported to, and then recorded by, police as a matter of course. And there is evidence to support this view.

On the reporting side, perhaps the most thorough survey ever undertaken was that conducted throughout the USA by the National Opinion Research Centre of Chicago University in 1967.[14] Questionnaires were sent to 10,000 households throughout the continental United States (selected on the basis that every household had an equal chance of being included) with the following results:

Percentage of cases in which police not notified

Auto theft	11
Robbery	35
Aggravated assault	35
Larceny ($50 and over)	40
Burglary	42
Sex offences (other than rape)	49
Family crimes	50
Simple assault	54
Malicious mischief	62
Larceny (under $50)	63
Fraud	74

It has been shown in other studies that the very high rate of notification of auto theft is due entirely to the need to do this for insurance purposes. As to robbery, although the rate of 65 per cent is somewhat lower than might be expected, it is felt, firstly, that the rate for *mugging* could well be considerably higher than this,[15] and, secondly, it does indicate that the 'scope' for an increase in respect of this particular area of the dark figure is relatively limited.[16]

On the recording side, a Departmental Committee on Detective Work and Procedure pointed out in 1938 that:

> These differences of (police) practice will not materially affect the
> statistics of what may be regarded as 'serious' crime.

while, more specifically, Hood and Sparks (1970: 38) tell us that

> in 1966 New York Police Commissioner Leary found that only 22
> per cent of auto theft and rape, 45 per cent of aggravated assault,
> and 54 per cent of larceny were properly recorded — as against 92
> per cent of robbery . . .

and also that:

> Goldman's enquiry into arrested offenders taken to juvenile court in
> certain areas of eastern USA revealed that, with one or two isolated
> exceptions . . . robbery was the only crime with a committal rate of
> 100 per cent. This, of course, is *entirely in line with what one might
> expect* [my italics] .

Unless the ultra-pessimistic and ultimately totally relativist position is
adopted of insisting that the existence of an unknown number of unreported offences renders *any* form of criminological research meaningless[17] then the best that can be done is to take note of the fact that the
figures do not reflect the true position, and hope that, at least as far
as the serious crime of robbery is concerned, this will not affect too
critically any comparisons that may be made. It is to such comparisons
that we now turn.

The statistics relating to robbery and mugging

Four sets of statistics will be looked at here:

(i)   Robbery in London, 1877–1977.[18]
(ii) Robbery in London as compared to the rest of England and Wales,
1957–1977.[19]
(iii) Robbery in London as compared to All Indictable Crime, 1957–
1977.
(iv) Mugging in London as compared to Robbery, 1957–1977.

(i) Robbery in London, 1877–1977

Figure 4.3 illustrates the growth of recorded robbery in London over

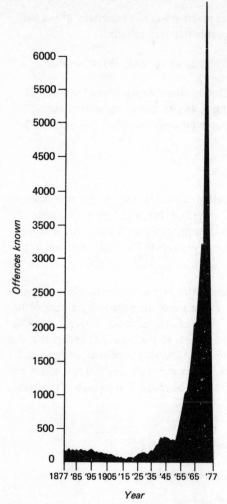

Figure 4.3 Robbery in the MPD, 1877–1977

the past century. It is not being suggested that such a graph is especially meaningful, if only because changes of so many kinds have taken place during the period in question. There has, for example, been a substantial increase in population;[20] two world wars must have had an overall, if unmeasurable, effect;[21] there have been boundary changes, such as when the Metropolitan Police District incorporated an area formerly the responsibility of the Essex Constabulary in 1968; most important of all, there have been a number of alterations in recording practice –

such as those which took place following the introduction of the 1968 Theft Act.[22] On top of all this, as Bernard Crick (1974: 24) points out:

> Long-term historical comparisons are difficult not merely because of the lack of figures, but also because it is probable that our general tolerance of, in particular, violent crime, grows less, so that things that once went unreported, now figure in both police investigation and in statistics of incidents and of convictions.

But none of this, it is suggested, can begin to explain why the apparent pattern of robbery has changed so dramatically, particularly in more recent years. The 'dark figure' and similar considerations may offer some explanation, but they certainly cannot account totally for an apparent increase of something like 25,000 per cent in less than fifty years. Moreover, although it is difficult not to be attracted by the argument of Daniel Bell (1961) (ably supported by Bernard Crick (1974)) that it is 'obvious' that there *must* have been more crime 150 years or so ago than there is now, it is, at least in the case of robbery, simply not supported by the only facts that are available.

While Tobias (1972: 308) may conclude that 'there seem to be adequate grounds on which to decide that the statistics of crime in the nineteenth century are of very little use', his only evidence tends to be based on the well-publicised activities of infamous individual criminals such as Jonathan Wild and Dick Turpin, and there is really very little other than subjective speculation to dispute the figures as they stand.[23]

To emphasise the general point still further we might turn once again to *Robbery in London* (McClintock and Gibson, 1961) which begins:

> In 1959 there were six times as many robberies in London as in 1939. Crimes of robbery recorded by the Metropolitan Police rose rapidly during the war, fluctuated between 1945 and 1955 and since then have risen *very steeply indeed* [my italics] .

All this is confirmed, of course, by Figure 4.3, but the *real* point is that the total robbery figure of 671 which caused McClintock, and others, such concern as recently as 1959, has now risen to well over 6,000.[24]

(ii) Robbery in London as compared to the rest of England and Wales, 1957-1977

There is considerable evidence to support the contention that robbery has always (that is to say since official records began) been mainly an urban problem. The 1839 *Report of the Royal Commission on a Constabulary Force* contains many quotations from the statements of magistrates and others emphasising the urban connections of most criminals, while, as Tobias (1972: 75/6) points out, contemporary writers of the mid nineteenth century had no doubt that the criminal class was substantially a phenomenon of the large towns. J. T. Burt wrote in 1863, for example, that the large towns were the nurseries and hiding places of criminal classes, and that dense populations gave shelter to the criminals, while the Rev. J. Clay, Chaplain of Preston Gaol, had written in his *1849 Report*:

> It is not manufacturing Manchester, but multitudinous Manchester, which gives birth to whatever criminality may be imputable to it. It is the large town to which both idle profligates and practised villains resort as a likely field for the indulgence of sensuality or the prosecution of schemes of plunder. It is the large town in which disorder and crime are generated.

If the larger towns have always had obvious advantages for criminal activity, by way of greater opportunity for crime and greater opportunity for escape after its committal, the argument can certainly be projected to include robbery in more recent times. In 1959 McClintock found that 35 per cent of all robbery in England and Wales was committed in London, and that a further 15 per cent was to be found in the six next largest provincial cities. In total, therefore, the seven largest cities accounted for half the national total, and since they contained only 27 per cent of the total population, their robbery rate was actually almost three times that of the rest of the country.

Taking the London area alone, of course, the difference would be even more marked. As pointed out by Radzinowicz:[25]

> The incidence of robbery in London is higher again than the average rate for the six largest provincial towns. Moreover, study of the kinds of robbery committed there and of the spoils secured would, in all probability, also reveal that London is the scene of the most daring and profitable exploits. At the same time its experience may be regarded as representing, in a concentrated form, the developing trends in the other cities. The metropolitan area is thus particularly well suited for a detailed investigation of the whole subject, in view both of its intrinsic importance and of its wider significance.

Indeed, the trend towards a concentration of robbery within the Metropolitan Police District has continued to the present day, as the following figures show:

		London	Rest of England and Wales
1959	Robberies	671	1,229
	Population (approx.)	8,250,000	38,000,000
	Rate per 100,000	8	3
1977	Robberies	6,826	6,904
	Population (approx.)	7,500,000	41,000,000
	Rate per 100,000	91	17

This would seem to indicate two things — firstly, in confirmation of the findings of McClintock and others, that the robbery rate is far higher in London than elsewhere, and, secondly, that this differential is progressively widening. Such a trend is illustrated by Figure 4.4 which gives a clear indication of just how London has 'forged ahead' over the past twenty years.

(iii) Robbery in London as compared to All Indictable Crime, 1957–1977

If the increase in London robberies had been at a rate equally applicable to all other categories of indictable crime then this might indicate some sort of breakdown of the forces of law and order within the Metropolitan Police District. In fact, it can be seen from Figure 4.5 that this has not been the case. Since 1957 all indictable crime has, indeed, increased at a steady rate, *but* the increase in robbery has been a great deal steeper. It would not be possible for anyone to make an authoritative statement as to just why this should be so, but it must be at least feasible that potential criminals have made a conscious decision to concentrate on, or turn to, robbery — as opposed, say, to burglary or autocrime — presumably because robbery is felt to be 'easier' and/ or more 'rewarding' in either a financial or psychological sense.[26] In any event, what can be said is that in the Metropolitan Police District, whereas for every indictable crime known to police in 1957 there are now 4, for every robbery known to police in 1957 there are now 17.

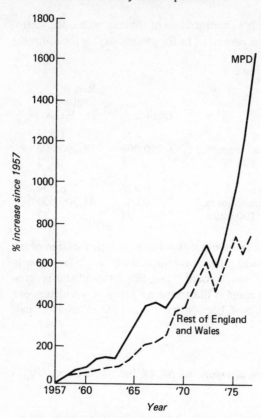

Figure 4.4 Robbery in the MPD compared with the rest of England and Wales: percentage increases, 1957–77

(iv) Mugging in London as compared to Robbery, 1957–1977

If robbery in London has, in recent years, 'accelerated' at a rate far in excess of that for indictable crime as a whole, the specialised category of mugging has experienced an even more marked deterioration. Figure 4.6, for example, shows that whereas, as we have just seen, for every robbery known to police in 1957 there are now 17, the corresponding figure for mugging is 27 – which, by any standards, must surely rate as a truly remarkable increase over a period of only twenty years.

Furthermore, if the reasonable and logical course is adopted of extracting the mugging figures from the totals for robbery as a whole, then the relative increase in the rate of mugging is highlighted still

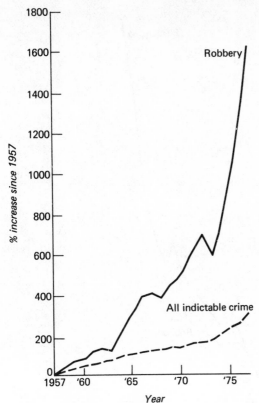

Figure 4.5 Robbery in the MPD compared with all indictable crime: percentage increases, 1957–77.

further. This is illustrated by Figure 4.7: obviously the situation with regard to mugging stays the same as before but, with the mugging figures extracted, it can be seen that there has been a considerable reduction in the level of percentage change for all other robbery.

For convenience the comparative increases in the Metropolitan Police District over the past twenty years for all indictable crime, robbery, and mugging have been summarised in Table 4.1.

To emphasise the point still further, a comparison can again be made with McClintock. In 1959 he wrote:

A second group of robberies which give rise to considerable anxiety comprises the sudden attacks in the open on ordinary passers-by: these crimes cause a feeling of insecurity disproportionate to their numbers. (1961: 16)

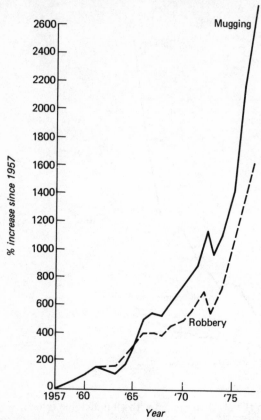

Figure 4.6 Mugging in the MPD compared with robbery: percentage increases, 1957–1977

Table 4.1 *Number of crimes known to police in 1977 for every one crime known in 1957 (MPD only)*

Category	Number
All Indictable Crime	4
Robbery (other than mugging)	12
All Robbery	17
Mugging only	27

He is, as we have seen in chapter 2, referring here to precisely the type of crime we would now term 'mugging', and his anxiety stemmed from an annual total of 162 such offences in the Metropolitan Police District

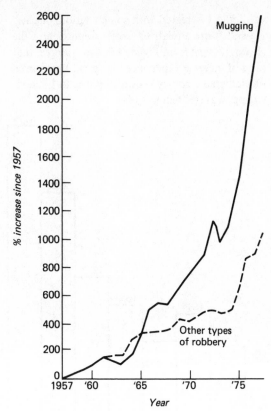

Figure 4.7 Mugging in the MPD compared with other types of robbery
percentage increases, 1957–1977

as a whole. In 1975, just sixteen years later, there were twice as many
muggings as this *on 'L' District alone.*

Summary

Whatever conclusions may be drawn from sets of facts and figures, it
seems clear that they are always likely to form an important background to more detailed research into causes, effects, developments,
trends and explanations. It is for such reasons that the statistics relating
to robbery and mugging have been examined so closely here. But even
if these provide a 'dramatic' initial impact it is important to stress not
only that, for the good reasons which have already been discussed at

some length, the figures should be treated with some caution, but also that even today mugging still forms a relatively small proportion of the total volume of crime. It can be seen from Figure 4.8, for example, that despite the very high rates of increase experienced in recent years, even by 1977, of the 569,000 indictable crimes known to police in London, the total number of muggings was still below 4,000.

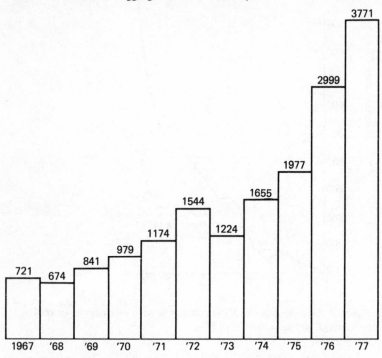

Figure 4.8 Mugging in the MPD: crimes known to police, 1967–77

Moreover, statistics prove absolutely nothing in themselves. Certainly it would be unwise to look at the various graphs and diagrams contained in this chapter and to assume at once that modern society is doomed — as Hunt (1975: 40) appears to be arguing when he tells us that

> violent crimes continue to multiply, the harried police manage to solve a smaller proportion of them than ever, the court calendars and prisons are choked and unmanageable, and great cities slowly sink into medieval savagery.

But the fact remains that, of the 'serious' crimes, robbery is numerically the largest category (there are about 150 murders and about the same number of rapes committed in the Metropolitan Police District each year), while, as an attempt has here been made to show, of the different classes of robbery it is in respect of mugging that the most serious deterioration has recently taken place. Indeed, there can be no denying that *the statistics are available* to support the arguments of those who contend, for example, that 'the streets of London are becoming like New York'. If there is to be any hope at all of halting this statistically obvious trend, then a precise knowledge of the background and the meaning of mugging is surely an essential prerequisite. This is the objective of the next, and main, part of this study, for which the words of Crick (1974: 21, 38) provide a fitting introduction:

> Many people, not simply addicted writers of letters to the press, seem convinced that 'this kind of violence' — whatever particular and small incident they are worrying about at the time — is unique to our times and if not checked will escalate, that 'one thing leads to another', that there is a linear progression from disorder in the classroom to disorder in the streets, from mugging and rape to riot and revolution . . . . I have not denied the existence of such violence, only sought to put it in proportion. If we believe it morally wrong but do not believe that it urgently threatens the fabric of civilised society, then we have time coolly and rationally both to study its causes and to act experimentally.

[5]   A study of mugging in London during the 1970s

Introduction

The intention throughout has been to conduct an in-depth study which, both in absolute and comparative terms, could provide a basis for those more general sociological considerations discussed at length in Part 2.[1] Once it had been decided to study mugging in the Metropolitan Police District, and that the general method of approach would be to examine in detail the original crime sheets (Forms 478) submitted by Districts,[2] the only remaining problem was that of choosing, firstly, which particular crimes should be analysed and, secondly, exactly what information should be collected.

As to the choice of sample, it had to be accepted that all information collected about offences or offenders would very quickly become dated. It was hoped and expected that this would actually have very little effect on the production of a worthwhile and meaningful study but, at the same time, it was felt that it would be preferable to extend any choice of sample over a fairly lengthy period of time (in the hope that it would then include a wide range of changing circumstances and practices), rather than concentrate on a continuous period of, say, six months which could conceivably prove unrepresentative in terms of such factors as hours of darkness, identifiable trends or particular methods of operation.[3]

Since there was clearly a limit to the number of offences which could adequately be analysed, there was a further choice to be made as to whether to sample by time alone or also by area. A small pilot survey was therefore carried out, as a result of which it was decided to include *all* muggings occurring throughout the *whole* of the Metropolitan Police District for the months of February and August[4] during the four years 1971, 1972, 1973 and 1974.

A working definition of 'mugging' has been discussed at some length in chapter 2, but a further consideration should be mentioned at this point. Due to the inevitable timelag in submitting crime reports to the central statistical department, the published number of muggings for any given month will *include* certain cases 'left over' from previous months and *exclude* certain other cases, especially those occurring right at the end of the period, or in which it is felt an arrest may be imminent. This factor has been taken fully into account in order to establish a 'true' total for each individual month, since it was felt that only on this basis could meaningful comparisons be made.[5]

As far as this study is concerned the number of muggings in any given month therefore comprises:

the published total of 'Robberies in the open following sudden attack' (of private property only, and *not* following even a brief association)
minus
those cases which were found to have taken place during a previous month,
plus
those cases for which (and for whatever reason) the crime sheet had not arrived in time for inclusion.[6]

The actual numbers involved are as indicated by the following table, from which it can be seen that the total sample to be analysed amounts to 1,010.

Table 5.1 *Mugging sample: monthly breakdown*

Month	Published 'mugging' totals	Occurred in previous months	Subsequently recorded	Revised totals
Feb. 1971	107	– 7	+ 3	103
Aug. 1971	113	– 3	+14	124
Feb. 1972	139	– 9	+ 9	139
Aug. 1972	166	–10	+12	168
Feb. 1973	125	–15	+14	124
Aug. 1973	96	– 4	+17	109
Feb. 1974	115	– 4	+ 5	116
Aug. 1974	132	–26	+21	127
Totals	993	–78	+95	1,010

In passing, it is felt that the wide variation between the published and the 'true' totals ought to be stressed. Taking the eight months as a whole, the 'true' total is 1,010 as compared to the published total of 993. This represents an error of only about 2 per cent, but it can be seen that for certain specific months the difference is much greater. The point is well illustrated by a comparison between August 1973 and August 1974. On the basis of the published figures the increase involved amounts to almost 40 per cent − yet, once the appropriate additions and subtractions in respect of previous and subsequent months have been made, this figure shrinks to a very much more 'reasonable' 16 per cent. Clearly this is a factor which ought to be taken into account whenever monthly (and possibly even annual) comparisons are being made.

Turning to what information should be collected it was decided simply to gather every item of information generally available and which promised to throw any light at all on the type of crime being studied.[7] For each of the 1,010 muggings in question, therefore, data was recorded on specially prepared 'field sheets' under each of the following headings:

Date As such this is of little value but does, of course, enable an analysis to be carried out in respect of the day of the week on which the crimes occurred.

Time of day An essential piece of information since, in combination with the previous heading, it can give an indication of possible patterns of attack.

Number/sex of attackers In particular this gives an indication of the involvement of 'gangs'.[8]

Age of attackers The categories used relate mainly to the legal definitions of 'Children' and 'Young Persons', and then to the somewhat arbitrary cut-off point of under or over the age of 21.[9] Since all reported cases for the months in question − not merely those involving an arrest − are included, there were naturally a number of 'not knowns'.

Arrests Simply an indication of the number of persons arrested for the particular offence in question. It might be noted that a single arrest out of any number of assailants still rates as a case 'cleared up'.[10]

Sex and age of person attacked As in the case of 'attackers', except that a further breakdown relating to 'more than 50' (not relevant to attackers) was included.[11]

Injury Whether 'Fatal', 'Serious', 'Slight', or 'None'. The distinction between 'Serious' and 'Slight' is rather arbitrary but, as far as any Metropolitan Police classification is concerned, normally relates to whether or not a visit to hospital has been necessary.

Weapon Self-explanatory.

Location Since, by definition, muggings are committed 'in the open' this category was perhaps unnecessary. However, it was possible that a pattern could emerge relating, say, to parks or towpaths.

Report number This refers to the police divisional serial number of the crime sheet in question. It therefore gives an indication of area, and also provides a means of tracing the offence should further research prove necessary.

Stolen The amount of cash, type of article, and stated value of that article.[12]

Since some 500,000 indictable crimes come to the notice of the Metropolitan Police each year it proved to be a considerable undertaking even to extract the 1,010 relevant crime sheets, especially since, once all the information for the month in question had been recorded, the crime sheets submitted during the following three months[13] were perused in order to cater for any 'late entries'.[14] Eventually, however, this task was completed to produce the raw data which will here be reviewed in three separate ways. Firstly, since the sample was deliberately chosen both to cover a lengthy period of time and also to point to any differences between summer and winter, the eight individual months will be compared one against the other. Secondly, taking the sample of 1,010 muggings as a whole, the data relating to each of the separate headings will be analysed in some detail in the expectation of being able to produce a picture of the 'typical' mugging. Thirdly, and most important of all, comparisons will be made with other appropriate studies in order to identify areas of similarity or change.

'Internal' comparisons

Tables of totals for each of the eight months under each of the eleven headings may be found in Appendix 3. These have been analysed in some depth in an attempt both to identify seasonal variations and also to establish what changes, if any, had taken place in the pattern of mugging throughout the period February 1971 to August 1974. In general terms the sample was found to be homogeneous, and only under the following headlines were there any variations (albeit not statistically significant)[15] which were worthy of even passing reference.

(i) *Winter/summer*

Time of day The two sets of data may be plotted as in Figure 5.1.

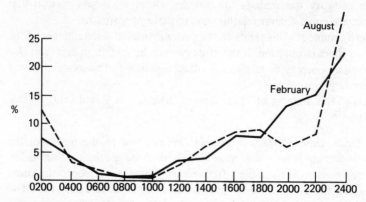

Figure 5.1 Mugging sample by time of day: February compared with August

It can be seen that between 0400 and 1800 the pattern is almost identical, but that in August there were far fewer offences committed between 1800 and 2200 (88 or 16.7 per cent as opposed to 143 or 29.7 per cent in February) — a trend which is in fact counterbalanced by totals for the period 2200 to 0200 (259 or 49 per cent as opposed to 170 or 35.3 per cent in February). In other words, shorter periods of darkness do not, as might be expected, mean fewer muggings, they simply mean that about the same number of muggings will be concentrated into a shorter period of time.

Sex of victim The percentage breakdown here is as follows:

February   Male 77.2%   Female 22.8%
August   Male 83.9%   Female 16.1%

Although the difference is not marked, there is at least some evidence here of the generally more 'vulnerable' female being at comparatively greater risk in winter-time.[16]

Cases cleared up Here the figures are:

February   156 out of 482, or 32.4%
August   142 out of 528, or 26.9%

Statistically speaking this could certainly be a chance variation: however, 14 *more* clear-ups from a total of 46 *less* cases could possibly lend support to the hypothesis that during the winter, with fewer other commitments and with less likelihood of holiday absences, police are likely to be able to devote more of their attention to the investigation of street crime.

(ii) *1971-74*

Size of group There is an indication that there had been a move away from group, as opposed to individual, involvement. For the sample as a whole, the attack was perpetrated by two or more persons in 73.4 per cent of cases. This proportion has, however, been progressively reducing as follows:

Feb./Aug. 1971	81.5%
Feb./Aug. 1972	78.5%
Feb./Aug. 1973	73.9%
Feb./Aug. 1974	61.7%

Sex of victim It would appear that females comprise an increasingly greater proportion of those attacked, the figures being:

Feb./Aug. 1971	8.3%
Feb./Aug. 1972	16.6%
Feb./Aug. 1973	20.2%
Feb./Aug. 1974	32.1%

Cases cleared up As shown by the following figures, after remaining at much the same level during 1971, 1972 and 1973, the clear-up rate reduced substantially in 1974:

Feb./Aug. 1971	31.7%
Feb./Aug. 1972	30.9%
Feb./Aug. 1973	31.8%
Feb./Aug. 1974	23.5%[17]

It should be stressed that none of the above findings is statistically significant: moreover, the other eight 'seasonal comparisons', and the other eight 'period comparisons' *not* specifically mentioned reveal little or no meaningful variation. All things considered, therefore, it was felt that the 1,010 muggings could be treated as a single homogeneous sample, and could be analysed accordingly.

Muggings described[18]

Once all the data had been collected it was used first of all in a straightforward descriptive sense. For each heading appropriate breakdowns were established and illustrative graphs prepared. These may be found on the following pages. Each would appear to be largely self-explanatory, though an 'interpretation' has been included in each case.

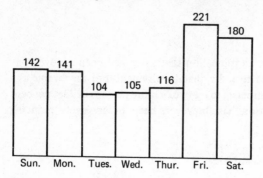

Figure 5.2 Mugging sample: day of week

Relatively few offences were committed on Tuesdays, Wednesdays or Thursdays. Fridays account for some 40 per cent of the total. Presumably this is a reflection of such factors as Friday traditionally being pay-day, and weekends normally being the time for social functions and therefore for greater interaction between groups or individuals.

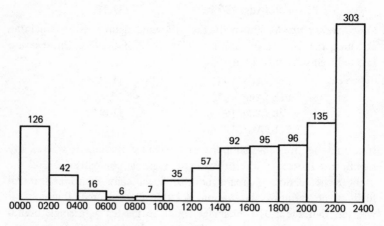

Figure 5.3 Mugging sample: time of day

Not surprisingly, it would appear that very few muggings are committed between 4.00 a.m. and 10.00 a.m. There is then a gradual build-up until 10.00 p.m., when there occurs the greatest concentration of offences in the two-hour period up to midnight. The frequently mentioned factor of pub closing times could well have a considerable bearing here.

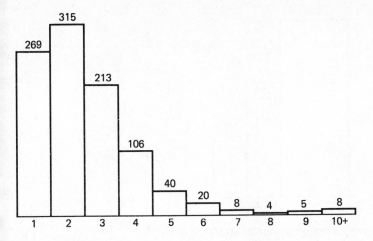

Figure 5.4 Mugging sample: attackers, size of group

A group of two is the most common formation with a single individual being the next most likely. In almost 20 per cent of cases the group comprised four or more: putting this in another way, in four cases out of five there was *not* what one could reasonably term a gang involvement.

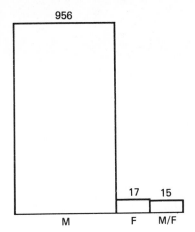

Figure 5.5 Mugging sample: attackers, sex

The vast majority of assailants are male. In less than 2 per cent of cases were females alone involved. This probably comes as no great surprise, though one might have expected to find a greater mixed (i.e. male and female together) involvement.

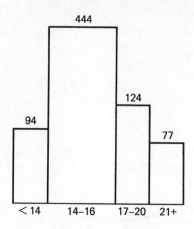

Figure 5.6 Mugging sample: attackers, age

Mugging is very clearly an adolescent crime. Of the 739 cases in which the victim was able to judge the assailant's age, 538 (72.7 per cent) were under the age of 17, and only 77 (10.4 per cent) were over the age of 21. This is without doubt one of the most significant findings, and is a theme which will be expanded upon in due course.

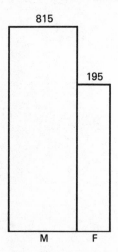

Figure 5.7 Mugging sample: victims, sex

This is perhaps the most surprising finding. Despite the presumed greater 'vulnerability' of females, more than 80 per cent of victims were in fact male. If nothing else this surely indicates that the average mugger is not simply after an 'easy catch'.

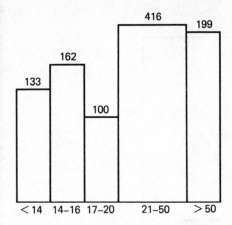

Figure 5.8 Mugging sample: victims, age

This presents a rather complex picture, but it can be seen that, whereas only about 10 per cent of assailants were over the age of 21, about 60 per cent of victims came within this age group. As to the involvement of the over-50s, this amounted to virtually 0 per cent of assailants and about 20 per cent of victims. This differential will be discussed in much greater detail later in this chapter.

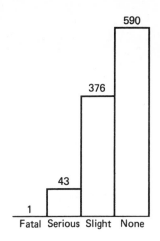

Figure 5.9 Mugging sample: victims, degree of injury

Over half the victims received no form of injury. In only 44 cases was hospitalisation required. This includes one fatality, which would of course be recorded by police as a murder.

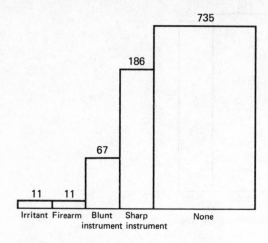

Figure 5.10 Mugging sample: weapon used

Somewhat surprisingly, in almost three-quarters of the cases no weapon was used. Sharp instruments (for example knives or razors) were far more common than blunt (for example clubs or coshes), while the use of a firearm was rare.

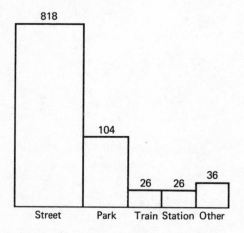

Figure 5.11 Mugging sample: location

Roughly 80 per cent of attacks occurred in the street, 10 per cent in a park and 10 per cent elsewhere. One might perhaps have expected relatively more offences to have taken place in secluded parks rather than in public thoroughfares, but otherwise the result is unsurprising.

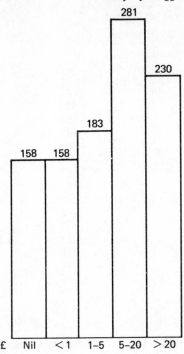

Figure 5.12 Mugging sample: stolen value

In almost exactly half the cases the value of cash or property stolen amounted to less than £5. Though the effects of inflation must obviously be borne in mind, there is a clear indication here that substantial monetary gain is not a normal outcome.

There are two further factors — locality and race — which, both from a descriptive and a sociological point of view, proved to be of such interest and importance that they were eventually analysed in some depth. The detailed results of these studies are discussed in chapters 6 and 7, but a brief review will also be included here.

Locality The sample of 1,010 muggings was found to be distributed between the various Metropolitan Police Districts as follows:

Table 5.2 *Mugging sample: district distribution*

'A' District	16
'B' District	35
'C' District	98
'D' District	43

Table 5.2 cont.

'E'	District	43
'F'	District	39
'G'	District	50
'H'	District	41
'J'	District	19
'K'	District	54
'L'	District	149
'M'	District	36
'N'	District	48
'P'	District	57
'Q'	District	50
'R'	District	19
'S'	District	15
'T'	District	20
'V'	District	11
'W'	District	61
'X'	District	41
'Y'	District	46
'Z'	District	19
	Total	1,010

It can be seen that the variation is very wide. 'C'[19], which in terms of acreage is in fact one of the smallest Districts, and especially 'L', stand out well ahead of the rest, while a number of Districts (notably 'V') are obviously well below the average — which is about 44. If such an analysis is pursued just slightly further the differences become even more marked. For example, during August 1972 there were 24 muggings in 'L', and not a single one in either 'S' or 'V'. Moreover, the vast majority of the total for 'L' Division as a whole occurred, in fact, on the very much smaller *Division* of 'LD' (Brixton).

At this stage, it is perhaps sufficient to state the obvious conclusion that locality appears to have a very marked bearing on the likelihood of a mugging occurring.

Race Initially, a conscious decision was taken to avoid this issue for reasons such as the following:
(a) The race of assailants, or even of victims, is not universally recorded (or known) by police.[20]
(b) If, say, four out of a 'gang' of six assailants are known to be black West Indians, and the other two white, then difficulties in analysis could clearly arise.[21]
(c) There are a number of problems relating to 'controls'. For example,

national census figures are based on country of birth or parentage, police recording practice normally on colour of skin.[22]

(d) Race is a factor which has not been included in a number of studies which it was anticipated might be used for comparison purposes.[23]

From an initial perusal of the crime sheets, however, it quickly became obvious that race is one of the most important considerations relating to the crime of mugging, and one which most certainly should be analysed in some depth in a study of this nature. This has now been done and the main findings included in chapter 7. In order to complete the picture of a typical mugging, however, the essential results will also be set out here.

As stated above, police recording of race is effectively based on colour of skin. It is, in fact, expressed in terms of 'Identity Codes'[24] as follows:

IC 1 White-skinned European type
IC 2 Dark-skinned European type
IC 3 Negroid type
IC 4 Asian type
IC 5 Oriental type
IC 6 Arabian type

The sample of 1,010 muggings was analysed on such a basis to produce results as indicated in Table 5.3. Clearly, there is at least some evidence here to support the contention that mugging mainly consists of 'blacks attacking whites'.[25]

Table 5.3 *Mugging sample: identity-code breakdown*[26]

	Assailants	Victims
IC 1	222 (30%)	882 (88%)
IC 2	67 (9%)	23 (2%)
IC 3	429 (58%)	52 (5%)
IC 4	19 (3%)	49 (5%)
IC 5	1 (–)	2 (–)
IC 6	1 (–)	2 (–)

Summary of Results

Generalising from the chosen sample of 1,010 muggings the following pattern has emerged:

Attacker The attacker is almost certain to be male and is likely to be alone or in a small group of two or three. The chances are high that he will be under the age of 21, and more often than not he will be black.

Victim Somewhat surprisingly, the victim of a mugging is normally male. He is likely to be over the age of 21, and therefore older than his assailant, and in the majority of cases he will be white.

Circumstances Although a substantial minority take place in parks or other types of open space, most muggings occur in the street. It is on a Friday or a Saturday that an attack is most likely to take place, particularly between the hours of 10.00 p.m. and midnight.

Result Injury to a victim is a distinct possibility, while it is unlikely that the attacker will ever be apprehended by police, or that the stolen property will ever be recovered.

Figure 5.13 A typical mugging

Comparison with other studies

As emphasised in chapter 1, it would appear that very little detailed research into mugging (whether in London or elsewhere) has previously been carried out — the one notable exception being *Robbery in London*.[27] The obvious plan of comparing my own results with those of McClintock has therefore been adopted and, indeed, forms a major part of this chapter and consequently of the study as a whole. Before so doing, however, it is felt that brief mention should be made of certain other sources of information against which a number of appropriate comparisons can usefully be made. These are:

(a) Henry Mayhew, *London Labour and the London Poor*;
(b) Morton M. Hunt, *The Mugging*;
(c) T. Sellin and M. E. Wolfgang, *The Measurement of Delinquency*.

(a) *Henry Mayhew*

From Henry Mayhew's description of 'highway robberies' as they occurred more than a hundred years ago may be extracted information on the following five factors:

(i) *Time of day* 'generally done at dusk, and rarely during the day'. Today this would be more like 'done at dusk or, more generally, late at night'.

(ii) *Size of group* 'often done by one person, at other times by two or more in company'. This would describe exactly those results obtained from the present study.

(iii) *Sex of attackers* 'by young men'. As we have seen, in general terms this is certainly still true.

(iv) *Age of attackers* Depending on the precise method of attack employed, Mayhew describes the typical assailant of the 1860s as being 'from nineteen years and upwards', 'from twenty-five and upwards', or 'from thirty to forty years of age'. In the 1970s almost all London muggers are younger than 21, with the great majority being under the age of 17.

(v) *Victim* 'a person who has a watch or noticed carrying money on his person'. Small amounts of money found on a person purely as a matter of chance now appear to be very much the order of the day.

Although it must be stressed once again that Mayhew's findings are distinctly impressionistic, there is at least some evidence here to suggest that over the past hundred years or so the pattern of street crime has made a significant movement in the direction of youthful involvement in indiscriminate attacks.

(b) *Morton M. Hunt*

As pointed out earlier, Morton M. Hunt's style in his book *The Mugging* is extremely journalistic, while his statements appear to be based on personal feelings rather than on a precise analysis of the available data. Nevertheless, there are a number of what might be termed 'surface' comparisons which might help to throw some light on the basic differences, if any, between muggings in an American city (in the 1960s) and muggings in London (in the 1970s).

(i) *Time of day* 'Those who are on the sidewalks late at night are three times as likely to be victimised as those who stay indoors after dark.' Although the meaning of this statement is not altogether clear, it appears to confirm yet again that mugging is mainly a night-time offence.

(ii) *Sex of attackers* '94 per cent of all persons arrested for robbery are males'. As we have seen, in this study the figure is actually 98 per cent.

(iii) *Age of attackers* 'three-quarters of all persons arrested for robbery are juveniles, youths or young adults under twenty-five'. In this study assailants under the age of 25 represent over 80 per cent of the total.

(iv) *Age of victims* 'the elderly being too slow-moving to escape and too feeble to offer effective resistance or counterattack, and hence being selected as victims more often than the young'. Perhaps surprisingly, this is not confirmed by the present study, in which victims over the age of 50 account for only about 20 per cent of the overall total.

(v) *Dress of victims* 'the man or woman whose clothing indicates that he or she has at least a modest income, and is therefore likely to be carrying a fair amount of cash, is particularly prone to attack'. This approximates to Mayhew's findings but is not supported by my own research.

(vi) *Numbers* 'A person walking alone is far more apt to be a target than one walking with a companion, even when the latter is elderly and frail.' This finding is confirmed by the present study which shows that only a very small proportion of victims were not alone at the time of the attack.

(vii) *Race* 'Non-white muggers most often choose white strangers as their victims.' Whatever the precise reasons for this phenomenon it would appear this is one of the main characteristics of mugging both in New York and in London.

Clearly, there is a high level of agreement between Hunt's conclusions and my own, especially in terms of assailants (male, young and black). Once again, however, there is some evidence to suggest that, in London in the 1970s, there was a definite move towards indiscriminate attacks, with very little heed being paid to such obvious factors as extreme old age or supposed affluence.

(c) *Sellin and Wolfgang*

As pointed out in chapter 1, the specific research into robbery contained in Sellin and Wolfgang's *The Measurement of Delinquency* has little direct relevance to this study, firstly because the sample selected was so small, and secondly because it relates to juveniles only and to arrested persons only. Nevertheless, from the following extract it may again be seen, in passing, that there appears to be much in common between juvenile robbery in the USA and mugging in London:

> the total property loss is but 354 dollars and the mean, median and mode are only 5 dollars . . . the range is from 5 cents to 66 dollars, and only four cases produced a loss of over 20 dollars . . . . All but one of the 27 offences occurred in the street or in the open, to which the offenders had legal access . . . . There was one victim per robbery except in two cases, each of which had four victims . . . . In 14, or 52 per cent, of the cases the victims were juvenile, in 12 they were adult, and, in one case with four victims, they were mixed juvenile and adult . . . . Verbal threats only were employed in one case, a knife in 4, a blunt instrument or physical force in 23, and a gun in only one.

F. H. McClintock

As pointed out above, it was felt from the beginning that comparison with Professor McClintock's work would prove to be an important part of the study. *Robbery in London* was published in 1961 and relates, in the main, to robberies which occurred in London in 1950 and 1957. The very latest figures quoted are the provisional totals for 1960 and since, as shown in chapter 4, the really dramatic increases have taken place since that time, there arose the obvious opportunity of trying to establish whether crimes of this type had changed in 'quality' as well as in quantity over the period in question.

Mainly because mugging was specifically included in only a small part of McClintock's research there are a great many findings both in his work and mine which cannot in fact be compared. It was felt, however, that comparisons could usefully be made under each of the following headings:

> Day of week
> Time of day
> Age of attackers[28]
> Sex of victim
> Location
> Stolen value

Firstly, a series of chi-square tests were carried out in order to establish whether or not there was a significant difference between the results obtained in 1950-57 and those of the present study. The findings may be summarised as follows:

	Value	v	Significance level exceeded	
Day of week	16.86	6	.990	16.81
Time of day	33.99	7	.999	24.32
Age of attackers	580.96	1	.999	10.83
Sex of victim	17.09	1	.999	10.83
Location	21.86	2	.999	10.83
Stolen value	10.97	5	(.950	11.07)

Although it must be accepted that the chi-square is statistically a somewhat unsophisticated test, there is a strong indication here that under each heading (other than 'Stolen value') the probability of the difference between the two sets of findings having come about by chance is slight and, in most cases, negligible. In other words, for five of the six mugging characteristics analysed a statistically significant change has taken place.

The next step was to establish the direction and exact extent of these changes. It was felt that, in the first instance, the best way of doing this would be visually — by plotting side by side the results obtained by McClintock in 1950 and 1957, and by myself from the sample of muggings which occurred during the period 1971-74. The resultant diagrams, together with appropriate comment, may be found on this and the following pages.

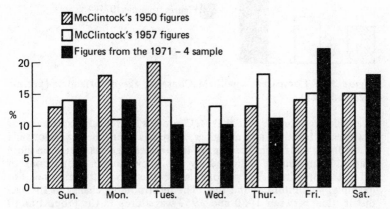

Figure 5.14 Comparisons with McClintock: day of week

Although comparisons under this heading are unlikely to hold much significance, it is interesting to note that while at one time the greatest number of attacks occurred on a Tuesday, this is now the 'safest' day of all. There has been a definite swing towards Fridays and Saturdays which together now account for about 40 per cent of the total as compared to only about 30 per cent in 1950-57.

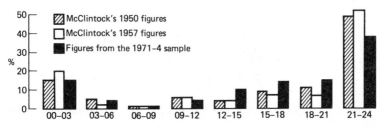

Figure 5.15 Comparisons with McClintock: time of day

Here there has been a broadly similar pattern throughout the period in question. There has in fact been a slight reduction in the proportion of offences occurring during the hours of darkness, though the six-hour period between 8.00 p.m. and 2.00 a.m. still accounts for many more attacks than the other eighteen hours put together.

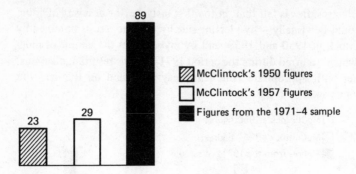

Figure 5.16 Comparisons with McClintock: age of offenders (percentage under 21)

Even allowing for the fact that McClintock's figures refer to robbery as a whole, rather than just muggings, there has clearly been a major shift of emphasis under this heading. In fact, the change has been even more marked than can be indicated by the above simple proportions of offences committed by persons under the age of twenty-one. For example, McClintock found that 'The most notable change in the age-distribution between 1950 and 1957 was a drop in the proportion of juveniles and a rise in the proportion aged between seventeen and twenty-one', and even surmised, 'It may be that, as this group grows older, the average age of those convicted of robbery will increase'. In fact, for the 1970s sample more than 70 per cent of assailants were under the age of seventeen.

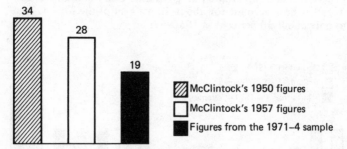

Figure 5.17 Comparisons with McClintock: sex of victims (percentage female)

As pointed out in 'Muggings described', one of the most surprising findings of this research was that, despite the presumed greater 'vulnerability' of females, more than 80 per cent of victims were in fact male. It can now be seen from the above graph that since 1950 there seems to have been a marked drift away from female involvement as victims.

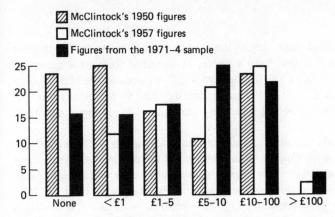

Figure 5.18 Comparisons with McClintock: stolen value

McClintock concluded that 'In most of the cases in which cash and personal belongings were taken the main object was the cash, and the stealing of personal property such as the contents of handbags, wallets and cases, was incidental.' There is nothing to suggest that this does not still apply today. The slight move towards a higher stolen value is no doubt due to the effects of inflation: indeed, it is interesting to note that the proportion of offences in which less than £5 was stolen was about the same in the 1970s as in 1950.

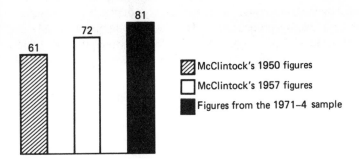

Figure 5.19 Comparisons with McClintock: location (percentage in street)

Over 30 per cent of the muggings studied by McClintock took place in parks, commons, country lanes or footpaths. By the 1970s about four muggings in five were committed in the street. (Of course, this change may be explained at least partially by the extensive building of roads which has taken place in the interim period — that is to say there are simply fewer country lanes and footpaths in existence.)

Summary

Having gained some idea of the extent of the problem in the previous chapter, it has now been possible, by means of studying a randomly-chosen sample of 1,010 muggings which occurred in the Metropolitan Police District in the 1970s, to identify some of the more important characteristics involved, and thus to produce a description of a 'typical' mugging.

Comparisons with the work of Henry Mayhew and Morton M. Hunt have lent some support to the view that in London in recent years there has been a definite move towards youthful involvement in indiscriminate attacks, and this has been confirmed by comparisons with McClintock's far more relevant study. The reduction in the age of offenders is particularly marked but, in addition, the concentration on male victims, the considerable reduction in real terms of the average stolen value, and perhaps even the move away from relatively 'out-of-the-way' venues such as parks and country lanes, all seem to give at least some indication that planned muggings based on the expectation of pecuniary reward have now largely given way to *ad hoc* opportunist attacks.

The questions 'What is a mugging?' and 'What is the extent of the problem?' have been answered. Now we must turn to the even more important task of trying to answer such questions as 'For what reasons do muggings take place?', 'Why is it that mugging has increased so dramatically in recent years?', and 'To what type of person does mugging appear an attractive proposition?'. These will be discussed initially in terms of ecology, deprivation, and race, before an attempt is then made to answer the most important question of all: 'What can be done to alleviate the problem?'.

Part II

Part II

[6] Theories of deviance

Introduction

Part I of this study has been almost exclusively descriptive: so far little attempt has been made at explanation, but now, as a first tentative step in that direction, this chapter now looks at a number of those existing sociological theories which may possibly help to explain the existence of, or the recent increase in, mugging in London.

Two particular approaches immediately come to mind. Firstly, since it has already been shown that the geographical distribution of mugging throughout the Metropolitan Police District is by no means uniform, it would seem appropriate to take a brief look at human or social ecology which

> is concerned with the relationships which exist between people who share a common habitat or local territory and which are distinctly related to the character of the territory itself; it is a study of social structure in relation to the local environment.[1]

Secondly, if only because the offender's lack of material resources is so frequently put forward as an adequate explanation for mugging (or, indeed, any other type of crime), it would seem only proper to spend a little time discussing a few of the many theories stemming initially from a concern with poverty or deprivation.

Social ecology

It has frequently been demonstrated (indeed, statistically it is beyond dispute) that crime is predominantly an urban problem, and when it comes to a study of crime or delinquency in an urban area the relationship between what is sometimes called the 'social geography' of the city and the location of offences,[2] provides one obvious point of departure in any attempt at explanation.

The search for such a relationship by making use of what is normally termed an ecological approach, the basic tenet of which is that certain areas of a city produce not only a majority of lawbreakers but a more than average number in proportion to their population, has had a long and distinguished history. Well over a hundred years ago, for example, Henry Mayhew, with the use of maps and statistical correlations,[3] not only pointed out that crime is concentrated in certain areas, but also specified which particular kinds of crime were to be found in which particular areas within the city.[4] It has been pointed out by Terence Morris (1957: 42-52) that the approach was, in fact, implicit in A. M. Guerry's material even earlier than this, but there can be no doubt that it reached its zenith between the two world wars at the hands of Clifford Shaw and Henry D. McKay who developed the pioneer work of the famous Chicago school of urban sociologists under the guidance of Robert Park.

The word 'ecology'[5] was originally borrowed from the field of biology by Park and his followers because it incorporated such ideas as 'symbiosis' or the habitual living together of organisms of different species in a biotic balance. Park's whole approach in fact depended explicitly upon a fully organic model of society, borrowing directly the language and the concepts of plant and animal ecology.

It was an intriguing and even revolutionary notion at the time, and it has continued to command the interest of social scientists to this day: as a directly productive theory, however, it has long since ceased to exert much influence on the mainstream of sociological thinking. But it should be remembered that even Shaw and McKay did not rely over-much on Park's fullblown biotic model. For them, as for various other members of the Chicago school, the adaptation of ecology as a sociological theory depended upon relating the commission of crime to a number of distinct zones radiating — rather like the growth rings of a tree trunk — from the centre of the city in a series of concentric circles.[6]

These can be categorised in the following way:

Zone 1   The 'Loop' or central business district.
Zone 2   The zone of transition containing the rooming house district, the underworld dens, the brothels, Chinatown, the Ghetto, and 'Little Sicily'.
Zone 3   The zone of working men's homes.

Zone 4   The residential zone of apartment houses (flats), residential hotels and, on the edge, single family dwellings.
Zone 5   The commuters' zone, i.e. respectable suburbia.

On such a basis,[7] the claim is that a particular pattern of delinquency can be associated with each separate zone to give a fairly steady progression from very high to very low as one travels from the city centre to the outskirts. But it was the zone next to the central business district which predominantly concerned the ecologists for it was here they claimed invariably to find the main concentration of delinquents.

The formal characteristics of this 'zone of transition' are described by Morris (1957: 19) as:

> physical deterioration, overcrowding, a mobile population and a proximity to the areas of industry and commerce. Its social characteristics are primarily a lack of informal agencies of social control whereby the norms accepted by the wider society may be maintained.

Furthermore, it was found by Shaw and McKay that while the population of such areas changed in the course of time, being replaced by new waves of immigrants and transients, the delinquency rate remained stable. This, in fact, may be thought of as the key concept of the ecological approach since it implies that there are certain pervading social influences which continue to operate in isolation and to imprint themselves upon successive groups of inhabitants; in other words, it points to the importance of environmental as opposed to psychological factors in the moulding of the delinquent.

Ecological studies of more recent years

Many studies along ecological lines have been carried out over the past forty or fifty years but since most of these, beginning with Andrew Lind's 1931 research in Honolulu, have been reviewed to such good effect by Terence Morris (1957), there would seem little point in repeating the exercise here. However, there is one further study, carried out since Morris's book was published, which is certainly worthy of mention.

In 1963–66 John Rex and Robert Moore found in Sparkbrook (Birmingham) a zone of transition subculture which offered positive advantages to the criminal, particularly since the landlord 'asks no questions', their main conclusion being that:

> there is a class struggle over the use of houses and that this class struggle is the central process of the city as a social unit. In saying this we follow Max Weber who saw that class struggle was apt to emerge wherever people in a market situation enjoyed differential access to property and that such class struggles might therefore arise not merely around the use of the means of industrial production, but around the control of domestic property. (1967: 273-4)

Having identified seven types of 'housing class' they confirm that the zone of transition is simply that area of the city where the least privileged 'housing class' lives. Moreover, the housing situation of the zone of transition — typified by the lodging-house — is illegitimate from the point of view of the public authorities, and also has a low status in the city's scale of values. The obvious long-term solution of the resultant tension would be to re-house the lodging-house tenants in other types of accommodation, but the general housing shortage precludes this, leaving as the only alternative the segregation of the problem area from the rest of the city.[8]

Rex and Moore's approach is especially useful since it not only provides some further explanation of the emergence and continuing existence of the zone of transition (or delinquency area), but, by introducing the notion of housing classes, it suggests a specific link between the ecological approach and the theories of social deprivation which will be discussed later in this chapter.[9] For as Rex tells us:

> Life in the zone of transition has a very recognisable quality and those who have ever known it recognise it when they see it again. It is a life of squalor, of under-privilege and of conflict and for those who work there professionally it means sitting with clients in dreary church halls, offices and club rooms trying to solve their personal problems and trying to reconcile the attainment of their ends with those of others. It is a world far from the functionally integrated social system which sociologists are too fond of discussing. Only as sociologists begin to understand it will they begin to understand what the city is like on the underside. (1973: 98)

Social ecology and the present study

It was very much in line with this philosophy that a simplified version of the ecological approach was employed in relation to the current project. Before turning to the results obtained, however, two important distinctions must be resolved. The first of these relates to the difference between 'crime commission' and 'delinquent residence', that is to say between the location of *offences* and the location of *offenders.* There are arguments in favour of using either of these methods,[10] but here — mainly due to the ready availability of the data — it is the former which will be employed.[11]

The second distinction which must be borne in mind relates to whether population, rateable value or area on the one hand, offences or court appearances on the other, should be used to establish the 'delinquency rate' of a given zone. Morris gives due consideration to this matter and concludes that although density of crime per acre is open to certain objections such as:

> If the areas compared are of similar size and are equally densely developed, then the rate undoubtedly reflects the concentration of crime in a physical sense. If, however, an area contains large expanses of parkland or water, the rate may give a false notion of dispersion, whereas crimes may be highly concentrated in a particular part of the area.

it is at least a realistic measure since it reflects the differences in the frequency of crimes between one area and another in a way which other rates do not. This then is the method which will be employed here in the adapted form of 'muggings per square mile'.[12]

Having made these decisions, the next and most important step was of course to plot the location of each of the 1,010 muggings on a map of the Metropolitan Police District. The result of this exercise can be seen in Figure 6.1, while in Figure 6.2 the ecological concept of radiating zones has been superimposed. Even visually the concentration of offences towards the centre shows up to good effect, but to emphasise this still more Table 6.1 shows, in numerical terms, the breakdown of muggings per square mile by zone. It can be seen at once that there is considerable support here for Schmid's traditionalist view that 'there is a general tendency for most crimes to decrease more or less in direct proportion to the distance from the centre of the city' (1960: 666), that is to say one of the basic hypotheses of the ecological approach is confirmed inasmuch as the mugging rate of the inner area is forty or fifty times that of the 'commuter zone'.

But before becoming too involved in the implications of such a

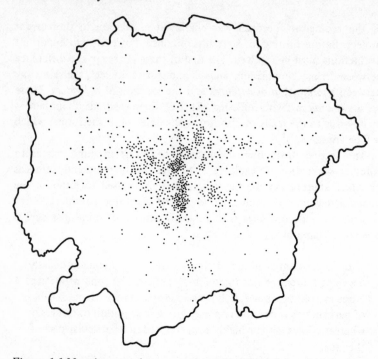

Figure 6.1 Mugging sample: geographical distribution

finding it will be as well to look rather more closely at the dot maps themselves. Even from casual observation it is clear that, although the grouping of offences is certainly biased towards the centre, there are two particular areas where the concentration is greatest: this is illustrated to greater effect by the 'isobar' method of Figure 6.3. It can easily be demonstrated, in fact, that the two areas concerned, 'C' District (or the West End) and 'L' District (London Borough of Lambeth), have a combined 'mugging index' of well over 100 as compared to a figure of only about 1.3 for the Metropolitan Police District as a whole. It would seem logical, then, to concentrate any further research on those areas rather than on the entire zone of transition within which there are demonstrably wide variations in the delinquency rate between one locality and another.[13]

One final consideration must be taken into account at this point: it is felt that in comparing the West End with Lambeth there is a crucial difference in the relationship between the place of commission of the offence and the place of residence of the offender. It is obvious that 'potential delinquents' will travel to places like Oxford Street, Regent

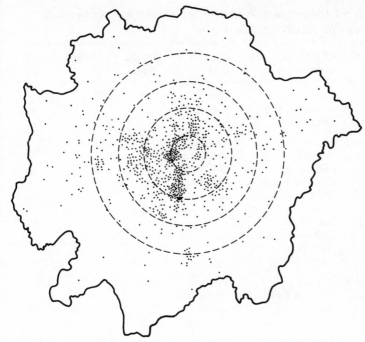

Figure 6.2 Mugging sample: geographical distribution by zone

Street and Piccadilly Circus to commit crimes, but that this is unlikely to be the case in the sidestreets of Brixton. What is being suggested in fact is that the proportion of muggings committed by *residents* of 'L' District is likely to be much higher than indicated by the 'L' District total, and the proportion on 'C' District much lower. Unfortunately, it has not been possible to put this hypothesis specifically to the test, and as far as can be ascertained there is no other independent evidence that can be quoted. There is no doubt, though, that teams of pickpockets, handbag snatchers and shoplifters frequently 'raid' the West End for comparatively easy pickings,[14] and it would seem not unreasonable to assume that this is likely to happen in the case of mugging too. In any event, it was on this surmise that it was decided to concentrate subsequent research on 'L' District alone which, even on the basis of the mugging figures as they stand, can easily be isolated as the greatest 'problem area'.

Social Ecology: A Review

In the course of the discussion so far, a number of drawbacks to the

Table 6.1 *Mugging sample: comparison of zones by reference to the Chicago School descriptions*

Zone	Chicago School description	Typical area	Square Miles	Muggings	Average
Zone 1	The 'Loop' or central business district	City West End	10	105	10.5
Zone 2	The zone of transition containing the rooming house district, the underworld dens, the brothels, Chinatown, the Ghetto and 'Little Sicily'	Lambeth Southwark Islington Camden	70	557	8.0
Zone 3	The zone of working mens' homes	Catford Norbury Leyton Finchley	120	172	1.4
Zone 4	The residential zone of apartment houses (flats), residential hotels and, on the edge, single family dwellings	Bromley Woodford Croydon Barnet	180	86	0.5
Zone 5	The commuters' zone, i.e. respectable suburbia	Biggin Hill Cheshunt Ruislip Esher	406	90	0.2

ecological approach have already become apparent: the time has now come to be rather more precise. Criticisms of the approach in general, and of the 'zonal hypothesis' in particular, include allegations that zones are looked at too much as facts rather than as a model (there are many reasons, notably topographical, why there can be no precise relationship between criminality and the city centre): that the approach is simply another form of determinism in that the suggestion is made that crime is determined by geography: that, if the theory is correct, why is everyone in the zone of transition not a criminal: that, in describing the

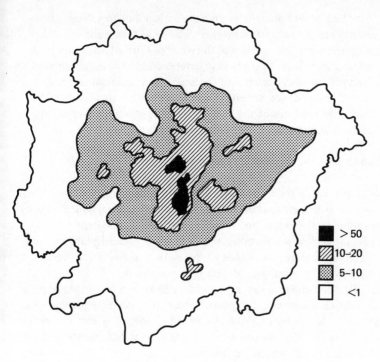

Figure 6.3 Mugging sample; distribution per square mile

symptoms of social disorganisation, the significance of stable patterns
of stable organisations are ignored: and that little attempt is made to
explain why delinquency areas came into being in the first place.

But there can be no doubt that *the* most telling criticism of social
ecology is that the geographical distribution of crime within a city is
no more and no less than one would expect. In itself it tells us nothing;
it is simply an indirect method of ascertaining where what we might
term social deprivation is at its highest level. The zone of transition is,
as it were, a necessary but not sufficient condition for an 'outbreak' of
delinquency.[15] As Morris (1957: 17, 130) confirms:

The natural area as a cultural isolate is to a considerable degree the
coincidental product of the economic differentiation between different physical areas. No one aspiring to the highest levels of social
status in the city chooses to live in an area dominated by industry
and commerce (a) because the smoke, grime and noise are physically
unpleasant, and (b) because rentals are proportionately lower and to

live there would give the impression of inability to validate, in money terms, the status to which a claim has been made . . . . The suggestion implicit in much of the work of Clifford Shaw and his collaborators is that the physical deterioration of a neighbourhood is somehow vitally related to the problem of delinquency and crime. The evidence, at least from Croydon, suggests that the physical characteristics of the area are of little relevance save as an indirect determinant of the social status of an area.

In essence, the argument is simply that:

(a) 'Slums' are likely to be located near the centre of any city or urban area since it is there that the housing and other facilities will, almost by definition, be the oldest, and therefore the most dilapidated.
(b) People of low social status, that is to say the 'social problem group' – including delinquents – tend to live in these slums simply because it is the only type of accommodation they can afford.
(c) QED, 'delinquent areas' as defined by Shaw will be located near the city centres. Moreover, the pervasiveness of these delinquency areas, emphasised so strongly by the traditional ecologists, is merely a reflection of the fact that no one other than 'potential delinquents' will ever be attracted to the area in the first place.

In other words, the ecological approach is based on something of a spurious correlation. There is in fact no *direct* causal connection between particular areas and delinquency: the area does not mould the individual, it simply attracts persons of a certain type because of factors such as the relative cheapness of the available housing.

As Taylor, Walton and Young (1973: 116) put it:

The most important implication of the use of biological analogies in explaining the development of housing zones in the city, and natural areas of delinquency, is the implication that the inhabitants of these zones and areas live where they do because of some personal characteristics they possess or because of some natural (and inevitable) feature of human selection.

But, as G. C. Holland (1843: 138) reminds us:

Families are not huddled together into dark ill-ventilated rooms from any peculiar pleasure it affords. They may indeed have become insensible of the inconvenience and wretchedness of such situations, but slender and uncertain means do not enable them to command more comfortable abodes. They are fixed there by circumstances.

Hence it may be concluded that social ecology *as such* is hardly worthy of further consideration — if only because it can so easily be subsumed under other, more meaningful, headings. For example, 'social dis-organisation or the lack of community effort' stressed by the ecologists is reflected in Merton's 'anomie', while the fact that 'Crime and delin-quency seemed to become part and parcel of the social traditions of these areas and were handed down through successive generations of inhabitants very much in the same way that language and other customs are transmitted'[16] is, of course, very reminiscent of Sutherland's 'dif-ferential association'.[17] Most important of all, since it has been argued that the ecological distribution is merely a reflection, or an indirect measure, of social deprivation, *this* is the topic which should be the subject of any further investigation.

Delinquency and deprivation

The apparent connection between poverty and crime has, of course, been a recurring theme in sociological thinking. It was certainly pointed to by Henry Mayhew in the mid nineteenth century,[18] while in the 1890s and early 1900s the pioneer social surveys of men such as Charles Booth[19] and B. S. Rowntree set the scene, as it were, for a wealth of similar studies and countless poverty/crime theories in later years.

One would instinctively assume that the writings of Marx would prove to be a profitable source of study. In fact he had little more than a passing interest in crime as such.[20] For him, crime was simply a 'strug-gle of the isolated individual against the prevailing conditions'. However (as W. G. Carson (1971: 7) tells us), to Marx's apostle Frederick Engels the apparent increase in crime (in 1848) was neither surprising, nor difficult, to explain; it was simply one manifestation of the exploitation of the proletariat by the emergent bourgeoisie, prospering under the principle of untrammelled competition:

There is no cause for surprise if the workers, treated as brutes, actually become such; or if they can maintain their consciousness of manhood only by cherishing the most glowing hatred, the most unbroken inward rebellion against the bourgeoisie in power. (1892: ch. 5).

This is an extreme view; and, in any case, the object of this chapter is not to develop specific political theories, or discuss in detail such matters as class consciousness. Nor are we talking today, as was Engels in 1848, of people being obliged to throw offal, garbage and excrement into the streets, or breathing putrefied air: rather, in the British tradition of social pragmatism, we are more interested here in the findings of researchers such as Sir Cyril Burt, who in the 1920s concluded that

> The correlation between the figures for juvenile delinquency and several statistical assessments of other social conditions are sufficient to show that the connection of childish offences with poverty and its concomitants is significantly high.

and that the figures

> indicate plainly that it is the poor, overcrowded, insanitary house-holds where families are huge, where the children are dependent solely on the state for their education, and where the parents are largely dependent on charity and relief for their own maintenance, that juvenile delinquency is most rife.

Carson (1971: 12) sees this as 'reflecting the extent to which poverty had become an accepted part of British criminology's standard explanatory repertoire'. The tradition has not died, indeed in many ways it can be said to be the very essence of sociology:[21] though today the sentiment is more likely to be expressed in terms of the mugger himself being a victim. (An excellent example of what is meant by this is the film *Clockwork Orange*: but see also the illustration on p. 119.) This being so, clearly some attempt must be made to sift the available evidence in order to establish what credence should be given to such a contention in a study of this kind.

Problems of definition

Before we can even begin to consider the precise relationship between delinquency and deprivation, thought must be given to the critically important question of definitions.

Let us start with deprivation. At the turn of the century Seebohm Rowntree defined families whose 'total earnings are insufficient to obtain the minimum necessaries for the maintenance of merely physical

"*To the shrewd observer, they're both crying for help, of course!*"

efficiency as being in primary poverty' (1901). For him the poverty line for a family of two parents and three children was precisely 17s 8d per week, made up of 12s 9d for food, 2s 3d for clothing, 1s 10d for fuel and 10d for household sundries. What, though, should be set as the poverty line today? It would not be an exaggeration to say that so many factors would have to be taken into account that it would be almost an impossible undertaking. As Peter Townsend puts it:

> the underlying work of developing a comprehensive definition of poverty in operational terms which can be applied in different countries and regions and which can permit a measurement of a kind sensitive enough to show the short-term effect on the numbers in poverty of, say, an increase in unemployment, an unusually large increase in prices, or the stepping-up in value of social security benefits, is still in a very early stage. This remains true despite a longish history of empirical work in some countries. (1974: 21)

But the problem of quantifying what constitutes a realistic poverty line need not concern us overmuch here. What is far more important is the very fact that 'poverty has emerged as an important social issue in many developed countries':[22] though it must quickly be added that the view of writers such as Peter Marris and Martin Rein (1974: ch. 1, 2) that primary poverty, in Rowntree's sense, is still prevalent in Britain today, is totally rejected. How can we realistically talk of 'poverty' when 'within a generation the possession of a television set in Britain has changed from being a doubtful privilege of a tiny minority to being an expected right of 95 per cent of the population'.[23] Surely 'poverty' can *only* be thought of in terms of the needs, aspirations, socially defined status and cultural conditioning of the individual in question.

While no one (presumably) would suggest that a Lambeth slum-dweller is in any sense 'worse-off' than, say, an impoverished Indian peasant eking out the barest of existences on the outskirts of Calcutta, there can be no doubt that he does indeed have a very low rating on the scale of values against which he should currently be measured.[24] Hence, we are interested not so much in deprivation as in *relative* deprivation.

This is a concept which has been studied in some depth by a number of writers. For long it had been assumed that primary poverty and social insecurity were at the roots of a great proportion of crime: it was all the more bewildering, then, that crime should continue to rise with the tide of post-war prosperity and social security.[25] The possibility had to be allowed for that affluence can itself be a cause of crime. It might even be argued, perhaps, that a high crime rate can be used as an index of economic success.[26]

As partial explanations of this phenomenon the theories of people such as Thorstein Veblen (conspicuous consumption),[27] J. K. Galbraith (*The Affluent Society*), and particularly W. G. Runciman (*Relative Deprivation and Social Justice*) were developed — the pervading theme of all their work having been summarised by Stephen Cotgrove as follows:

> It is not poverty alone which generates radicalism. On the contrary, stable poverty tends to be associated with conservatism. It is the awareness of the possibilities of betterment which accompanies industrialisation, which is explosive. It is relative deprivation not absolute poverty which generates discontent. (1967: 279)

Perhaps even more important is the meaning which is to be given to 'delinquency'. The basic question, 'What is a crime?', is central to *any* criminological study, and for this reason has already been discussed at some length in chapter 4: when it comes to equating crime (or delinquency) with deprivation, however, the additional danger of a circular argument, or even a self-fulfilling prophecy, must always be borne firmly in mind. The question that really needs to be answered is: 'Is delinquency linked *by definition* with poverty?'. (In this connection see the illustration on p. 121.)

SKINHEAD BASHING

34 *Is this Society's attitude to the unsuccessful? (A Punch cartoon.)*

We have already seen that the apparent level of crime at any given point in time is influenced by a great number of factors, many of which can be grouped under the general heading of the 'dark figure' of crime:[28] what we are now interested in is not so much how good a reflection of the actual amount of 'crime' are the published statistics, but rather what is — or what should be — termed a 'crime' in the first place.

For one thing there is a definite risk that a 'deviant', 'delinquent', or 'criminal' will be defined as such simply because he acts differently from other members of the dominant culture. For example Dennis Chapman, in his *Sociology and the Stereotype of the Criminal*, argues that most studies of crime and the offender take as their starting-point a stereotype of the criminal which is a social and legal artifact. This is clearly reflected in the first four points of his eleven-point thesis:

1   That any behaviour that has a disapproved form also has objectively identical forms that are neutral or approved.
2   That if a behaviour is seen as goal-seeking then the choice of the form of behaviour between objectively identical forms – approved, neutral or disapproved – may depend on chance, knowledge, learning or training.
3   That apart from the factor of conviction there is no difference between criminals and non-criminals.
4   That criminal behaviour is general, but the incidence of conviction is controlled in part by chance and in part by social processes which divide society into the criminal and non-criminal classes, the former corresponding to, roughly, the poor and the underprivileged.

Thus:

members of the middle class are substantially immune from prosecution if they commit offences and, if prosecuted, receive treatment that is sympathetic rather than hostile and punishments that do not identify them permanently as criminal.

This theme has been developed by the social reaction, or labelling, theorists such as Howard Becker,[29] Edwin Lemert and Edwin Schur – who encapsulates the whole approach in his questions, 'Deviant to whom?' 'Deviant from what?'. As Taylor, Walton and Young (1975: 141) point out:

The ultimate preoccupation of this group of theorists is with the way in which being labelled deviant by a social audience, or by an agency of social control, can change one's conception of self, and possibly lead to a situation where, even if there was no initial commitment to deviation, there may still be a progressive turn to such commitment.

Deviance is seen, in fact, as a quality that lies not in behaviour itself but in the interaction between the person who commits an act and those who respond to it.

In much the same vein David Matza stresses the similarity of larger societal values and the values embodied in 'delinquent ideology'. He, too, attacks rigid or hard deterministic views of deviant action and, in refuting notions of the pathology of deviant phenomena, stresses the similarity between deviancy and any other type of action.[30] Indeed, a number of supposedly delinquent values are closely akin to those embodied in the leisure activities of the dominant society. It is simply that 'deviants' exhibit a 'bad sense of timing'.[31]

Following on from this, it is John Mays (1963: 58) who asks the crucial question, 'Are we all delinquent?', and points out that

> the idea that there is a law-respecting, peaceable, moral majority and a desperate, lawless, tough, unfeeling unscrupulous subhuman minority on the other hand, is nonsense.

His main contention is that delinquency as a form of subculturally prescribed behaviour during boyhood results in almost *every* boy committing offences of one type or another. Here, of course, we come very near to the type of theory exemplified by Edwin Sutherland's concept of white-collar crime — 'crimes committed by persons of respectability and high social status in the course of their occupations' (1960: 41). Certainly every job has its perks and few individuals have failed to succumb to such temptations as 'borrowing' stationery, or making 'free' telephone calls. In this sense, therefore, crime is endemic and not epidemic in character: we are indeed all criminals.

Earlier in this chapter it was suggested that the geographical distribution of crime could be predicted in the sense that social problem areas are (for largely economic reasons) almost certain to be located near the centre of a city: and

$$\text{problem area} = \text{conflict} = \text{delinquency}.$$

From only a slightly different standpoint it is now being argued that the 'social distribution' of crime can also be predicted for the simple reason that it is only deprived individuals of low social status who are ever labelled as deviant in the first place: their delinquency can be explained in terms of their social milieu. Unfortunately, for most practical purposes such an approach does not get us very far, and at some point we must settle for a given definition of crime (or delinquency) even if this *does* mean accepting that 'crime' simply denotes a failure to adapt to means legitimised by, and upheld on behalf of, the 'ruling' middle and upper classes.

Certainly British criminologists have always tended to regard the published statistics as social facts *par excellence*.[32] What is more, since this study is mainly concerned with the practicalities associated with a particular type of crime — as opposed to the theory of delinquency in general — there would seem little point in pursuing further what are mainly semantic arguments. Rather we must extract ourselves from what Stuart Hall has termed a 'spiral of definition', and return to the main theme of attempting to establish to what extent 'true' or 'natural' crime (in the Durkheimian sense) — which, if only to enable further progress to be made, is taken to include mugging — can be associated with deprivation.

Delinquency, deprivation and mugging in the Metropolitan Police District

The idea of a single cause of crime is today rightly discredited — what Sir Cyril Burt was the first to call 'the principle of multiple causation' having become firmly established[33] — but even if poverty is not *the* cause of crime there would certainly appear to be a close correlation between the two. Perhaps, as we have just seen, this is largely a matter of definition; perhaps it is the sheer middle-class bias of most sociologists which makes them talk (as does Morris) of larceny amongst working-class adults resulting in an almost Hobbesian situation of a war of all against all; perhaps it is due to the very nature of the delinquent sub-culture itself,[34] but, whatever the reason it is felt that few would express surprise at, for example, the finding of Hunt (1975: 33) that:

> In the case of muggings, the medical and biological factors are of little or no relevance, but all the rest are. Nearly all muggers come from urban slums, where poverty, filth, and disease are prevalent, and where family life is often harsh and hostile.

In line with such a finding the next step in this study should clearly be to establish the level of deprivation experienced by people living in that area already identified as the one in which substantially the greatest proportion of muggings occur, that is to say the London Borough of Lambeth.[35] Can it now be demonstrated that residents here are 'relatively deprived' in comparison with other Boroughs within the Metropolitan Police District?

Relative deprivation in the London Borough of Lambeth

The London Borough of Lambeth extends from Waterloo Bridge in the north to Streatham in the south, from Clapham in the west to

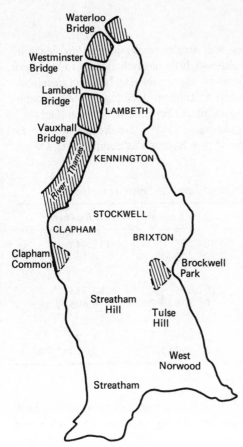

Figure 6.4 The London Borough of Lambeth

Norwood in the east. It is bounded to the north and west by the river Thames and includes two small areas of parkland (*vide* Figure 6.4).

For any 'index of deprivation' much must depend on subjective judgment while, as far as Lambeth is concerned, a further consideration was the type of information readily available from the latest national census held in 1971.[36] In this respect the following three factors appeared particularly relevant and will therefore be investigated here,

        (a) level of unemployment;
        (b) how overcrowded?;
        (c) household amenities.

(a) *Level of unemployment*

Apart from being an obvious indicator of 'social deprivation', it should also be pointed out that — although little research appears to have been carried out on the exact level of any correlation between unemployment and crime — a number of eminent sociologists (for example, Mannheim) have pointed to an apparent connection between the two.

As far as Lambeth is concerned, Table 6.2 indicates the relevant statistics for males resident in the Borough as compared to Greater London as a whole.

Table 6.2 *London Borough of Lambeth: male employment*

	Greater London	*LB Lambeth*
Total male population	2,774,505	112,445
Economically active	2,305,450 (83.1%)	94,190 (83.8%)
of which		
Employed	2,197,075	87,585
Unemployed	108,375 (4.7%)	6,605 (7.0%)
of which		
Sick	23,825	1,225
Other	84,550 (3.7%)	5,380 (5.7%)

(Source: 1971 National Census, part I, table 18)

The important totals are those for the unemployed (non-sick) — Lambeth's proportion of 5.7 per cent being exceeded only by Tower Hamlets. In actual numbers, Lambeth's total of 'unemployed, non-sick, economically active males' is easily the highest of any of the 32 London Boroughs.

As for males under the age of twenty-one, the statistics are as shown in Table 6.3. This is to say that in Lambeth (in 1971) one in ten economically active males under the age of twenty-one was unemployed.

It seems beyond dispute, then, that at least as far as unemployment is concerned, the London Borough of Lambeth can indeed be rated a socially deprived area.

(b) *How overcrowded?*

The level of overcrowding is likely to have a significant bearing on the general living standards experienced by residents of a given area. Certainly

Table 6.3 *London borough of Lambeth: employment of males under 21*

	Greater London	LB Lambeth
Male population 15–20	293,660	12,460
Economically active	183,475 (62.5%)	8,160 (65.5%)
of which		
Employed	168,970	7,280
Unemployed	14,505 (7.9%)	880 (10.8%)
of which		
Sick	995	45
Other	13,510 (7.4%)	835 (10.2%)

(Source: 1971 National Census, part I, table 18)

it is a factor closely linked with the urban sociologists' conflict model of the city,[37] and more particularly with Pahl's concept of 'the struggle for social space'.[38]

In terms of persons per hectare the position in 1971 was as follows:

Greater London   47.18
LB Lambeth   112.77,

the Lambeth figure being exceeded by only four of the thirty-one other Boroughs. (Moreover, the Stockwell ward of Lambeth had 192.99 persons per hectare – a total exceeded by only 12 of the 649 wards in the entire Greater London area.)

Sheer density of population, however, is by no means the whole story. Factors such as the number of high-rise flats must have a considerable influence, and a more telling indicator would therefore be the number of families sharing individual dwelling units. This is shown by Table 6.4. It can be seen that in Lambeth there are 3,615 dwellings which contain three or more families. This represents about 10 per cent of the total for Greater London as a whole (as compared to only about 4 per cent of dwellings of all types) and demonstrates very clearly that Lambeth is indeed very badly off in this respect.

(c) *Household amenities*

Under this heading we now come directly into line with Rex and Moore's notion of 'housing classes'. For example, one obvious measure of the relative affluence of an area is the number of persons living in

Table 6.4 *London Borough of Lambeth: number of
households in occupation of dwelling*

	Greater London	LB Lambeth
0	52,565 (2.1%)	1,875 (1.9%)
1	2,305,650 (92.2%)	84,385 (86.8%)
2	105,935 (4.2%)	7,410 (7.6%)
3	24,685 (1.0%)	2,525 (2.6%)
4	7,345 (0.3%)	630 (0.6%)
5	2,740 (0.1%)	260 (0.3%)
6+	2,395 (0.1%)	200 (0.2%)

Source: 1971 National Census, part II, table 21)

owner/occupier premises as a proportion of all tenures. Here the
figures are:

> Greater London: 3,202,145 out of 7,206,560 (44.4%)
> LB Lambeth: 69,320 out of 298,615 (23.2%).

As the almost direct converse, of course, we have the proportion of
persons living in rented accommodation, namely:

> Greater London: 3,963,295 out of 7,206,560 (55.1%)
> LB Lambeth: 225,090 out of 298,615 (75.4%).

In other words, in order to be in line with the rest of Greater London
one would have 'expected' Lambeth to have had some 164,000 persons[39] living in rented accommodation: in fact this total was exceeded
by more than 60,000.

The 'housing deprivation' experienced by residents of LB Lambeth
is even more clearly illustrated (as in table 6.5) by the level of available
amenities. It can be seen that, for every one of the categories shown,
Lambeth compares unfavourably even with the relatively poor standard
of amenities found throughout the rest of London.

In terms of 'housing class', then, as for the two previous headings,
there can be little doubt that Lambeth is indeed one of the most deprived
of London Boroughs, and we can therefore say that for this area at least
the connection between delinquency and deprivation has been proved.

Summary

This chapter has done no more than scratch the surface of a topic
which constitutes one of the main cornerstones of sociological thinking

Table 6.5 *London Borough of Lambeth: household amenities*

	Greater London	*LB Lambeth*
Hot water		
Exclusive use	2,302,265 (86.8%)	89,435 (79.9%)
Shared use	144,895 (5.5%)	9,630 (8.6%)
None	204,655 (7.7%)	12,875 (11.5%)
Fixed bath/shower		
Exclusive use	2,137,400 (80.6%)	79,485 (71.0%)
Shared use	271,905 (10.3%)	19.125 (17.1%)
None	242,515 (9.1%)	13.330 (11.9%)
WC		
Inside exclusive use	2,162,915 (81.6%)	83,815 (74.9%)
Inside shared use	269,610 (10.2%)	19,210 (17.2%)
Outside exclusive use	179,765 (6.8%)	7,045 (6.3%)
Outside shared use	35,200 (1.3%)	1,640 (1.5%)
None	4,330 (0.2%)	230 (0.2%)
Hot water +		
Fixed bath/shower +	2,007,775 (75.7%)	73,340 (65.5%)
Inside WC		

(Source: 1971 National Census, part III, table 25).

— that actions are moulded more by an individual's position in society than by his own psychological make-up. A full review of this theme is simply not possible in a work of this kind, and no more has been attempted than to mention some of the more relevant theories as a guide to further reading.

There is, however, one further approach which should briefly be mentioned at this point, mainly because it illustrates particularly well the concept of 'opportunity structure' which is common to almost all those theories of ecology, poverty, deprivation, or inequality mentioned in this chapter: that is to say the explanatory model suggested by R. K. Merton.[40] He defines five logically possible types of response to the situation we all find ourselves in, namely:

		Culture goals	*Means*	
I	Conformity	+	—	
II	Innovation	+	—	
III	Ritualism	—	+	
IV	Retreatism	—	—	
V	Rebellion	±	±	*(cont.)*

(where + = acceptance, — = elimination, and ± = rejection
and substitution of new goals and standards. 'Innovation'
is the delinquent solution)

As a criticism of this approach it has often been claimed that no allowance is made for change, and that it classifies but does not explain:
nevertheless, it does seem to provide an excellent framework for considering many of the points made in this chapter, not least the relative
deprivation which has played such a central role in the discussion. For,
as John Gunn (1973: 77) tells us:

> The attraction of Merton's theory is that in some measure it has
> been predictive, because it suggests that if a society sets its goals at
> more and more unrealistic levels, more and more members will
> experience frustration and turn to innovation . . . . Furthermore it
> suggests that increasing affluence in a society is not necessarily
> associated with a diminishing crime rate.

As to why it is violence, such as mugging, which so often emerges
as the delinquent solution, is a point elaborated by Wolfgang and
Ferracuti:

> when multiplied by thousands, congested, and transmitted over
> generations, poverty becomes a culture. The expectations of social
> intercourse change, and irritable, frustrated parents often become
> neglectful and aggressive. Their children inherit a *subculture of
> violence* where physically aggressive responses are either expected or
> required by all members sharing not only the tenement's plumbing
> but also its system of values. (1967: 9)

Almost all the available evidence points to this direct, if not necessarily
causal, relationship, while as far as the London Borough of Lambeth is
concerned we have now seen that, in terms of deprivation, the necessary
preconditions for the emergence of violence are certainly present. However, it seems likely that *within* the Borough it is members of the
coloured population who will experience the very worst of what has
clearly been shown to be a 'bad deal'.

The real problem is how the overall opportunity structure can be
improved to enable everyone to take an equal share in society. This
becomes especially noticeable when we begin to consider the question
of race, for, as Michael Harloe puts it:

the picture derived from census migration data is a familiar one of a high concentration of newly or recently arrived coloured population living in markedly worse housing conditions than their white working-class equivalents. (1973: 319)

It is to the special problems of these coloured immigrants that we must now turn.

[7] Race

Introduction

Few subjects are likely to provoke more heated discussion and argument than the question of race,[1] yet it would scarcely be an exaggeration to say that no one is prepared to state the known facts for fear of being labelled racist. An excellent example of this tendency is provided by the apparent horror with which certain individuals and organisations greeted the news that questions about ethnic backgrounds might possibly be included in the next (1981) national census:[2] just why this should be so is by no means clear since the product would be the totally neutral one of establishing the size of Britain's black population, and with the parents' country of birth becoming increasingly unreliable as an indicator (as more and more immigrants born in Britain have their own children), a straightforward 'head count' becomes the only answer.[3] Again, in 1972 the Select Committee on Race Relations and Immigration, in the course of a discussion on crime rates, remarked that '*If* [my italics] coloured people were disproportionately involved in crime, colour prejudice would be strengthened and race relations embittered'. 'Ignorance is bliss' it would seem, though this is not to deny that there *is* a very real difficulty involved: this has been expressed in the Metropolitan Police 'Memorandum to the Select Committee on Race Relations and Immigration', issued in March 1976, as follows:

> A dilemma at the heart of race relations is whether to expose experience and facts to public debate, and therefore risk feeding prejudice, or stifle experience and facts and risk loss of definition of social problems and consequent apathy in their resolution.
> (paragraph 28)

In the considered opinion of this writer it achieves absolutely nothing to withhold *any* fact that may be available. If more time were spent on tackling the actual problem of involvement in crime, whether by white citizen or black, and less on side issues such as definitions and the fear of hurting people's feelings, then it is very likely that far more could be achieved.

The statistics

It has already been shown (in chapter 5) that, of the sample studied, a very high proportion of assailants were described by their victim as 'coloured', 'black', 'West Indian', or the like, and were therefore designated Identity Code 3 — 'Negroid type'. The actual figures are 429 out of 739, or 58 per cent. High as this proportion may appear it is by no means wildly out of line with the general trend. For example, the latest available figures for the Metropolitan Police District as a whole show that, of those persons arrested[4] for all forms of indictable crime during 1976, 13 per cent were Identity Code 3, while for robbery only this proportion rises to 28 per cent, the full breakdown for these, and certain other categories of crime, being as follows:[5]

Table 7.1 *1976 arrests: percentage breakdown by identity code*

	IC1	IC2	IC3	IC4	IC5	IC6
All crimes of violence	70	3	22	3	1	1
Robbery only	68	2	28	2	0	0
Burglary	83	1	14	1	0	0
Autocrime	85	2	10	2	0	0
Shoplifting	67	7	12	5	2	7
All indictable crime	78	3	13	3	1	2

Moreover, on 'L' District alone the figure for Identity Code 3 involvement in robbery was 61 per cent, while it might also be of interest to note that in the USA the relevant statistics are: arrests for all categories of crime — some 26 per cent described as Negro; for robbery only, 63 per cent, and for robbery in urban areas, 66 per cent.

There can be little dispute then that, in absolute terms, robbery must be classed as predominantly a 'black crime'. However, it must also be stressed that the task of assessing exactly the *comparative* level of West Indian involvement is bedevilled by a number of factors, not the least of which is the absence of precise knowledge about the size of the West Indian population.[6] Taking Great Britain as a whole, it is

currently estimated that one person in every thirty is black: in London
the official figure is about double this,[7] while there can be little doubt
that in certain areas the proportion is very much higher still. As far as
'L' District, that is to say the London Borough of Lambeth, is concerned, the 1971 Census shows the relevant statistics to be as follows:

Born outside UK
      Greater London − 1,113,275 out of 7,452,345 (14.9%)
      LB Lambeth   −   60,550 out of   307,515 (19.7%)[8]

Born in 'New Commonwealth' countries
      Greater London − 476,485 out of 7,452,345 (6.4%)
      LB Lambeth   −   33,475 out of   307,515 (10.9%)[9]

Born in West Indies
      Greater London − 128,795 out of 7,452,345 (1.7%)
      LB Lambeth   −   16,650 out of   307,515 (5.4%)[10]

In other words, in 1971 in the Greater London area, of every hundred
residents fifteen were born outside the United Kingdom − of which
two were born in the West Indies, and four in other New Commonwealth countries. Of every hundred people living in the London Borough
of Lambeth, on the other hand, twenty were born outside the United
Kingdom − of which five were born in the West Indies, and six in
other New Commonwealth countries.[11]

Moreover, since these figures are based upon country of birth, they
do not accurately indicate the true number of black residents. The
figures may include a number of white people born in the New Commonwealth − they do not include black citizens born in Britain. The
Community Relations Commission have suggested that an approximation of the true number of black residents can be obtained by increasing the census figure by half as much again. If we apply this rule, we
arrive at an estimated figure of 50,000 black inhabitants in Lambeth,
25,000 of whom are of West Indian origin. Comparison with a GLC
Research Memorandum (No. 425), published in March 1973, indicates
that this is the very best estimate that can be made.[12]

In very broad terms, then, we find that in Lambeth West Indian
residents who (even allowing for a certain amount of casual 'immigration' from other Boroughs) almost certainly make up less than 10
per cent of the total population, are thought to be responsible for
something like 50 per cent of the known robberies. As T. C. Jones,

one-time Statistical Adviser to the Metropolitan Police, puts it in an unpublished paper entitled 'Crime and Race' (1974):

> Quite clearly there is a very high involvement in robbery and theft
> from the person on the part of West Indian-type persons both under
> and over 17 when compared to that of the rest of the population.
> Despite the difficulties in making these comparisons, and whatever
> the social, environmental, or other reasons may be for this pheno-
> menon, there can be no doubt that this is the case.

Putting all of this in a slightly different way, since in Lambeth a black West Indian is at least seven or eight times as likely to commit a robbery as a white person, there would appear to be every justification for the comment made in the Metropolitan Police 'Memorandum to the Select Committee on Race Relations and Immigration' (March 1976) that:

> already our experience has taught us the fallibility of the assertion
> that crime rates amongst those of West Indian origin are no higher
> than those of the population at large. (paragraph 26)

At the same time it is of the utmost importance to appreciate that there is not *necessarily* a direct link between blackness and criminality. As Morton M. Hunt (1975: 33) tells us:

> To the bigoted white, the astoundingly high rate of Negro criminal-
> ity seems proof of a racial tendency towards violent crime, but there
> is no scientific evidence whatever that criminal behaviour is coded
> into the genetic material.

A hint of the factors which might help to explain the apparent correlation is provided, again, by the Metropolitan Police Memorandum:

> It is no part of our position that there is a causal link between
> ethnic origin and crime. What our records do suggest is that London's
> black citizens, among whom those of West Indian origin predomin-
> ate, are disproportionately involved in many forms of crime. But in
> view of their heavy concentration in areas of urban stress, which are
> themselves high crime areas, and in view of the disproportionate
> numbers of young people in the West Indian population, this pattern
> is not surprising. (paragraph 25)

As Wolfgang and Ferracuti (1967) tell us, when the untoward aspects of urban life are found amongst Italians, Germans, Poles, or almost any other group, *their* crime rates are similarly high: 'Relative deprivation and social disqualification are thus dramatically chained to despair and delinquency'.

Historical background

There have been Negroes in England for more than four hundred years: indeed, it has been estimated that towards the end of the eighteenth century they already made up something like 2 per cent of the population of London.[13] However, the present coloured population derives almost entirely from immigration which has taken place since the Second World War — starting with 492 Jamaicans who boarded the SS *Empire Windrush* in June 1948 as a result of encouragement given to West Indians to come and do jobs which no white worker wanted. The weather might not be very good, the people not very friendly, the employers not very generous; but at least there was work to be had. Not that this original shipload of West Indians proved in any sense to be the first wave of an army of 'unarmed invaders' for, despite the widely-realised labour shortage in Britain, no more than 2,000 or so (at the very most) West Indians arrived each year prior to 1954.[14] This was mainly due to the fact that the typical West Indian migrant greatly preferred the United States to Great Britain. As Dilip Hiro (1971: 9) puts it:

> [America] was nearer; it was richer; it already had a large established West Indian community. And, once the West Indian passed the literacy test and medical examination, it was easy to gain entry.

To the obvious regret of almost everyone concerned such a state of affairs was not to last. For many years the British West Indies had been included in the immigration quota for Britain (a generous and never fully subscribed 65,000 a year). But, after the war, West Indian migration to America rose to such a degree that it was decided to modify the law. The resulting McCarran-Walter Act — signed by President Truman in 1952 — had the effect of separating the British West Indies from Britain, and allotting an entirely separate, and totally 'inadequate', quota of only eight hundred to the entire area.[15] This amounted to virtually a total ban on West Indian migration to America, and they were therefore obliged to seek other outlets. In particular they now looked to Britain with its 'open door' policy[16] as their country of settlement. Before the McCarran-Walter Act, for every West Indian emigrating to Britain at least nine went to America: after the passing of the Act this ratio was reversed. In 1954 about 9,000 West Indians came to Britain and by the following year even this total had been trebled.

As to the basic causes of such migration, it is customary to talk in terms of the 'push' factors which stimulate people to leave their native land, and the 'pull' factors which attract them to the receiving country. In the case of the West Indian, and more particularly the Jamaican, the principal push factors have always been poor opportunities and a population growing at a rate which the economy simply has not been able to sustain: the overriding pull factor has been employment opportunity in English industrial towns (though the notion of Britain being the 'mother country' should not be discounted completely). Overall the position is well summarised by Daniel Lawrence when he tells us that:

> the strong sense of identity with Britain, coupled with the right of free entry which Jamaicans enjoyed until 1962, made this country a logical choice for would-be migrants at a time when we were short of labour and the McCarran-Walter Act had made migration to the United States so difficult. (1974: 18)

The West Indian in Britain

But what happens once they arrive in this country? Clearly the life they can lead depends to a very large extent on the reception they receive from the existing inhabitants:[17] frequently this reception is decidedly cool, amounting in fact to discrimination[18] — sometimes unconscious, sometimes subtle, often overt. As described by Lawrence:

> Instead of a society in which hard work and ambition brought high incomes and security they found that discrimination often made it difficult for them to obtain jobs. Instead of an open and friendly welcome they found prejudice and sometimes open hostility. Experiences of rejection have been felt most strongly by the Jamaicans. Their strong sense of identity with Britain produced higher expectations and probably greater exposure to circumstances in which prejudice and discrimination were encountered. (1974: 196).

This applies particularly in the fields of employment, housing and education. Daniel puts it thus:

> Today, Britain's coloured people . . . no longer consist overwhelmingly of male adult workers leading more or less celibate lives in lodgings and hostels; today the majority are living as families and their basic concerns are, therefore, precisely the same as those of the rest of the population: a decent home at a fair price, a steady income for the breadwinner from a job appropriate to his skills, and good education and fair opportunities for their children. (1968: 10)

In the field of employment there is much evidence to indicate a general unwillingness to employ coloured workers except when adequate alternative sources of labour are unobtainable.[19] Indeed, Peter Wright, in his study of *The Coloured Worker in British Industry*, (1968: 49) suggests that coloured workers do not even get the jobs Englishmen won't take — 'he may only get those which foreign workers do not want either'.

Although some have argued that many coloured immigrants have (or at least had) rather a poor command of the English language[20] and lack some of the individual skills of native workers, and therefore that one might expect them to be concentrated in the poorest paid and least attractive jobs,[21] this does not account for the known discrimination against qualified black immigrants, or indeed the lower level of discrimination experienced by unskilled *white* immigrants. In this connection some very interesting evidence is provided by a study sponsored by the Race Relations Board and the National Committee for Commonwealth Immigrants in 1966–67, and published under the title *Racial Discrimination in Britain* (Daniel, 1968). Investigators selected a sample of firms suspected of discrimination and sent three testers to them to enquire about or apply for jobs. These testers (one of them English) were carefully selected as being of similar age and of good appearance. Both white alien and coloured testers spoke English fluently, but with a sufficiently pronounced accent to make them readily identifiable as non-English. As to the results obtained, in only one of the forty firms tested was the coloured immigrant tester told that a vacancy existed or offered a job. The English tester had fifteen offers and the Hungarian ten. On two further occasions the coloured immigrant had his details taken for further reference, was asked to call back, or was told something should be available shortly. This occurred fifteen times for the English tester, and seven times for the Hungarian. Thus the incidence of discrimination on the part of the forty firms may be summarised as follows:

Number of cases where no jobs available for anyone	10
Number of cases where employment possible	30
Discrimination against English tester	0
Discrimination against Hungarian tester	13
Discrimination against coloured tester	27

When it comes to housing, the coloured immigrant always finds himself at the end of the queue, and can usually obtain accommodation only in those 'zones of transition'[22] where, as we have seen, 'the housing is least desired and the existing population least organised to repel strangers'[23] — almost certainly to become either a lodging-house landlord or lodging-house tenant. As Sheila Patterson (1963) puts it:

the West Indians have evolved their own solution to the problems of living space by buying up deteriorating property much of which has ceased to seem a sound investment proposition to local investors, and by filling it with fifteen or twenty-five people instead of two to three English families who formerly lived there. (18–19)

Hence, in her study of Notting Hill in 1964 Pearl Jephcott found that 87 of 155 households had the sole use of one room only, 'and that was generally a small one'.[24]

Again, the PEP study[25] provides some interesting evidence. The three testers applied to sixty landlords who had not barred coloured tenants in advance.[26] In half the applications, they adopted professional roles with appropriate levels of income, and seeking corresponding accommodation (the West Indian was a hospital registrar, the Hungarian an accountant, and the Englishman a school teacher). In the other half they claimed working-class occupations (bus conductor, van driver and builder's labourer respectively). The outcome was:

Occasions when all three applicants were given similar information.	15
West Indian told accommodation taken; both others told it was vacant.	38
West Indian asked for higher rent than both other applicants.	4

West Indian and Hungarian told accommoda-   2
tion taken: Englishman told it was vacant.
West Indian and Hungarian asked for higher   1
rent than Englishman.

This shows that in applications to landlords who professed not to discriminate, in three cases out of four some kind of colour discrimination
did in fact occur. Moreover, this probably underestimates the true
situation for, among the fifteen occasions on which the West Indian
received a similar response, there were instances such as when the
Englishman was told, 'Come round quickly, I've got a West Indian
coming at 7 p.m., so get here by 6.30.'
    Landlords' reactions when they were approached by telephone were
similar in that, on only 46 occasions out of 120, were all three appli-
cants given similar information. Thus Daniel reports:

> The figures combined show that the West Indian experienced dis-
> crimination in two thirds of his total of 180 applications to land-
> lords whose advertisements did not specifically exclude him in
> advance. (1968: 156)

When it comes to education, the position is so well described by
Tony Jefferson and John Clarke in their unpublished study 'Down
These Mean Streets . . . . The Meaning of Mugging' (1973: 3–4), that
little more need be added:[27]

> to be West Indian has meant to have additional problems: the
> problems of 'identity', of racism, of an ignored or misrepresented
> cultural heritage, of having to take culturally biased intelligence
> tests, and of being educationally misplaced. . . . Where teachers are
> not openly racist they may be either unwittingly or patronisingly
> so with, as a consequence, low expectations of their West Indian
> charges. Text books, more or less overtly, perpetuate racist myths:
> the curriculum usually ignores West Indian culture or, where the
> effort is made, often presents it through 'white eyes', owing to the
> shortage of West Indian teachers. West Indian patois, unacceptable
> and incomprehensible to white middle-class ears, is held to necessitate
> remedial language classes. All this takes its toll of West Indian
> children and many become 'self-fulfilling prophecies': poorly motiv-
> ated with low self-expectations they become low achievers; confused
> and made anxious by a grudging, qualified or patronising acceptance

they become, according to disposition, listless and apathetic, or more commonly frustrated and hostile.

All in all, as Mark Abrams tells us in his introduction to Daniel's *Racial Discrimination in Britain*:

> all but those with totally closed minds must accept the fact that in Britain today discrimination against coloured members of the population operates in many fields ... (p. 13)

Indeed, it would appear that this fact has long since been 'officially' acknowledged by the passing of appropriate legislation. In 1964 the general election manifesto of the Labour party declared that it would 'legislate against racial discrimination and incitement in public places and give special help to local authorities in areas where immigrants have settled', and this ultimately led to the passing of the 1965 Race Relations Act which declared unlawful any discrimination on grounds of colour, race, or ethnic or national origin in certain places of public resort (hotels, restaurants, public houses, theatres, dance halls, swimming pools, public transport, etc.); it also prevented the enforcement of racial restrictions on the transfer of tenancies and penalised incitement to racial hatred.

To secure compliance with the provisions of the Act, a Race Relations Board was set up consisting of a chairman and two other members appointed by the Home Secretary. This Board was constituted in February 1966,[28] and it immediately set about the task of setting up local conciliation committees in those areas with substantial immigrant populations.[29] All of this was re-enforced and extended by the Race Relations Act of 1968, while in 1976 a new Act came into force which widened the definition of discrimination to include not only intentional racial discrimination[30] but also victimisation of anyone who makes a complaint, and indirect discrimination where practices and procedures which apply to everyone have the unjustifiable effect of putting people of a particular racial group[31] at a disadvantage. Apart from dealing with discrimination in detail in relation to employment, education, the provision of goods, facilities, services and premises, discriminatory practices and advertising, it also created the Commission for Racial Equality — which replaced the Race Relations Board — to assist individual complainants.

If, and when, discrimination does still occur, the main 'losers' are obviously the immigrants themselves; but this is by no means the only consideration. For instance, one of the principal justifications for opposing discrimination is, to quote Abrams's introduction to Daniel, the democratic one:

> if we truly believe in democracy then our commitment is to a society in which all members are able to develop their potential to the full for the benefit of society and the individual; and the starting point for this is the right of every individual to full and equal opportunity in all spheres of life — economic and social as well as political. To deny the right to a minority of our fellow citizens amounts to a total rejection of the principles of democracy. (1968: 13)

while it is important to remember that the indigenous population is also crucially affected. In employment, for example, the outcome of discrimination is the wasteful use of coloured manpower: trained teachers as railway guards, qualified accountants as wages clerks. Clearly, from the point of view of the community as a whole, such misuse of available and potential skills and abilities ought to be totally unacceptable. In housing, too, discrimination has led to the establishment of coloured 'ghettos' where, because of overcrowding and landlord neglect, the opportunities for structural modernisation of older dwellings have been wasted; while in education the tendency to look on coloured immigrants merely as 'a drain on the system' must inevitably have represented a serious misuse of scarce resources.

Responses to racial tensions

From a number of points of view, then, it is suggested that everything possible should be done to reduce the incidence of racial discrimination. But discrimination is only a symptom: the real 'disease' is the inability of many sections of the black and white communities to live side by side in harmony.[32] What, then, are the responses actually adopted by the two 'sides'?

As far as some sections of the indigenous population are concerned, the existing legislation to restrict further immigrant entry is viewed as inadequate, and such feelings have spilled over into race riots and impassioned pleas for repatriation. For the coloured immigrant, the main options are assimilation, acceptance, development of a defensive West Indian consciousness,[33] or involvement in small-scale crime.[34] Let us now look at each of these factors in more detail.

On the question of legislation, after a full debate on coloured immigrants at the Conservative Party Conference in the autumn of 1961, the Commonwealth Immigrants Act was introduced, and was passed in 1962. By the time the 1964 general election was fought the Labour Party, despite its initial opposition, had accepted the principle of restriction on the number of new coloured immigrants. Rumours of the impending restrictions created a 'beat the ban' rush, the peak being reached in the first half of 1962, when more than 34,000 West Indians arrived in Britain as immigrants. Following the passing of the Act the intake dropped to around 5,000 or less a year, consisting mainly of dependants of immigrants already here.

In the event such restrictions did little to dampen feelings which were already running dangerously high. As Lawrence (1974: 24) tells us, 'the absence of overt conflict should not be confused with a state of racial harmony', but, from time to time, even overt conflict does rear its head. By the mid 1950s, throughout the country, small groups of bored youngsters and frustrated troublemakers had begun to express their feelings by such actions as breaking the windows of dwellings occupied by immigrants, or beating up the occasional coloured pedestrian who happened to cross their path on a Saturday night. But, in London at least, the term 'race riot' was established most firmly in people's minds by the events which took place in Notting Hill in 1958, described by Hiro (1971: 39-40) in the following terms:[35]

> Shortly before midnight, a crowd of two hundred whites attacked coloureds' houses near Bramley Road. One house was set alight and two others were pelted with bricks and milk bottles.
>
> Another house had a bicycle thrown through its window. In the fighting that ensued iron railings, bicycle chains and choppers were used.
>
> The next day, a Sunday, a mob of five or seven hundred, shouting 'We'll get the blacks', 'Lynch the blacks', and using knives, bottles, crowbars and dustbins attacked coloureds' houses. Another mob of a hundred youths, armed with knives, sticks and bars, gathered under the arches of Latimer Road station. There were also attacks and fights on the Harrow Road and Kensal Rise.
>
> Similar incidents occurred on the next two days. Only when rain fell on Wednesday did the violent activity subside. But when the sun shone again the next day, racialist shouting and bottle-throwing revived, and with it came petrol-bomb attacks on coloured people's

homes in Notting Hill and Paddington. The attackers' intention was to root out the blacks, then assault them . . .

[the West Indians] were made to realise that they were not 'overseas British' now living in Britain, but were Black men and women living in a white society. With this, a new chapter in the racial history of Britain began.

The plea to 'send the blacks home where they came from' gained much of its momentum from these disturbances but, as is well known, it was left to Mr Enoch Powell to make it a truly national issue when, on 20 April 1968, he made his 'river of blood' speech,[36] and later outlined his scheme for the repatriation of 600,000 to 700,000 immigrants.

This is a theme which has now been taken up by the National Front, where the dividing line between fear and aggression is often difficult to distinguish:[37] although the literature of this political movement includes pious condemnation of race hatred, virtually every word is calculated to promote racial tension and fears, while its posters feature grotesque Negro-faced caricatures which somehow manage to escape prosecution under the Race Relations Act.

The National Front has gained support by exploiting genuine concern about immigration and its future development,[38] such anxieties having been accentuated by the disillusion felt by many people over raging inflation, increasing unemployment, poor housing and economic stagnation. For those people who believe that Britain is 'suffering from drift, confusion and the lack of strong leadership, the Front offers crystal-clear certainties and solutions'.[39] The Front's policy on race is ostensibly straightforward: it calls for the 'repatriation by the most humane means possible of those coloured immigrants already here together with their descendants and dependents'.

There is nothing new about the concept of repatriation, indeed it is always likely to appear an obvious and outwardly simple solution to the 'problem' of unwanted immigrants. As Hiro (1971: 3) has pointed out: 'The repatriation of blacks in England was first ordered by the Privy Council of Queen Elizabeth I in 1596 and concerned "divers blackamoors" who had "crept into the realm since the trouble between her Highness and the King of Spain" '. A similar solution was also proposed for the mainly freed but unemployed slaves who had become concentrated in the common lodging houses for the destitute in the St Giles area of London, while, following the 1919 racial disturbances in Cardiff and elsewhere, there was another outcry for the repatriation of coloured people in general. In each of these instances some of those involved did take advantage of free passages home: it is by no means certain, however, that this would prove to be the case today.

Why this should be so is not immediately obvious, since several studies have provided evidence to show that a high proportion of coloured immigrants had no intention of settling permanently in Britain when they first arrived.[40] Moreover, with the discovery that Britain was by no means the 'land of milk and honey' they had confidently expected, it might well be imagined that they would be keener than ever to return to their homeland. There are at least two reasons why things have not often worked out quite in this way. Firstly, there may well be many who simply cannot afford to make the return journey. For these, Powell's policy of assisted repatriation might have a limited appeal. But far more crucial is the fact that few immigrants would wish to go home virtually empty-handed. To quote Lawrence:

> To go home with only a little more, or perhaps even less, money
> than one set out with is an open admission of defeat. It could
> involve a loss of face and would almost certainly mean the period
> spent in Britain, with its attendant humiliation in many cases, had
> been unprofitable and wasted. Moreover it could place the immi-
> grant at an actual disadvantage on his return: he might, for instance,
> even find it difficult to get a job. (1974: 33)

From a general point of view there is the additional consideration that if a scheme of repatriation was to be enforced there would be an immediate loss of a large and important part of this country's work-force. West Indians first came to this country in any numbers specifically at the request of organisations such as London Transport: clearly if, as suggested by Powell, hundreds of thousands of immigrants are made to leave then the public transport and hospital systems, not to mention a host of other individual industries and firms, would experience very considerable problems, at least in the short term.

It can be seen, then, that all the 'white man's solutions' (whether appropriate legislation, race riots or repatriation) amount to an attempt to drive the blacks away so that the problem no longer exists. For the black man, of course, such measures represent no solution at all: his main concern is to find ways of being able to live with the resentment and discrimination with which he is confronted.[41] One possible approach is assimilation: giving up, as it were, his West Indian identity and accepting totally the lifestyle and culture of the white man. Apart from the mental trauma involved, this is also likely to lead to attempts at physical changes such as hair straightening or even lightening of the skin,[42] though here the difficulties are obvious, as Lawrence (1974: 60) points out:

> It may not be easy, but it is nevertheless possible for a man to change his religion or his language − not so his skin colour. He may be proud of it or ashamed of it but, like it or not, there is nothing that can be done about it. The sons of rich men may become poor and the sons of Jews, Gentiles; the sons of radicals may become con-servatives and ignorant men, wise − but the children of black parents must always remain black. It is this which makes the distinction so invidious.

A second, and related, option is acceptance of the status of second-class citizenship: 'to take not the white man's identity, but the white man's definition of West Indian identity'.[43] Psychologically this may prove even more difficult than assimilation and, in practice, is often based on the projection of achievement aspirations on the second generation.[44] A third possibility is to rely on the development of a largely defensive West Indian consciousness. It had become obvious from the time of the Notting Hill riots that coloured immigrants would do well to 'stick together', while 'Black power' demonstrations in other countries (notably the USA)[45] must have had some influence, particularly on the younger West Indians, in providing some sort of reference point for fighting their way out of the desperate situation in which, in their own eyes at least, they found themselves. A final possibility is to become involved in small-scale crime which, to a dis-illusioned West Indian youth, can often appear to offer not only more income but also more status than a conventional job. Mugging clearly comes under this heading, and it is therefore the one which will be expanded upon at length in the next, and final, chapter. There is, however, one further aspect of racial integration, which has already been touched upon briefly, but which is of such importance that it should now be dèalt with in more detail: namely, the special problems associated with the second-generation immigrant.

The second generation

If coloured immigrants in general find themselves at a serious dis-advantage as compared to the indigenous population, this applies with even greater force to their children. Those coming from the West Indies to join their parents are confronted with an additional set of problems inasmuch as they have to readjust not only to their parents but also to a nuclear rather than the traditional extended family,[46] perhaps to half-brothers and sisters and to British society itself. Those born to West Indian parents in this country, on the other hand, are almost certain to react differently to what one might loosely call the racialism with which they are confronted. As Jefferson and Clarke (1973: 13) put it:

> Whereas their parents have never suffered the subtle racial inequalities of the British educational system, were 'invited' here (albeit to take the heaviest, dirtiest and lowest paid jobs), eventually found accommodation (albeit substandard and decaying), and were left relatively unharassed by the police and public, the picture for their children is radically different. Their education has made them more expectant and aspirant, while simultaneously, through a subtle and pervasive (although often unwitting) racism, robbing them of the means (a firm identity, self-respect and the qualifications) of achieving their higher aspirations; this situation is compounded by the job market, where even *white* unqualified working-class youths are 'virtually unemployable', by homelessness, and by a changed 'mood' noticeable both in the public and the police.

Moreover, of the options open to their parents, assimilation has proved almost impossible, while for the young black, acceptance of second-class citizenship is simply not an alternative. Only the development of a distinctive West Indian consciousness and, to an even greater extent, involvement in small-scale crime appear to offer any sort of solution to their problems.[47] As mentioned above, this will be dealt with at much greater length — and will also be put into its proper context — later. However, there is a specific piece of evidence concerning the impact of the second generation which might conveniently be included at this point.

We have seen that net West Indian migration into this country first assumed significant proportions following the passing of the 1952 McCarran-Walter Act, and came to something of a halt with the passing of the Commonwealth Immigrants Act of 1962. The actual totals (to the nearest thousand) have been as follows:

1952 — 2,000
1953 — 2,000

1954 – 10,000
1955 – 27,000
1956 – 29,000
1957 – 23,000
1958 – 15,000
1959 – 16,000
1960 – 50,000
1961 – 66,000
1962 – 32,000

We have also seen that the greatest concentration of West Indians (especially Jamaicans) in London is in Lambeth. If we add to this the fact that mugging is a crime committed mainly by 14–16-year-olds,[48] then the 'second generation' thesis, would suggest a significant increase in the proportion of muggings occurring in Lambeth as from about 1969 (i.e. 1955 + 14) onwards. Figure 7.1 illustrates that this has indeed proved to be the case. In 1970, almost precisely at the time one would have predicted, mugging in Lambeth proportionately doubled from about 8 per cent to about 16 per cent – at which level it has since remained.[49]

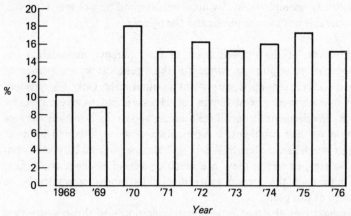

Figure 7.1 Mugging: 'L' District as a percentage of the MPD, 1968–76

(The breakdown for the years prior to 1968 not available)

As a summary of this chapter as a whole, and of the second-generation thesis in particular, a final, if rather long, quotation from Jefferson and Clarke (1973: 23) gives an excellent 'ideal-type' pen-picture of the career development of a West Indian youth:

He leaves school at the earliest opportunity without qualifications and with a firm belief that White Society has taken no real interest in his educational welfare. His prospects, which he can see only too clearly, are a series of 'dead-end' jobs, interspersed with long periods of unemployment or more-or-less continuous unemployment. Underemployed or unemployed (and virtually unemployable) he rows with his parents who do not fully appreciate the changed nature of the employment situation (from the full employment of the early 1950s to the technological unemployment of the late 1960s) nor the child's hostile response to this situation resulting from his very different aspirations. The parents blame the child, the more harshly since their hopes were heavily centred on his succeeding where they failed. A result of this row, or series of rows (exacerbated by the overcrowded accommodation), is that the youth leaves home. On the move from friend to friend or sleeping rough and isolated from parents, much time is spent on the streets. Here he comes into contact with the police. They probably see him as idle, apathetic and, in some vague way, a threat, in his constant bored loitering. Especially if it is late at night they will probably stop and search him — just to let him know they want no trouble. Ironically, this harassment and intimidation, oft-repeated, has the reverse effect. The youth learns, from such experiences, to fear and hate the police.

So, poor, bored, homeless and increasingly alienated, since the only official agents of society he comes into contact with are bureaucratic officials in the Social Security and Youth Employment Office (who will often make him feel it is his fault for not having a job, begrudge him his money and 'free' time and often keep him running around after jobs they know he has little chance of getting simply to keep him occupied) and the hated police, he can become desperate. At this point crime can become an option since it is a 'solution', at least temporarily, to his problem.

It is to a closer analysis of this 'solution' that we must now turn.

[8] Conclusions and recommendations

Introduction

The reasons for embarking upon this study were set out in some detail in the General Introduction, but, in essence, reduce to the fact that while mugging[1] can be described as an extremely serious category of crime, it is nevertheless one on which very little research appears to have been carried out. Thus, the core of this analysis has been descriptive in that a close study has been made of a random sample of muggings within the Metropolitan Police District, the results of which, together with comparisons made with those very few earlier studies which proved at all relevant, have provided a factual basis for further more detailed and comparative study and research. The aim of such a method is, as Glaser and Strauss put it in their *Discovery of Grounded Theory: Strategies for Qualitative Research* (1968: 24), 'constantly to work outwards from the data, always to endeavour to generalise specific explanations to other situations'.

So far it has been shown that mugging is a problem, that it is an increasing problem, and that it is an increasing *social* problem: but what of the causes, structures and meanings of the phenomena being studied? Certainly no attempt has been, or will be, made to derive a totally new social theory. In a work of this kind this would be overambitious. The aim has been to look anew at the problems involved in the light of the specific data collected in order to isolate, and to offer an explanation of, the distinctive features associated with that type of crime we call 'mugging'.

Taylor, Walton and Young (1973: 237)[2] tell us of students 'bothered by the "unreality" of criminological studies, by which they meant the lack of sustained connection between theories and statistics about crime'. It is hoped that this criticism could not be levelled at this study: nevertheless, it is fully appreciated that there remain a number of 'untied ends' and the object of this final chapter is therefore to review, and in some instances to expand upon, what has so far been said; to introduce a number of additional concepts which, although of considerable relevance, have yet to be put into their correct context; and, most importantly, to discuss in terms of social policy a range of possible measures which could perhaps be taken if an attempt is to be made to alleviate some of the problems involved. Such a procedure will be categorised under the four headings thought to be most appropriate, namely, 'facts', 'causes', 'meaning' and 'some possible solutions'.

Facts

In chapters 3, 4 and 5 it has been shown that robbery in general, and mugging in particular, are viewed by members of the public as very serious crimes indeed,[3] and that, even though the mass media play an important part in the dissemination and reinforcement of this attitude, there can be little doubt that any fear an individual may have of personally being mugged is far from groundless. Details of the vast increase experienced in London have been discussed at length in chapter 4, where it was stated that

> the *real* point is that the total figure of 671 which caused McClintock, and others, such concern as recently as 1959, has now risen to well over 6,000.

This represents something like a tenfold increase in less than two decades, with the figure doubling at the rate of about once every four or five years. Within the totals for robbery as a whole, the proportion of muggings is becoming progressively greater, and there seems little likelihood of this trend being reversed: indeed, if the American experience is taken into account, it becomes obvious that there is room for a considerable further expansion. The annual mugging total for England and Wales is not recorded,[4] but on the basis of the 1977 Metropolitan Police District figure of some 3,700 this is most unlikely to be in excess of 20,000.[5] In the United States there were 175,000 recorded muggings as long ago as in 1970, at which time the average American citizen's chance of being mugged was about 1 in 1,200 — though as Hunt (1975: 31) tells us:

> If the city-dweller lives in or near high-crime slums, or travels through them, and if he has at least some of the traits of the likely victim,

his present chances of being mugged in any given year must be several times greater than this – at a conservative guess, around one in 100.

In London as a whole one's 'yearly average chance' of being mugged is currently in the order of one in 2,000, though in certain more vulnerable areas this undoubtedly rises to at least one in 1,000, and quite possibly one in 500.

Moreover, this takes no account of unreported attacks. Chapter 4 deals at length with the 'dark figure' of crime, but it should now be added that, although one of the very reasons for undertaking a study of mugging was because it was felt that such a crime, being generally considered so serious, is more likely to be reported by the victim, it is possible that, as mugging loses its 'novelty value', such an argument may now apply far less forcibly than it did five years ago. Certainly, the general feeling amongst most criminologists of today appears to be that the published statistics bear less and less of a direct relationship to the amount of crime actually committed. For example, recent (1977) estimates of the size of the dark figure have ranged as high as 90 per cent (Sparks, Genn and Dodd, 1978), or even 95 per cent (Radzinowicz, 1977). Some commentators, indeed, feel that even estimates such as these err on the side of caution[6] (while, as C. H. Rolph tells us,[7] the much used 'tip of the iceberg' analogy is no good, because the iceberg tip varies precisely in proportion to its submerged mass, which the crime tip does not). All in all, although it still seems certain that the mugging statistics for London are not bedevilled by anything like the same level of unknown offences as indictable crime as a whole, it might well be that, in certain isolated areas, the annual chance of being robbed of one's personal belongings in a random attack by a stranger in the street would prove to be something in the order of one in 200, or even more.

There is, unfortunately, no way in which one can be more precise. Radzinowicz (1977: 17) estimates that 'less than a dozen countries, most of them small, can offer anything approximating to full and reliable statistics', and England and Wales is not one of them: which is precisely why the bulk of the statistical side of this study has been concentrated on a randomly chosen, relatively small, but therefore manageable, sample of muggings in respect of which precise details were readily available. The method of selection and the results obtained are explained and discussed in chapter 5: a considerable amount of useful data is contained therein, of which the following points are perhaps most worthy of note.

Definitely the most surprising finding was that, despite the presumed greater 'vulnerability' of females, more than 80 per cent of victims were in fact male; perhaps the most striking was that about three-quarters of all assailants were under the age of seventeen. On comparing these results with those of McClintock some twenty years earlier[8] it was found that the percentage of male victims had not changed all that dramatically,[9] but that the change in the age structure of assailants has been such that it is a factor worth emphasising. For instance, McClintock's study shows that in London in 1950, 23 per cent of convicted robbers were under the age of twenty-one, and even by 1957 this proportion had risen only to 29 per cent. By the late 1960s the proportion of arrested robbers under the age of twenty-one first reached 50 per cent, while, in the present study, the figure in respect of mugging is no less than 89 per cent.[10]

As an extension of these comparisons, an analysis has now been carried out of the age on arrest for robbery in the Metropolitan Police District since the war. Concentrating (for the sake of simplicity) on the percentage under or over the age of twenty-one the change as between the first five years after the war, and the past five years, has been as follows:[11]

	under 21	%	over 21	%	(total)
1946–50	377	35	697	65	(1,074)
1972–76	5,170	61	3,307	39	(8,477)

This means that, since the war, arrests for robbery of persons over the age of twenty-one have increased fivefold, and of persons under the age of twenty-one no less than fourteenfold. (It should be noted that such differences are not explained by changes in the age structure of the general population. The age groupings employed in the national census do not, unfortunately, tie in directly with those used here, but the proportion of the (most appropriate) 10–19 age-group was about 12 per cent in 1951, and rose to only 13 per cent in 1971.)[12]

Concern about the involvement of juveniles in crime is, of course, no new phenomenon. Consider, for example, the following passage:

The number of children and young persons arrested continues to increase. Much has been said and written during the year on this subject and the view seems to be widely held that the number of arrests is no indication of a greater prevalence of crime amongst the young. Various reasons are put forward to account for the rise in the figures. The first is that the number of children of the ages in question in this country has increased in the last few years . . . . The second reason offered is that police vigilance is greater and that a greater number of arrests are made in proportion to offences than formerly . . . . Yet another explanation given is that people are less reluctant to bring young people to justice now than they used to be . . . . While it may be that the cumulative effect of these three causes all operating in the same direction has had a substantial effect on the figures, there is no means of checking the extent of such effect, and, whatever allowances and explanations may be made, there is no escape from the fact that *the juvenile crime figures are far higher than they ought to be and that the position shows no sign of improvement.* [my italics]

The point is that this appeared in the *Report of the Commissioner of Police of the Metropolis* for the year 1936! Of the three 'explanations' offered at that time, the possibility that 'people are less reluctant to bring young people to justice now than they used to be' would, now as then, be almost impossible to test. However, the contention that 'the number of children of the ages in question in this country has increased in the last few years' has already been discounted (see above), while there are a number of arguments to contradict the theory that 'police vigilance is greater and that a greater number of arrests are made in proportion to offences than formerly'. For example, it can easily be demonstrated that the proportion of arrests to offences has *reduced* in recent years,[13] while on 'L' District – which in chapters 6 and 7 has already been isolated as having the greatest concentration of muggings – any suggestion that the apparent level of mugging is simply a function of police activity[14] must be at least partly disproved by Table 8.1, which indicates clear-up rates (for robbery as a whole) in respect of each police district during 1975. It can be seen that only one District ('X') had a lower clear-up rate than 'L' – an indication, one would imagine, that police respond to (and are overwhelmed by) the problem rather than cause it.

One further theory should be discounted at this point: the idea that juveniles commit only 'petty' crime. In an unpublished paper dated September 1974 and entitled 'Juvenile Crime (A "Vicious Perplexity")', Peter Marshall, then Commander of the Metropolitan Police Community Relations Branch, now Commissioner of the City of London Police, wrote:

Table 8.1 *Robbery in the MPD: clear-up rates by District, 1975*

'A' District	38%
'B' District	21%
'C' District	32%
'D' District	31%
'E' District	24%
'F' District	23%
'G' District	22%
'H' District	30%
'J' District	30%
'K' District	18%
'L' District	17%
'M' District	34%
'N' District	22%
'P' District	22%
'Q' District	22%
'R' District	36%
'S' District	42%
'T' District	40%
'V' District	35%
'W' District	23%
'X' District	15%
'Y' District	33%
'Z' District	33%
'MPD'	26%

Some [juvenile crime] may be petty and some may be committed by youthful psychological casualties, but closer examination shows the steepest increases in categories of crime which only the blinkered observer would describe as 'petty' or 'childish'. (p. 3)

Specifically as far as mugging is concerned the following example, based on the official police report, would most certainly support such a contention.[15] In 1974, on a Friday evening in February, a 21-year-old female was surrounded by a gang of seven other females as she walked along a street in Lambeth. When she tried to escape she was held and threatened with a piece of wood and a burning cigarette, whilst a demand for her to hand over her money was made. With the assistance of a male passer-by she eventually managed to escape and make her way to some flats. Unbeknown to her, the seven attackers had followed her there and as she entered the stairway they attacked again, punching her about the face and head whilst pulling at her bag. In the struggle her purse, containing just 37 pence and some house keys, fell to the ground and was picked up by the attackers, who then ran off leaving the victim to telephone the police. In due course all seven were identified, arrested, and appeared before the Lambeth Juvenile Court. Six had previous criminal records, three had previous convictions for robbery. Their ages were 16, 15, 15, 13, 13, 12 and 10![16]

Causes

Today the idea of a single cause of crime has been discredited, and what Sir Cyril Burt was the first to call the 'principle of multiple causation' has become firmly established. To take one example, Lord Pakenham, in his 1958 *Causes of Crime*, identified and listed nine broad headings, as follows:

Natural Endowment;
The Influence of the Family;
The Influence of the School or Club;
The Atmosphere of the Times;
Economic and Social Conditions;
Religious Atmosphere;
Effectiveness or Otherwise of the Police;
Penal Treatment;
'X' Characteristics of the Criminal

Many of these are of indisputable importance and some have already been discussed in detail — but many others might have been included: Burt (1925), for instance, listed no fewer than *170* distinct conditions, every one of which was considered conducive to delinquency.

But whenever such categorisations are considered, it is important to remember, as pointed out by Albert Cohen (1955), that 'causes' must not be confused with 'factors'. Race provides a good case in point: we have seen that, as far as muggings are concerned, race is certainly a factor which must be taken into account, but is, in no sense, a 'cause'. Bearing this distinction in mind, the main factors involved in mugging have been the subject-matter of this study, and have already been discussed at some length: as to causes, there are one or two specific 'theories' which should be mentioned at this point — one of the most frequently raised being the effect of war.

This is a theme which has been taken up by a number of writers, although, as far as mugging in London is concerned, it can easily be shown that there is little or no substance in the contention of Mays (1963: 31), supported by many others, that

> There is therefore a strong *prima facie* case for connecting the general upset in family and social life during the war years with the anti-social behaviour of young people who, at a particularly suscep- tible and sensitive stage of their psychological development, had to endure exceptionally adverse conditions. If this is true, and the evidence points strongly in favour of this theory, then these sub- sequently abnormal delinquent youngsters are to be thought of more as victims of circumstances than as being exceptionally depraved or vicious.

Firstly, it was shown in chapter 4 that the period of the late 1940s and early 1950s has been about the only time during the past fifty years when mugging actually reduced. Secondly, the vast acceleration in the number of muggings in recent years has now categorically proved that such theories about the adverse effects of the Second World War must surely have been wrong.

Change in family structure and attitudes is a closely related topic, and here the war *has* had something of a delayed effect in so far as the post-war birth bulge (aided by the influx of mainly young immigrants) has produced what Terence Morris calls a 'striking change in the demo- graphic profile of the nation';[17] that is to say, there are simply more young people about these days than there were in the interwar years.[18] There is also the question of 'working mothers'. The effect on family life, and more particularly on the children, of absent mothers is far too wide a topic to discuss at length here: it seems likely, however, that it is a factor which must have had some bearing on the increase in delin- quency,[19] while, as Robert Wilson tells us in his *New Society* article entitled 'Crime and Punishment in England':

> Though it may pain the sophisticated to encounter such apparently Victorian sentiments, it seems inescapable that we have witnessed a change in the moral quality of family life that has had, along with other factors, a profound effect on the general level of public safety and security.

All the available evidence suggests that this has indeed been the case, and it is a theme to which we will be returning later. In general, how- ever, it is more plausible to consider the causes of mugging as being deep-rooted in the social structure, rather than to single out particular causes as having an autonomous influence. Even less would it be possible to quantify the 'weighting' which should be allocated to each. The most that can be said is that crime is a product of a large number, and great variety, of factors which cannot be organised into general propositions having no exceptions. In other words, no 'scientific' theory of criminal behaviour is possible. Indeed, to end this section in a somewhat humorous vein, however 'scientific' one tried to be in analysing the causes of mugging, it is doubtful whether the results achieved would be any real improvement on this cartoon.

This is six parts need, to three parts social protest, to one part sheer enjoyment.

Meaning

If precise causes are difficult, if not impossible, to identify, what of the 'meaning' of mugging? Here we come to the heart of the matter if only because an action is, in itself, unlikely to have any significance until, and unless, it is put into its social context.[20] For something publicly viewed as seriously as mugging, because the overall picture is so complex, it is perhaps even more important to realise that only through a knowledge of the significance, or meaning, of the action taken can a true understanding of the phenomenon in question be acquired.

With this in mind, the approach that will here be adopted will be to concentrate on two specific examples, firstly of how a criminologist, or other 'outside observer', might view mugging, and, secondly, the significance the mugger himself might attach to his actions. It is stressed that the two examples are by no means exhaustive and are simply used as explanatory models, partly to give an indication of the range of alternative meanings that can be ascribed to the same set of actions, but more particularly as a vehicle for focusing attention on some of the more important factors which must be taken into consideration in a study of this kind.[21]

(i) *Mugging as simply one aspect of a violent society*

A number of commentators have identified the later 1960s and early 1970s as a period of 'law and order crisis', and accord the 'mugging explosion' a prominent position in its development,[22] Steve Chibnall, for example, points to the convergence of themes as illustrated in Figure 8.1.

As Chibnall (1977: 121) sees it:

> In Gunman, Bomber, and Thug are the shadowy and half-recognised spectres of anomie, the chaos of expectation, the disruption of the taken for granted. This is the key to understanding the peculiar generality of the law-and-order crisis, the reason why it becomes inseparable from the anxiety engendered when gasmen, miners, and electricity workers withdraw their labour, behaviour which, although perfectly legal, carries the connotations of lawlessness.

It is just such a theme which has been developed by the mugging research group at the University of Birmingham, whose members tackle the problem in terms of thresholds — 'boundaries staking out progressively societal tolerance limits' — as illustrated in Figure 8.2.

The crossing of the Permissiveness threshold, they argue, threatens to undermine social *authority* (moral standards); the crossing of the Legality threshold threatens to undermine social *legitimacy* (parliamentary channels); and the crossing of the Extreme Violence threshold threatens to undermine social *control* (the State itself). In their view there has been an increasing tendency for events to be pushed beyond such thresholds: between 1966 and 1970, they suggest, the threshold of Permissiveness was dominant; from 1970 onwards, the threshold of Legality was dominant; and since 1972, the threshold of Extreme Violence has been dominant.[23]

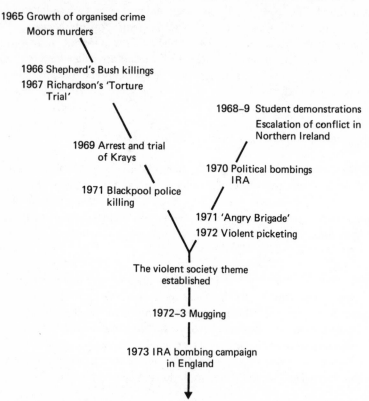

Figure 8.1 Criminal and political violence: convergence of themes

I would argue that this represents an extreme and overly confident view of the impending crisis of Western capitalist society, inasmuch as mugging is seen as a relatively unimportant symptom of a general drift towards what might be described as a Hobbesian state of eternal conflict. However, their view is not without some supporting evidence. For instance, as an extension of Chibnall's point quoted above, there can now be little doubt that the trade union consciousness (stemming from a realisation of the strength of the worker if collectively organised) has at least the potential to become a revolutionary consciousness:[24] while it could be contended that the recent expansion of the National Front movement can most usefully be seen as a manifestation of the desire of extremists to make maximum political

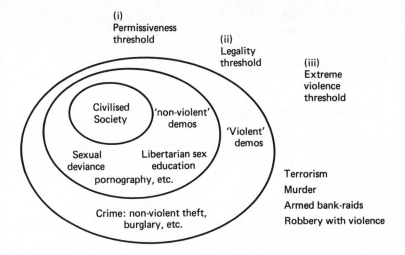

Figure 8.2 Criminal and political violence: thresholds

capital out of violence in general and mugging by coloured youths in particular.[25]

Such developments are arguably the kind which *could* lead to total anarchy, but this does not alter the fact that the case presented by the writers discussed above is surely exaggerated. The grouping together of trade union militancy, terrorist bombings, and the growth of mugging, violent demonstrations and the like, has a certain attraction and stimulates fresh thought on the development of the phenomena involved. There are, however, two serious drawbacks. Firstly, it can be argued that society is *less* violent now than it has ever been. Tobias's contentions in this respect have already been discussed at some length in chapter 4,[26] while Bernard Crick (1974: 20) – arguing with conviction that organised society will *not* disintegrate – tells us that

> Even in our political and economic crises it is so depressingly more likely that things will shamble on, second-rate, dull, undemanding and a bit seedy, rather than oblige holders of alternative visions by breaking down for them.

Secondly, the 'Convergence of Violence' thesis is too simple. It claims to offer a useful guide to the direction in which society is currently heading, but, if it is able to offer any solutions at all, these are necessarily of a Utopian variety. In the short term such an ideological approach is unhelpful, and diverts attention from present problems and realistic strategies: what we really need to know is what, if anything, can be done about mugging *now*. Practical measures, not grand theory, must be given first priority.

(ii) *Mugging as a cultural option*

Whereas crimes such as burglary and fraud are almost entirely economic in nature, mugging is far better explained in terms of what might best be described as a 'cultural option':[27] for a certain type of person mugging is the 'done thing'; it indicates 'style' or *'machismo'*; or (as a young West Indian, interviewed by Jefferson and Clarke, put it), 'Tievin's freedom, man'. It is perhaps better thought of, therefore, not so much as criminal activity as an attempt to establish a social identity, and in this sense I would argue that mugging bears a close resemblance to the mods/rockers/hippies/skinheads and other similar phenomena. Certainly the 'preconditions' are likely to be very much the same: deprived background, restricted family life, limited education, substandard housing.[28] Thus, Tony Jefferson's description of a typical Ted of some ten years ago could easily apply to the typical mugger of today: (a) born in South London, (b) from the *lumpenproletariat*, (c) occupationally unskilled, semi-skilled or unemployed.[29] Or, again tying in very closely with the results of this study, Dick Hebdige characterises the Mods as being 'the dispossessed, the lower working class and principally the *young* lower working class'.[30]

The present eruption of soccer hooliganism displays many of the same trademarks: only through their favourite team can certain fans hope to find any semblance of 'success' in life. Should they be frustrated in this vicarious pleasure then there is likely to be trouble. As the young fan quoted by Chris Murray in his *New Society* article entitled 'The Soccer Hooligan's Honour System' puts it, 'It's just if your team get beat. Good supporters don't like a team getting beat, so we wait for the other supporters to come out and give it to them. Show them who's boss.'

Mugging can be seen then as an alternative to, perhaps even a development from, these various other forms of cultural option: why, though, is it a phenomenon which has recently come so dramatically to the fore? To some extent this may be a reflection of its being the current 'fashion', seized upon and augmented by the media[31] and caught in what might be termed a 'self-perpetuating escalation', described so well by Stanley

Cohen in his *Folk Devils and Moral Panics*, and by Ian Taylor (in terms of 'Soccer Consciousness and Soccer Hooliganism') as follows:

> As the scale of control increases, that is, as magistrates become more ready to sentence offenders and police become more willing to act (knowing they will obtain convictions), then by definition there develops an 'objective' demonstration of the scale of the problem. That is, more and more soccer hooligans appear in the criminal statistics and the need for further control is emphasized. (1971: 160)

But there are other, more deep-rooted, reasons. The results of the study outlined in chapter 5 show that the attacker is 'almost certain to be male and is likely to be alone or in a small group of two or three. The chances are high that he will be under the age of twenty-one, and more often than not he will be black', that is to say the four main characteristics of the typical mugger are:

> (a) male,
> (b) alone,
> (c) young,
> (d) black.

The description 'male',[32] and 'young',[33] is common to all those other cultural options of the type mentioned above. What, though, of (b) and (d)? Race was the subject of chapter 7 and only the main points need be recapitulated here, while the fact that the mugger is normally alone (or at the most in a group of two or three) can, and will, be analysed in terms of the demonstrable individualism of the typical West Indian.

I have argued that small-scale crime such as mugging is one of the few options available to members of the black population (particularly to second-generation immigrants) as a counter to the resentment and discrimination, notably in the fields of housing and education, with which they are frequently confronted. It should now be added that this will especially be the case in a generally deteriorating economic situation, which causes concern to all and an actual reduction in the standard of living of many. During such a period, to quote Lawrence,

> there can be little doubt that racial discrimination will appear more salient than in a stable or improving situation. There is a greater possibility that members of the white indigenous population will

feel resentful towards coloured people better placed than themselves. There is a greater possibility that preference will be given to
white people when scarce jobs are allocated. There is less possibility
that sufficiently strong action will be taken to ensure that coloured
people do not face discrimination when seeking jobs. (1974: 127)

Sheila Patterson (1963) expresses this same sentiment in terms of
discrimination being related to the 'degree of economic insecurity'
felt by the working population, and points out that this is no new
development. Kenneth Little, for instance, showed in *Negroes in Britain*
how discrimination against coloured seamen in Cardiff swelled in the
shipping industry's lean years from 1921 to 1938, while, in *The Coloured
Quarter*, Michael Banton showed that the only serious disturbance of
the first ten post-war years occurred in Liverpool where the level of
unemployment was relatively high.

We have seen that the original reason for the encouragement of
immigration was economic, in the sense that West Indians were required
to carry out certain jobs: it would appear that the converse also applies,
in that the fewer the jobs available the less that West Indian immigrants
are 'wanted'. Hence, when the moderate recession of 1956–58 came,
the West Indian workers were the first to experience redundancy even
in South London where the setback was relatively mild, and this
applied even more so in the late 1960s and early 1970s (at just the time
mugging was making such a dramatic advance), when Britain's economy
was such that the many problems 'normally' experienced by coloured
immigrants in this country were accentuated still further. If the 'urban
battleground' makes life difficult for many whites, the argument goes,
it becomes very difficult for the average black, and downright impossible for the average *young* black.[34] And, without homes or jobs, it is
hardly surprising that many become disillusioned and a few turn to
anti-social behaviour and even criminal activities. For this group, as
Jefferson and Clarke (1973: 23) tell us:

Mugging is the 'perfect' crime: needing no criminal knowledge or
skill to execute, it is both 'instrumental' (in that it can supplement
income) and 'expressive', with its violence, of the felt desperation
and hostility.

Of the points mentioned, it is felt that the last is by far the most
important. The actual financial gain from a mugging is normally so
small that it must be seen as totally incidental to the main object of the

operation, which, I would suggest, must therefore be to demonstrate toughness and masculinity,[35] and, even more crucially, to strike fear both individually and collectively into the white population who, again in the words of Jefferson and Clarke, 'have for so many centuries held (both literally and metaphorically) the whip hand'.

Just as the succession of youth cultures typified by the Mods and Rockers endeavoured to demonstrate their independence from the adult world, which exemplified what they saw as an overbearing and unjust society,[36] so the black youth sees mugging as an ideal means of 'getting his own back' on a society which he considers has done him no favours at all, and which is dominated by unfeeling and unsympathetic whites.[37] The *Evening News* leader of 15 January 1975 may have been exaggerating slightly to suggest that 'to be young and black in London is to be without hope', but it would be far more difficult to dispute its contention that 'A young and touchy generation of black boys and girls is seeking to avenge itself on a society which it regards as cold, complacent and hostile', or, indeed, the argument, as expressed by Linsay Mackie in a *Guardian* article of 1 September 1976, that 'going on the rampage will not solve the predicament of young blacks and nobody thinks it will. But the solutions to their plight are drearily few — and probably getting fewer in a society where the majority community is becoming increasingly short-tempered about the ethnic communities within it.'

Mugging could even be seen as a potent expression of 'black power' in the sense that it represents one of the very few means by which a member of the black population feels he can exert some sort of control over his own identity: but there is another, less ideological and more down-to-earth, reason why mugging has emerged as the perfect cultural option for disillusioned young West Indians. All the 'traditional' youth cultures quite clearly stem from the gregarious instinct of 'let's band together and show 'em who's boss'. Now, although it might be argued that this is precisely the point of movements such as Black Power, in fact, deep-rooted in West Indian culture is the motivation to 'go it alone'. This stems initially from the not so very far off days of slavery — when it was very much to the owner's advantage if he could keep slaves from communicating with each other,[38] and thus lessen the risk of a concerted uprising — and has since been perpetuated by such factors as the following recorded by Hiro:

the West Indian community in Britain was composed of many subcommunities, each one loyal to its own island of origin; and forging a single West Indian identity was not an easy task. Long distances between islands in the Caribbean — stretching across a crescent whose two ends are as far apart as London and Morocco — has fostered individual identities among islanders and inter-island rivalries. The British hegemony over the islands had further strengthened these tendencies by encouraging liaison between each island and the metropolitan country, and discouraging inter-island contacts. For instance it took ten weeks for a letter to travel directly from Jamaica to Trinidad but only a month if routed via Britain. (1971: 43)

From her 1963 study of Brixton, Sheila Patterson felt that the individual West Indian migrant's concentration on economic activities, high residential mobility and the intention to return home within a few years were all factors which had impeded the growth of a stable internal social organisation. In fact:

> The Somerleyton-Geneva Road area calls to mind Zorbaugh's de-
> scription of Chicago's near North side in the 1920s: 'an area of tran-
> sition, an anonymous rooming-house area without community
> tradition or much informal social control, a world where behaviour is
> impulsive rather than social . . . a world of atomised individuals or
> spirited nomads'. (1963: 184)

This is still the case today.[39] There *are* a certain number of West Indian Clubs and Associations to be found in Brixton, and other such areas, but the basic individualism of the West Indian when compared, for example, to the Asian immigrant remains apparent. The absence of a tradition of following a recognised leader (as suggested by Hiro); a lack of the support that Asians derive from a different religion, and a kin or locality-based network that helps members in distress (as sug-gested by Banton); or the strength and self-contained nature of Asian culture arising from a pattern of colonialism (as suggested by Jefferson and Clarke) are among the many reasons which may help to explain the difference between the two cultures but, in any event, going around in 'herds' — as in the case of soccer hooligans[40] — just does not seem to appeal to the average young second-generation West Indian. It is in activities such as mugging, with its inherent individualism, that he sees the perfect way of giving vent to the frustrations with which he is con-fronted and for which he blames a society dominated by the white man. With this in mind it should come as no great surprise that, as con-firmed by this study, something like 60 per cent of muggers are black and approaching 90 per cent of their victims are white, for, as Gerald Priestland puts it:

> At the root of all violence lies Man's ambition, rather than innate cruelty: his will not merely to survive in Schopenhauer's sense but to assert *his* definition of his own identity, and his impatience to assert it through the language of force when persuasion and argument have failed. I act, therefore I am. (1974: 133)

Some possible solutions

This final chapter has tended to concentrate on the 'suitability' of mugging as an activity to be indulged in by young West Indian immigrants. However, when it comes to suggesting possible solutions to what members of the public at least see as a very serious problem,[41] it is best to think in more general terms: we are, after all, attempting to analyse London muggings as a whole and not just those of one particular type, and, in any event (as shown in chapter 7), many of the longer-term 'solutions' to the specific problems associated with coloured immigrants (ranging from anti-discrimination legislation to restrictions on immigration and enforced repatriation) have already proved to be practically worthless.

As a first step in any 'anti-mugging campaign', we must not forget those simple measures which can be taken to reduce the likelihood of a particular mugging taking place, and high on any list of preventative measures must come the encouragement of potential victims *not* to frequent certain places at certain times.[42] To take a somewhat trite comparison, just as there is no football hooliganism every other week at Stamford Bridge, so there would be no (or at least very little) mugging if people did not put themselves at risk by going out at night, alone, along unlit streets, in localities such as Lambeth.[43] Police rightly have an aversion to what are popularly termed 'no-go' areas[44] (being eager to claim that their resources will be directed to those areas where they are most needed), but this is not quite what we are talking about here: one is simply arguing that a campaign should be mounted to advise people, especially the old and infirm, to consider their routes carefully, perhaps to carry a whistle or other warning device,[45] certainly to go about whenever possible in pairs or groups.[46]

Another of the possible 'simple solutions' would be to attempt to reduce the incidence of truancy. It is currently estimated by police and local authorities alike that more than a third of juvenile crime is committed by truants,[47] and many researchers have pointed to the relationship between absence from school and criminal activity. For example, in his 1975 analysis of the causal factors of juvenile theft, Belson found that an appreciable amount of stealing goes on during truancy, and that the frequency of playing truant is related to the amount of stealing done; while in a Metropolitan Police study of 106 persistent juvenile recidivists, no fewer than 89 were described as frequent or occasional truants.[48] It would be very difficult to prove, but the raising of the compulsory school-leaving age from 15 to 16 would appear to have much to answer for in this respect: the Inner London Education Authority now 'admits' to an overall average of 15 per cent of secondary school pupils being absent at any one time,[49] and in some London Boroughs the figure must certainly be well in excess of 20 per cent. Moreover, doubts are increasingly being expressed over the reliability of school records. How many children, for instance, are marked 'present' at the start of the day and then promptly disappear? It is stressed that one is not suggesting that truancy is necessarily a cause of delinquency, but that the two are certainly associated: and there is no doubt that mugging is a type of crime which is becoming increasingly concentrated amongst the very age group we are here considering. It could only be of help, therefore, if measures such as quicker action by schools to recognise and deter truants, harsher penalties for parents of persistent truants, and encouragement to the police to continue their 'truant sweeps'[50] were all introduced as soon as possible.

Practical measures such as the above could be introduced with almost immediate effect, but there is also much that can be done in the medium and long term. In this respect a useful framework is provided by the final report of the (US) National Commission on the Causes and Prevention of Violence,[51] published in 1969:

> We believe that the twin objectives of the social order must be to make violence both unnecessary and unrewarding. To make violence unnecessary, our institutions must be capable of providing justice for all who live under them − of giving all a satisfactory stake in the normal life of the community and the nation. To make violence unrewarding, our institutions must be able to control violence when it occurs, and to do so firmly, fairly and within the law.

As to making violence unrewarding, it is best to discuss separately those persons whose job it is to apprehend offenders (what Radzinowicz calls conventional protections, that is to say formal agencies of control such as the police), and those methods of dealing with offenders once they have been convicted. As to the first heading, if what we read in the papers is to be believed, a substantial improvement in the lot, and therefore, it is argued, in the number, of policemen in London would solve *all* our crime problems overnight.[52] Unfortunately, this is far from being the case: in fact it would be very difficult to produce any evidence to show in general terms that there is any sort of inverse relationship between the number of police available and the amount of crime committed. At the same time it is clearly totally inadequate that London, with a resident population (not to mention visitors) of something like 7.5 million, has only about 21,000 serving police officers.[53] If we exclude senior management, administrators, specialists and those on courses, sick or on annual leave, and then (in order to cater for a 24-hour-a-day, seven-day-a-week coverage) we divide the remainder by four, we find that at any one time London is being protected by only some two or three thousand patrolling policemen. Small wonder, then, that there are calls[54] for the Government to increase expenditure on the police service. Moreover, when it comes to the prevention of a specific category of crime such as mugging, the case for augmenting the police becomes even stronger. The deployment of extra police, both uniformed and plain clothes, in areas where street attacks have been taking place must obviously help to deter a potential offender: in particular, the setting up of 'mugging squads' has already met with some success,[55] and is an approach which should be encouraged.

The other half of any bid to 'make violence unrewarding' is far less clear-cut. In chapter 3 some evidence has already been produced to suggest that there is no inverse relationship between the severity of sentences passed and the number of robberies committed, and this conclusion is one supported by many modern criminologists. Punitive reaction to crime, the argument goes, has proved singularly unhelpful in the past and there is no reason to believe that it will serve society any better in the future. To rely on the criminal justice system will only isolate delinquents and make their integration into the community that much more difficult. Even fines can often encourage dishonesty by increasing delinquents' debts: detention centres and borstals are expensive, overcrowded, and for petty delinquents merely become a means of learning all there is to know about more serious crimes. Dennis Chapman (1968: 9) expresses it in the following way:

The present system of justice and punishment has the effect of making a small number of persons, drawn mainly from the poor, the ill-educated, and the unskilled into designated criminals. In prison they become socially isolated and culturally disorientated and often deteriorate intellectually, and on release are more vulnerable to petty misdemeanor and to detection and arrest than any other group. Once caught in the system, their disorientation is progressive.

Louis Blom-Cooper[56] even goes as far as to suggest:

> now that the Advisory Council on the Penal System has added a contemporary voice to the acknowledged futility of imprisonment we might start to dismantle our overcrowded, insanitary jails foisted on us by our Victorian ancestors.

But this is not everyone's view. Police especially are looking for more, not less, custodial accommodation for what they see as a growing hard-core of juvenile offenders who are resisting remedial care and from whom the community is entitled to expect some measure of protection; while the Criminal Injuries Compensation Board, in its annual report for 1976, expressed the view that too many courts were still imposing what its members saw as totally inadequate sentences for violent crime ('there seem to us to be too many cases in which an offender who has caused serious injuries is fined less than a week's take-home pay'). Or again, in mid 1977 (mainly as a reaction against the 1969 Children and Young Persons Act, which had shifted the emphasis away from institutional care for juvenile offenders and replaced it with treatment within the community), William Whitelaw, then the Conservative Party's spokesman for Home Affairs,[57] launched in the House of Commons a well-publicised campaign for the setting-up, on an ambitious scale, of attendance centres for delinquents, and of Army-style 'glasshouse' imprisonment aimed at giving 'a short, sharp and permanent shock to thugs who at the moment feel free to terrorise old people, thousands of whom are housebound not through physical disability but from fear of venturing into the streets'. There are, indeed, good arguments to be put on both sides of this very emotive subject, but on balance it is felt that tinkering (in whatever direction) with the penal system and/or the sentencing process is most unlikely to make any worthwhile contribution to the aim of reducing the amount of mugging in London.

Turning now to the second goal of 'making violence unnecessary', we come to possible long-term solutions — in other words to the key area of social policy. In this connection the highly relevant problem of social deprivation has been discussed at some length in chapter 6, and there is no doubt that when one reads of Paul Harrison's experience of an estate in Hackney, published in *New Society*, that

> The kids set about wrecking the place, standards deteriorate. And so on until the place becomes a noisy, dilapidated barracks, like one of the deeper circles of hell where the devil saves his manpower by using the souls to torment each other.

then the comment of the Eisenhower Commission that

> The way in which we can make the greatest progress towards reducing crime is by taking action necessary to improve the conditions of family and community life for all those who live in our cities, and especially for the poor who are concentrated in the ghetto slums.

clearly expresses an admirable sentiment. But just how can such an objective be achieved?

The two main alternatives are evolution and revolution. As to the latter possibility, Taylor, Walton and Young (1973), for instance, remind us that a 'criminal' is a product of such factors as the forced division of labour and inequalities of power, wealth and authority; is identified and labelled as a result of social reaction; is brought to trial and dealt with in the very name of society: so, for crime to be abolished, society itself must be subject to fundamental, that is to say revolutionary, change.[58] Certainly, the 'ultimate solution' of greater, if not complete, social equality is an extremely important consideration which must always be borne in mind, but this should not detract from the more modest aim of trying to find a counter to those forms of deviance – such as mugging – which are undisputedly against the best interests of the community as a whole.

But even if we reject revolution in favour of a process of more gradual evolution, one of the more obvious approaches, a simple injection of cash, is unlikely to provide even a temporary solution. In January 1975 the Government announced an allocation of £2 million (£1.25 million to London) for the youth service, in an attempt to 'deal with the growing problem of young West Indians without jobs or homes who turn to crime as a way of life'. It is evident from the crime figures quoted earlier in this chapter, and much more fully in chapter 4, that the attempt met with very little success.[59] Indeed, as suggested in chapter 6, even if the general economy of the country improved so dramatically that everyone's standard of living doubled, there is still no guarantee that the incidence of mugging would be affected in any way — America providing an excellent illustration of the fact that the price of increased affluence can often be increased vulnerability.

Fortunately, hopes for an improvement in the mugging situation are not entirely without foundation. Firstly, the sheer passing of time could well mean a vastly improved integration of what is probably *the* most problematic group, the second-generation West Indian 'immigrant'.[60] Secondly, there is one area where an injection of money, effort and good intention certainly *could* be of help, and that is in the provision of better leisure facilities. As we have seen, much juvenile delinquency stems from what are ostensibly leisure pursuits (mods, rockers, skinheads, soccer hooligans, etc.[61]), and there is clearly a demand for what Belson (1975: xvii) calls 'legal outlets for fun and excitement seeking':

> Such outlets should be forms of activity which are not only socially acceptable but are attractive to the kinds of boys already engaged in stealing or in excitement seeking activities that put them at risk.

The pattern of leisure pursuits is changing all the time,[62] but what members of the Centre for Contemporary Cultural Studies call 'pathetically inadequate facilities' remain. Not that this is a new problem: Morris, for example, quotes from a statement made by the Mayor of Croydon, as long ago as 1948, that 'another main cause [of juvenile crime] is lack of opportunity for and encouragement or guidance in the proper use of leisure' (1957), while Cohen (1973) talks of the Teds reacting 'not so much to adults, but the little that was offered in the 50s'.

It must be stressed that even if good youth clubs and the like were set up at every available opportunity there is, of course, no guarantee that anti-social behaviour such as mugging would take a dramatic turn for the better, but this nevertheless remains one area of real hope: certainly it would be very difficult not to agree with Paul Harrison (1975) when he suggests that

> Perhaps the easiest factor of all to change is facilities for play. If anyone is looking for more causes for urban aid to go to, then this should take a very high priority.

Summary

What all this amounts to is that, although the provision of a higher standard of living for all, the elimination of slums, and the full integration of racial minorities remain very worthwhile long-term aims, they are not sufficiently precise to be of much use in countering the current wave of mugging in London and elsewhere. Preventative measures carried out both by individuals and the formal agencies of control offer by far the best immediate hope, but we must also accept the fact that disillusioned youth always has been, and probably always will be, something of a problem, and that this has never applied more so than today. However, it is important to remember that the manifestation of this disillusionment in the committing of offences is not necessarily a bad thing. To take an extreme view, Radzinowicz feels that

> A society which would wholly repress crime would, in the process, have to repress all initiative, all non-conformity, all adaptation to change: there is cause to be thankful that no State has yet found a recipe for completely successful deterrence: if it had, human liberty would be at an end. (1977: 325)

while we must agree with Crick, that to denounce violence as such must surely be hypocritical when society itself has armies, police and prisons.[63]

What, then, is the answer? Mays (1963: 211) suggests that:

> The juvenile gang is not an evil phenomenon. If it indulges in excessively dangerous criminal acts it becomes undesirable. It must therefore be transformed. The good qualities must be retained, the undesirable results eliminated. Mere suppression will not achieve this end. We have to find outlets for these groups which are socially acceptable substitutes for the behaviour which in another context we deprecate. It is therefore an educational rather than a penal problem.

Such an aim could perhaps be achieved by providing adequate leisure facilities, whether these be associated with the local community, the church, professional football club, youth or any other type of organisation. For, if it is not possible to make the average working-class youth (black or white) feel he is not deprived in a general social sense, then it becomes all the more important to ensure that he has something to identify with on those occasions when he can demonstrate that he is capable of shaking free of the crushing social forces with which he feels he is surrounded.

But, before there can be *any* solution, there has to be a wider realisation that a problem exists. For, as Mays (1963: 149) tells us:

> In Britain, alas, there is a less admirable social convention tending towards the glossing over of unpalatable truths. We miscall it over here good manners and gentlemanly tact and like to pretend problems don't exist by refusing to face them in the open.

Police in particular are reluctant to talk about mugging, partly because they fear that what they say may be branded as racism, and partly because they feel that any exposure of violence will breed still more violence. That such a view is generally held was well demonstrated by the uproar which greeted the BBC television feature on Millwall football violence:[64] no one, it seemed, queried the facts as presented, but a great many people queried the desirability of making them generally known. But, at least as far as mugging in the Metropolitan Police District is concerned, the 'ignore it and it might go away' approach has clearly achieved absolutely nothing. Year after year the total rises and the Establishment expresses its concern. Perhaps we have, indeed, nothing too much to worry about, and mugging will prove to be just another fleeting phenomenon; perhaps there is nothing, short of social revolution, that can usefully be done anyway: but at least the facts should be made known to all, in the belief that a problem faced is a problem half way to being solved. This, it is hoped, will prove to be the main contribution of this study.

Appendices

Appendix 1 Sections dealing with robbery in the principal Acts concerned with larceny and related offences

1 The Larceny Act of 1861

Section 40. Whosoever shall rob any person, or shall steal any chattel, money, or valuable security from the person of another shall be guilty of felony, and being convicted thereof shall be liable, at the discretion of the court, to be kept in penal servitude for any term not exceeding fourteen years and not less than three years — or to be imprisoned for any term not exceeding two years, with or without hard labour, and with or without solitary confinement.

Section 41. If upon the trial of any person upon any indictment for robbery it shall appear to the jury upon the evidence that the defendant did not commit the crime of robbery, but that he did commit an assault with intent to rob, the defendant shall not by reason thereof be entitled to be acquitted, but the jury shall be at liberty to return as their verdict that the defendant is guilty of an assault with intent to rob; and thereupon such defendant shall be liable to be punished in the same manner as if he had been convicted upon an indictment for feloniously assaulting with intent to rob; and no person so tried as is herein lastly mentioned shall be liable to be afterward prosecuted for an assault with intent to commit the robbery for which he was so tried.

Section 42. Whosoever shall assault any person with intent to rob shall be guilty of felony, and being convicted thereof shall (save and except in the cases where a greater punishment is provided by this Act) be liable, at the discretion of the court, to be kept in penal servitude for the term of three years, or to be imprisoned for any term not exceeding two years, with or without hard labour, and with or without solitary confinement.

Section 43. Whoever shall, being armed with any offensive weapon or instrument, rob, or assault with intent to rob, any person, or shall, together with one or more other person or persons, rob, or assault with intent to rob, any person, or shall rob any person, and at the time of or immediately before or immediately after such robbery shall wound, beat, strike, or use any other personal violence to any person, shall be guilty of felony, and being convicted thereof shall be liable, at the discretion of the court, to be kept in penal servitude for life, or for any term not less than three years — or to be imprisoned for any term not exceeding two years, with or without hard labour, and with or without solitary confinement.

2 The Larceny Act of 1916

Section 23

(1) Every person who
    (a) being armed with any offensive weapon or instrument, or being together with one other person or more, robs, or assaults with intent to rob, any person;
    (b) robs any person and, at the time of or immediately before or immediately after such robbery, uses any personal violence to any person;
shall be guilty of felony and on conviction thereof liable to penal servitude for life, and, in addition, if a male, to be once privately whipped.

(2) Every person who robs any person shall be guilty of felony and on conviction thereof liable to penal servitude for any term not exceeding fourteen years.

(3) Every person who assaults any person with intent to rob shall be guilty of felony and on conviction thereof liable to penal servitude for any term not exceeding five years.

(*Note*: The punishments were amended by the *Criminal Justice Act of 1948* — penal servitude being abolished and replaced by imprisonment, and corporal punishment being abolished altogether.)

3 The Theft Act of 1968

Section 8

(1) A person is guilty of robbery if he steals, and immediately before or at the time of doing so, and in order to do so, he uses force on any person or puts or seeks to put any person in fear of being then and there subjected to force.

(2) A person guilty of robbery or of assault with intent to rob, shall on conviction or indictment be liable to imprisonment for life.

Appendix 2   Robbery

Table A2.1 *Crimes known, arrests, and methods of dealing with convicted 1832-1931 (b) England and Wales as a whole, 1932-76*

Year	Crimes known	Arrests	Cleared up	Mag. court	Tried	Acq'd	Death
1832		24		12	12	4	6
1833		15		1	14	3	5
1834		22		10	12	4	8
1835		30		16	14	3	10
1836		17		0	17	0	
1837		42		13	29	10	
1838		27		6	21	5	
1839		36		7	29	7	
1840		59		24	35	9	
1841		45		9	36	8	
1842		64		7	57	21	2[R]
1843		46		4	42	12	3[R]
1844		51		10	41	17	2[R]
1845		62		18	44	9	
1846		85		8	77	31	
1847		67		7	60	19	
1848		117		9	108	26	
1849		49		1	48	10	2[R]
1850		66		1	65	19	
1851		116		37	79	25	
1852		64		18	46	11	
1853		60		18	42	9	
1854		66		12	54	15	
1855		72		16	56	14	
1856		107		9	98	22	
1857		90		17	73	19	
1858		116		14	102	21	1[R]
1859		127		17	110	15	1[R]
1860	43	60		4	56	10	
1861	58	84		1	83	16	
1862	140	163		3	160	40	
1863	85	86		0	86	20	
1864	95	119		1	118	41	
1865	118	146		2	144	44	
1866	123	134		2	132	51	
1867	115	134		0	134	43	
1868	130	187		61	126	44	
1869	147	208		62	146	38	
1870	107	143		41	102	33	
1871	97	158		43	115	58	
1872	72	100		5	95	35	

offenders, by year, for 1832-1976 (a) Metropolitan Police District,

Transportation				Penal servitude					
7	10	11–20	Life	3	4	5	7	10	11–20
			2						
1			5						
	4	7	5						
	5	4	2						
	3	15	1						
1		7	5						
	1	13							
	6	9	2						
5	14	15	1						
11	10	1							
18	10	6	2						
9	10	3	1						
12	8	9	1						
7	18		3						
6	3	2							
4	3	2							
2		5							
		3							
		10	2						
		7							
		3							
8	4	1							
2	1								
4									
3	14	9	3						
				5		10	8	10	2
				3		9	15	14	
						12	20	6	3
						17	25	2	
						3	16	6	
						7	18	8	
						11	23	4	1
						4	13	2	
						2	10	3	1
						6	17	1	1

(cont'd over)

Table A2.1 (*cont.*)

	Imprisonment								
Year	< ½	½-1	1-2	2-3	3-4	4-5	5-7	7-10	> 10
1832									
1833									
1834									
1835									
1836									
1837									
1838									
1839									
1840	5		3	2					
1841	3	3	10	1					
1842	1	2	7	4					
1843		5	6	3					
1844	3	2	3						
1855	8	3	6	1					
1845	1	2	6						
1846	6	11	1						
1847	12	16	17	1					
1848		3	9						
1849	1	3	10						
1850	7	12	6	1					
1851	5	11	8						
1852	2	7	8	7					
1853	4	8	11	9					
1854	4	6	15	14					
1855	2	8	32	22					
1856		12	16	19					
1857	4	9	35	29					
1858	2	14	26	39					
1859	4	7	12	20					
1860	4	6	31	19					
1861		10	31	48					
1862	6	7	17	1					
1863	4	4	27	1					
1864	1	12	45	1					
1865		6	26	2					
1866	3	16	44	2					
1867	1	7	39	2					
1868		3	61	5					
1869	3	5	38	4					
1870	2	4	31	4					
1871		4	24	7					
1872									

Borstal	Prob'n	Cor.Tr.	Det.C're	Susp.S.	Fine	Other	Flogging
						1	
						1	
						2	
						1	
						1	
						2	
						3	
						2	
							2
							1
							3
						3	8
						1	13
							13
							21
							10
							5
							19

(*cont'd over*)

Table A2.1 (*cont.*)

Year	Crimes known	Arrests	Cleared up	Mag. court	Tried	Acq'd	Death
1873	52	62		4	58	24	
1874	57	63		10	53	14	
1875	59	58		7	51	17	
1876	81	104		20	84	27	
1877	121	113		36	77	33	
1878	127	119		19	100	41	
1879	105	117		28	89	27	
1880	138	98		10	88	27	
1881	140	135		16	119	34	
1882	148	182		11	171	59	
1883	102	115		12	103	36	
1884	126	113		7	106	43	
1885	114	124		4	120	31	
1886	121	125		0	125	58	
1887	103	115		4	111	35	
1888	133	138		5	133	42	
1889	111	113		12	101	20	
1890	112	105		27	78	26	
1891	123	125		47	78	20	
1892	169	132		30	102	26	
1893	133	116		37	79	18	
1894	154	135		36	99	21	
1895	131	128		32	96	26	
1896	111	117		18	99	21	
1897	141	151		53	98	30	
1898	165	192		56	136	24	
1899	131	140		31	109	29	
1900	110	124		36	88	17	
1901	115	152		42	110	20	
1902	128	142		29	113	28	
1903	99	126		33	93	16	
1904	94	101		21	80	16	
1905	90	94		14	80	25	
1906	94	103		34	69	17	
1907	97	88		24	64	20	
1908	96	83		14	69	19	
1909	76	57		16	41	11	
1910	74	78		17	61	10	
1911	72	70		21	49	4	
1912	67	77		12	65	14	
1913	59	47		8	39	7	

Transportation				Penal servitude					
7	*10*	*11–20*	*Life*	*3*	*4*	*5*	*7*	*10*	*11–20*
						4	7	3	1
						3	14	4	1
						5	11	2	
						4	12	5	2
						4	10	4	
						1	12	3	1
						6	7	2	1
						10	4		
						24	5	3	
						25	3	3	3
						17	2	1	
						19	4	2	
						8	2	2	
						10	2	1	1
						8	1		
						7	1		
						9	1	3	
						5	2		
				1	1	1	2	1	
				5	3	8	3	2	
				3	2	4	5		1
				4	2	11	7	3	1
				7	3	3	2	1	
				6	3	6			3
				8	4	4	8		
				8	1	12	5	1	
				12	4	10	4	2	
				10	4	16	2		
				8	1	5	2	3	1
				7	4	10	5		
				6	5	12	2		
				7	2	8	3	1	
				9	2	15	4		
				8	3	11	3		
				7	4	6	1		
				6	1	3	4	2	
				6		1			
				2	1	9	1		
				2	2	7	4		
				5	3	3	2		
				4					

(*cont'd over*)

Table A2.1 (*cont.*)

				Imprisonment					
Year	< ½	½–1	1–2	2–3	3–4	4–5	5–7	7–10	> 10
1873	1	5	11	2					
1874	3	2	12						
1875	1	7	7	1					
1876	1	9	23						
1877	1	11	11						
1878	2	11	24	5					
1879	1	9	32	4					
1880		10	34	3					
1881	2	10	38	3					
1882	7	20	45	6					
1883	2	16	26	3					
1884	1	9	26	2					
1885	10	26	38	2					
1886	5	18	27	2					
1887	3	19	43	2					
1888	5	36	38	2					
1889	1	26	40						
1890	5	14	23	1					
1891	2	19	31						
1892	5	16	31						
1893	6	12	24						
1894	3	23	24						
1895		16	36						
1896	5	18	37						
1897	3	15	25						
1898	3	27	52						
1899	2	12	34						
1900	1	11	27						
1901	5	18	44	1					
1902	3	26	24	4					
1903	6	15	24	6					
1904	7	6	24	2					
1905	2	7	13						
1906	1	9	16	1					
1907	1	7	15	2					
1908	6	8	17	1					
1909	2	3	15	2					
1910	5	9	19	3					
1911	5	8	13						
1912	7	7	21						
1913	1	6	19						

Borstal	Prob'n	Cor.Tr.	Det.C're	Susp.S.	Fine	Other	Flogging
							10
							7
							3
						1	3
						3	5
							3
							4
							4
							6
							7
							13
							6
						1	2
						1	2
							7
						2	2
						1	15
						2	5
							3
						3	2
						4	9
							14
						2	14
							12
						1	8
						3	26
							16
							8
						2	8
						2	8
						1	2
						4	2
						3	2
						1	1
						2	
						1	
2							
						4	
1						2	
1						1	

(*cont'd over*)

Table A2.1 (*cont.*)

Year	Crimes known	Arrests	Cleared up	Mag. court	Tried	Acq'd	Death
1914	36	32		9	23	9	
1915	20	18		3	15	3	
1916	19	12		3	9	3	
1917	38	15		3	12	1	
1918	33	32		6	26	12	
1919	61	50		8	42	19	
1920	67	68		15	53	17	
1921	38	32		1	31	3	
1922	39	47		10	37	10	
1923	36	26		5	21	8	
1924	36	22		5	17	3	
1925	42	36		11	25	7	
1926	28	22		0	22	8	
1927	30	20		7	13	2	
1928	34	23		10	13	5	
1929	60	30		9	21	4	
1930	77	43		8	35	6	
1931	104	43		17	26	4	
1932	342	162		4	124	16	
1933	219	140		7	85	19	
1934	215	151		8	100	18	
1935	182	104		8	79	24	
1936	189	152		31	90	25	
1937	209		105	11	85	23	
1938	287		143	24	124	21	
1939	268			27	96		
1940	342			50	96		
1941	483			54	230		
1942	685			93	260		
1943	730			89	284		
1944	821			44	249		
1945	1033			57	355		
1946	921		391	59	369	59	
1947	979		411	58	378	57	
1948	1101		488	90	464	57	
1949	990	610	470	96	432	56	
1950	1021		527	175	440	55	
1951	800		364	174	295	41	
1952	1002		523	117	386	44	
1953	980		510	182	422	35	
1954	812		418	133	389	36	

Transportation				Penal servitude					
7	*10*	*11–20*	*Life*	*3*	*4*	*5*	*7*	*10*	*11–20*
				15	6	5	2		
				9	5	2	1	2	
				8	1	6			
				2				1	
				5		2			
				8	1		1	1	
				6	3	2	2		1
				33	19	13	10	5	
				46	13	19	7	2	
				41	33	16	13	8	2

(cont'd over)

Table A2.1 (*cont.*)

				Imprisonment					
Year	*< ½*	*½–1*	*1–2*	*2–3*	*3–4*	*4–5*	*5–7*	*7–10*	*> 10*
1914									
1915									
1916									
1917									
1918									
1919									
1920									
1921									
1922									
1923									
1924									
1925									
1926									
1927									
1928									
1929									
1930									
1931									
1932	12	22	37						
1933	5	23	12						
1934	15	23	17						
1935	11	14	16						
1936	10	13	15						
1937	3	14	15						
1938	8	26	16						
1939									
1940									
1941									
1942									
1943									
1944									
1945									
1946	28	46	69						
1947	19	49	83						
1948	10	54	129						
1949	10	45	75	58	12	15	7	3	
1950	9	35	73	53	45	28	9	8	2
1951	8	31	54		31	14	18		1
1952	7	39	72	54	29	31	13	8	3
1953	14	42	77	50	23	18	11	7	1
1954	6	29	69	54	22	16	9		

Borstal	Prob'n	Cor.Tr.	Det.C're	Susp.S.	Fine	Other	Flogging
4						5	61
2						5	42
6						6	28
5						6	12
11						9	8
15						4	10
26						13	17
40						47	33
30						53	49
37						64	21
46	35	28			6	36	
40	34	18			7	24	
50	16	11				20	
33	21	8			4	20	
57	37	13			4	33	
61	40	8			2	37	

(cont'd over)

Table A2.1 (*cont.*)

Year	Crimes known	Arrests	Cleared up	Mag. court	Tried	Acq'd	Death
1955	823		432	115	339	38	
1956	965		477	97	448	42	
1957	1194		573	108	616	83	
1958	1692		788	177	788	68	
1959	1900		879	263	906	120	
1960	2014		933	246	893	83	
1961	2349		922	212	868	79	
1962	2517		1076	245	1143	109	
1963	2483		1069	233	1162	127	
1964	3066		1182	216	1133	127	
1965	3736		1378	348	1308	158	
1966	4474		1662	317	1567	143	
1967	4564		1837	346	1785	189	
1968	4815		1902	412	1990	214	
1969	6041		2399	573	2226	201	
1970	6273		2634	590	2248	220	
1971	7465		3143	901	2580	306	
1972	8926		3813	1263	2703	349	
1973	7338		3374	1370	2328	294	
1974	8666		3466		2119	251	
1975	11311				2855	291	
1976	11611				3156	352	

Transportation				Penal servitude					
7	10	11–20	Life	3	4	5	7	10	11–20

(*cont'd over*)

Table A2.1 (*cont.*)

				Imprisonment				
Year	< ½	½–1	1–2	2–3	3–4	4–5	5–7	7–10	> 10
1955	9	39	72	51	19	14	10	1	
1956	9	45	86	54	35	19	14	5	
1957	11	59	139	62	19	14	12	1	1
1958	7	72	147	75	51	27	16	5	2
1959	22	111	205	93	27	31	17	8	3
1060	22	75	199	109	49	30	22	8	4
1961	17	71	154	109	49	37	20	8	4
1962	14	91	220	138	59	46	39	14	2
1963	20	90	173	150	66	46	19	19	2
1964	26	82	178	136	64	56	20	10	19
1965	34	83	184	156	57	66	40	17	6
1966	19	74	232	271	103	67	54	15	22
1967	18	76	258	241	96	85	53	29	5
1968	13	79	263	265	120	67	58	27	18
1969	35	85	288	275	120	79	60	21	14
1970	20	104	269	333	129	83	40	14	10
1971	22	112	315	391	144	100	56	40	17
1972	28	91	291	395	126	101	70	33	18
1973	20	80	245	357	129	93	56	54	16
1974	26	67	237	330	116	79	54	18	31
1975	50	98	311	485	193	106	79	41	15
1976	68	114	341	554	185	132	116	55	49

Borstal	Prob'n	Cor.Tr.	Det.C're	Susp.S.	Fine	Other	Flogging
41	20	8			5	12	
57	34	4			6	38	
73	77	14			12	39	
139	88	24			11	56	
126	59	16			14	54	
121	69	19			19	64	
129	75	8			22	86	
150	99	17			21	124	
159	101	8			29	153	
169	91	5	68		24	58	
203	115	7	98		33	51	
217	104	1	130		50	65	
335	160		117		48	75	
309	168		134	140	48	67	
430	160		156	156	48	98	
445	159		158	133	51	80	
443	188		171	120	56	99	
522	179		219	146	59	76	
405	129		159	132	62	97	
389	90		171	129	59	72	
580	99		168	196	42	101	
521	85		185	178	52	169	

Appendix 3

Table A3.1 *Day of the week*

	Mon.	Tue.	Wed.	Thur.	Fri.	Sat.	Sun.	Total
February 1971	11	10	14	12	24	15	17	103
August 1971	23	15	11	11	22	21	21	124
February 1972	17	14	13	20	30	28	17	139
August 1972	27	17	15	20	40	27	22	168
February 1973	11	11	10	19	33	24	16	124
August 1973	13	12	15	13	23	20	13	109
February 1974	20	13	12	13	20	20	18	116
August 1974	17	16	16	12	29	21	16	127
Total	139	108	106	120	221	176	140	1,010

Table A3.2 *Time of day*

	00.00	02.00	04.00	06.00	08.00	10.00	12.00	14.00	16.00	18.00	20.00	22.00	Total
February 1971	11	5	3	1	1	1	9	10	5	9	24	24	103
August 1971	22	10	4	1	0	6	10	10	12	6	11	32	124
February 1972	17	9	4	3	1	6	2	7	6	21	18	45	139
August 1972	22	3	0	0	1	5	12	15	20	13	21	56	168
February 1973	7	2	0	0	0	10	6	19	19	16	18	27	124
August 1973	19	0	2	0	0	2	7	10	7	5	15	42	109
February 1974	7	7	0	0	4	3	6	7	13	19	18	32	116
August 1974	21	6	3	1	0	2	5	14	13	7	10	45	127
Total	126	42	16	6	7	35	57	92	95	96	135	303	1,010

Table A3.3 *Number and sex of attackers*

	1F	2F	>2F	2 M/F	3M/F	>3 M/F	1M	2M	3M	4M	5M	6M	>6M	N/K	Total
February 1971	0	0	0	0	0	0	17	35	27	10	4	3	5	2	103
August 1971	0	0	0	1	1	0	25	39	21	22	8	1	6	0	124
February 1972	0	0	0	1	0	1	31	52	29	13	5	4	2	1	139
August 1972	1	1	0	2	0	0	35	58	30	20	8	4	6	3	168
February 1973	3	1	1	2	0	1	43	27	27	12	3	1	3	0	124
August 1973	0	0	3	1	1	0	20	36	25	8	5	2	2	6	109
February 1974	1	2	3	0	0	1	43	30	24	6	1	1	0	4	116
August 1974	0	0	1	1	0	2	50	26	28	8	2	1	2	6	127
Total	5	4	8	8	2	5	264	303	211	99	36	17	26	22	1,010

Table A3.4 *Age of attackers*

	< 14	14–17	18–21	>21	N/K	Total
February 1971	7	47	14	7	28	103
August 1971	11	49	15	12	37	124
February 1972	7	68	14	13	37	139
August 1972	12	88	18	9	41	168
February 1973	22	52	13	7	30	124
August 1973	16	43	15	7	28	109
February 1974	14	48	10	11	33	116
August 1974	5	49	25	11	37	127
Total	94	444	124	77	271	1,010

Table A3.5 *Sex of victims*

	M	F	Total
February 1971	92	11	103
August 1971	116	8	124
February 1972	110	29	139
August 1972	146	22	168
February 1973	95	29	124
August 1973	91	18	109
February 1974	75	41	116
August 1974	90	37	127
Total	815	195	1,010

Table A3.6 *Age of victims*

	<14	14–17	18–21	22–50	>50	Total
February 1971	9	28	13	37	16	103
August 1971	18	16	13	53	24	124
February 1972	8	23	10	61	37	139
August 1972	20	31	18	67	32	168
February 1973	29	28	11	36	20	124
August 1973	19	11	11	50	18	109
February 1974	19	10	8	49	30	116
August 1974	11	15	16	63	22	127
Total	133	162	100	416	199	1,010

Table A3.7 *Degree of injury*

	Fatal	*Serious*	*Slight*	*None*	*Total*
February 1971	0	3	43	57	103
August 1971	0	7	39	78	124
February 1972	0	9	58	72	139
August 1972	1	3	57	107	168
February 1973	0	5	37	82	124
August 1973	0	6	44	59	109
February 1974	0	4	48	64	116
August 1974	0	6	50	71	127
Total	1	43	376	590	1,010

Table A3.8 *Weapon used*

	Firearm	*Sharp*	*Blunt*	*Irritant*	*None*	*Total*
February 1971	0	21	12	0	70	103
August 1971	3	22	5	1	93	124
February 1972	1	27	10	4	97	139
August 1972	0	34	4	2	128	168
February 1973	3	28	14	2	77	124
August 1973	0	18	14	1	76	109
February 1974	1	12	4	1	98	116
August 1974	3	24	4	0	96	127
Total	11	186	67	11	735	1,010

Table A3.9 *Location*

	Street	*Park, etc.*	*Train*	*Station*	*Other*	*Total*
February 1971	87	9	1	2	4	103
August 1971	91	19	5	2	7	124
February 1972	116	4	3	11	5	139
August 1972	123	27	11	3	4	168
February 1973	102	14	2	3	3	124
August 1973	82	19	2	2	4	109
February 1974	103	5	1	1	6	116
August 1974	114	7	1	2	3	127
Total	818	104	26	26	36	1,010

Table A3.10 *Stolen value*

	Nil	≤£1	£1–5	£5–20	>£20	Total
February 1971	7	14	29	31	22	103
August 1971	17	22	19	36	30	124
February 1972	25	13	21	44	36	139
August, 1972	25	34	29	49	31	168
February 1973	25	29	21	30	19	124
August 1973	21	23	18	27	20	109
February 1974	16	12	23	31	34	116
August 1974	22	11	23	33	38	127
Total	158	158	183	281	230	1,010

Table A3.11 *Arrests and 'clear-ups'*

	Cases	'c/u'	%	Arrests	Arr. c/u
February 1971	103	36	35.6	82	2.3
August 1971	124	36	29.0	88	2.4
February 1972	139	47	33.8	100	2.1
August 1972	168	48	28.6	94	2.0
February 1973	124	47	37.9	83	1.8
August 1973	109	27	24.8	57	2.1
February 1974	116	26	22.4	46	1.8
August 1974	127	31	24.4	49	1.6
Total	1,010	298	29.5	599	2.0

Notes

1 General Introduction

1 Hood and Sparks (1970), p. 9.
2 A word which is, as we shall see, legally meaningless.
3 McClintock (1974), 'Phenomenological and Contextual Analysis'.
4 Ibid., p. 153.
5 McClintock (1974), 'Criminal violence in industrial society', unpublished paper.
6 Brodie (1970).
7 And which, in nine cases out of ten, might well not even have been reported to police. See chapter 3.
8 Pratt (unpublished paper, 1972).
9 Though, as will become apparent in part 2, a good deal of use was eventually made of their findings.
10 See chapter 5.
11 One of the main differences is that the official statistics give details only of those who have been arrested whereas, even when an arrest has not been made, the victim is likely to have at least some idea of the type of person who carried out the attack.
12 Many stores let shoplifters off with a verbal warning rather than go to all the trouble of reporting the offence to police.
13 Though, admittedly, mainly for insurance purposes.
14 It might be noted at this point that a number of questions were posed by an analysis of the statistics which proved impossible to pursue but which, it is suggested, would certainly justify further research. Precisely why, for example, did robbery in London 'take off' in the mid 1950s, both in absolute terms and in comparison to indictable crime as a whole? Why does there appear to have been a levelling off in the number of robberies every five years or so, to be followed immediately by a further surge upwards? Why did robbery increase at such an unprecedented rate in 1975, and why has this increase continued unabated ever since?
15 About the only exception here is homicide — which will eventually be classified as manslaughter, murder, infanticide, etc.
16 Designated G. 10 Branch.
17 Obviously, local police must be allowed some discretion in deciding whether a reported incident is in fact a crime see chapter 4.

18   As, for example, by McClintock himself.

2   Some definitions

1   'An Act to consolidate and amend the Statute Law of England and Ireland relating to Larceny and other similar offences.'

2   'An Act to consolidate and simplify the Law relating to Larceny triable on Indictment and Kindred Offences.'

3   Which had been set up on 2 February 1959 'to be a standing committee to examine such aspects of the criminal law of England and Wales as the Home Secretary may from time to time refer to the committee, to consider whether the law requires revision and to make recommendations'.

4   Though a person can, of course, be found guilty of theft on a charge of robbery.

5   Indeed, as a point of interest, when the Bill was before the House of Lords, Lord Wilberforce introduced an amendment (later withdrawn) that it should actually not be permissible 'to refer to any decisions of any Court prior to the passing of this Act'.

6   For a more comprehensive review of these elements see, for example, Butler and Mitchell (1972).

7   Though it could, of course, be charged as a separate offence in addition to the stealing.

8   Butler and Mitchell (1972).

9   A conviction for theft was substituted.

10   As will be apparent from some of the cases quoted in this section, the difference between 'robbery' and 'snatching' is one of the finest distinctions on the statute-book. The Criminal Law Revision Committee made special mention of this fact, while the Metropolitan Police Statistical Department, in their routine returns, have recently (as from 1974) gone as far as to combine 'robbery' with 'other violent theft' (i.e. 'snatches').

11   It might be noted that, although none of the authorities appear to comment on the fact, the rulings in the three cases cited here, and in *R* v *Gnosil*, do not appear to be wholly consistent. Moreover, it is probably true to say that even today, as in the eighteenth and nineteenth centuries, the final classification of a particular offence can often depend on a non-judicial 'on the spot' interpretation by one particular person – normally a police officer.

12   In any event – as pointed out in the *Criminal Law Review* – the force was apparently used only by one of the accused not involved in the actual stealing, and this would appear to be insufficient for two reasons. Firstly, since the postmaster was not himself subjected to any bodily harm as might have rendered his consent irrelevant, the action could not be described as 'force', and secondly, any force which might have been used was not used in the direct furtherance of the theft.

13   There seems little doubt that the term 'mugging' has been coined

very largely by the press for the benefit of a mass audience, and that in this way its usage has been established and enlarged. For a discussion of the role of the mass media as creators of deviance see chapter 3.

14 'Being a dictionary of "Colloquialisms and Catchphrases, Solecisms and Catechreses, Nicknames, Vulgarisms and such Americanisms as have been naturalised" '.

15 'Being "the Vocabularies of Crooks, Criminals, Racketeers, Beggars and Tramps, Convicts, the Commercial Underworld, the Drug Traffic, the White Slave Traffic, Spivs" ' (especially p. 455).

16 The word can be spelt in a number of different ways: the *Oxford English Dictionary* gives 'gar(r)otte'.

17 Walker (1965: 18).

18 A fact which seems particularly surprising when it is remembered that for the extremely rare crime of procuration a breakdown into eleven different sub-categories is required, and for buggery no fewer than sixteen.

19 The Professional Robber — 'a professional associating with other professionals, gaining a certain status in the criminal underworld and learning techniques by which to commit theft' (p. 63). The Opportunist Robber — 'the opportunist usually chooses targets which net him small amounts of money, often less than $20. Targets are chosen for their accessibility and vulnerability rather than the large amount of money they can provide' (p. 68). The Addict Robber — 'includes both heroin addicts and other regular users of drugs where crimes are related to their use of drugs . . . . He rarely thinks of a big score, wanting only enough money to get his next fix' (pp. 71-2). The Alcoholic Robber — 'rarely considers how much money he will steal or what he will do with it once he has it. Instead, his intoxicated state sometimes leads him to assault others and to take their money as an afterthought' (p. 78).

20 A point which has been expanded upon in chapter 1.

21 In other words, it would have been possible to carry out an investigation of *all* 'street robberies', regardless of type or motive. Conceivably (though doubtfully) this would have been more in line with the 'average person's' view of what constitutes a mugging. It would, however, have cut across what is, in this writer's view, the central concept of a *random* attack on an ordinary person in the street.

3 The attitudes of society

1 Note on back cover of Hunt's *The Mugging*.

2 The results are documented in considerable detail in Sellin and Wolfgang (1964). The techniques used have in fact been criticised by a number of writers such as Rose (1966: 414-21), and Walker (1971), particularly pp. 69-75, where he comes out firmly

in favour of the alternative method of 'criminotyping' suggested in McClintock and Avison (1968). (In essence the 125 police areas in the country are rated 1–9 on the basis of rates per 100,000 population for four groups of offences: violent and sexual offences together, breaking and entering offences, larceny, and 'selected serious crimes'. The worst area would rate 999/9, the best 111/1.) However, the indexing of crime is not the main point at issue here and such criticisms need concern us no further.

3   Both of about 250 persons.
4   The numbering of the categories is that used by Sellin and Wolf-gang.
5   The results from the student sample were much the same.
6   That is to say, the rating 10.64 or 6.73, looked at in isolation, relates to nothing in particular. Compared one with another, they indicate that the offence rated 10.64 is considered to be more than twice as 'serious' as that rated 6.73. This should become clearer later in this chapter when ratings for a number of completely different offences are quoted.
7   For example, under offence no. 18 (The offender robs a victim of $5 at gunpoint. The victim is shot and requires hospitalisation) the rating of the police sample was:

	Age of offender	
13	17	27
10.42	10.00	10.04

8   Though it must always be remembered, of course, that we are only talking here about a small sample of just one section, albeit an 'expert' section, of the community.
9   Adapted from Lenke (1974), pp. 86–7.
10 For both judges and police officers the sample·was fifteen.
11 Stuart Hall (1975).
12 Pratt, M. J. (1972), unpublished booklet.
13 According to Steve Chibnall (1977: 88) it was the shooting of three policemen in Shepherds Bush in August 1966 which 'introduced the "Violent Society" theme and saw the realignment of the British Press firmly behind the front-line troops in that war, the police. The liberalizing drift which had begun, imperceptibly, in the early sixties had been decisively corrected. Fresh battle lines had been drawn, deep-seated values and beliefs reaffirmed.'
14 See, for example, Himmelweit *et al.* (1958), and Klapper (1960).
15 The argument may be paraphrased as 'Television may not change a boy's intrinsic attitude to violence. But even one who thinks violence wrong is more likely, after being exposed to it on television, to kick other boys in the crotch as hard as he can, brand chests with cigarettes, bash heads against walls and have a go at rape.'
16 The word 'catharsis' which occurs quite frequently in the literature dealing with the mass media is defined in the *Oxford Illustrated Dictionary* as 'Purification of emotions by vicarious experience,

esp. through the drama'.

17 Though the difficulties involved have apparently done nothing to deter a vast army of researchers in the fields both of sociology and psychology.

18 Wilkins (1964), particularly pp. 59–65.

19 Or, as Steve Chibnall (1977: viii) puts it, 'in a highly differentiated society like Britain, the events which capture the interest of the media only become visible through their eyes. There is often no easy method of separating "sacred" facts from "free" comment.'

20 McClintock (undated paper on 'Violent Crime and the Media', p. 3)

21 Cohen (1973) particularly pp. 16–19 and 161–6. Indeed the whole question of 'moral panics' — under which heading mugging can most certainly be included — and the media coverage thereof is so comprehensively covered in this well-known study that the present writer feels unable to offer a great deal in the way of additional observations. (NB: 'A moral panic is when a society enters a sort of self-producing spiral — a moral tail-spin — about a troubling issue' (Hall: 1975).)

22 Op. cit., p. 4.

23 Though it could perhaps be argued that this was only because the idea was already simmering, ready to be taken up. This effect, particularly with regard to the National Front, is discussed in more detail in chapter 7.

24 This theme is expanded upon in Hall and Jefferson (1976: 75–9) — 'Some notes on the relationship between the societal control culture and the news media, and the construction of a law and order campaign'. In essence, the argument is that the media can be 'producers' as well as 'reproducers'.

25 This breakdown was mainly dependent upon the availability of statistics in existing publications: for example, the *Number of Persons Taken into Custody by the Metropolitan Police and the Result of Charges* was published annually from 1829, when the Metropolitan Police Force was first established, until 1892 (though only the figures for 1832 onwards are really usable). Figures relating to the Metropolitan Police District are further available for the years 1893 to 1931 from *Reports of the Commissioner of Police of the Metropolis*, also published annually, while in 1893 was started *Criminal Statistics for England and Wales* (Home Office, annually).

26 Fox (1960: 157).

27 Probation, corrective training and fines were measures first used against convicted robbers in 1949, detention centres in 1964, and suspended sentences in 1968 (see Appendix 3).

28 It is appreciated, of course, that many factors are involved — for example, the more lenient alternatives to acquittal now available — but it is felt that this does not invalidate the argument which follows.

29 'In extremis' such arguments are difficult to counter. For example,

the late Sir Ronald Howe, who was Deputy Commissioner of the Metropolitan Police from 1953 to 1957, was widely quoted as saying something like, 'I happened once to have lunch with Himmler, who told me that Hitler had asked what was *the* crime in Berlin. Himmler answered "housebreaking", and Hitler then said "Chop off the heads of the next six housebreakers". This they did. I am not advocating it here, but that stopped it!'

30   And this trend has continued. In 1976 the average was 3.18 years.

31   A sentence of five years or more being, by almost any standards, a substantial one.

32   The actual figures are: in the 1950s, an average of 18 a year out of 183 (9.8%); in the 1970s (up to 1975) an average of 106 a year out of 456 (23.2%).

33   Although this aspect was originally analysed in considerable depth, in the event it was found that the results obtained were only of passing relevance to the main theme of this thesis. Only the basic details have therefore been included here.

34   Following which a pamphlet entitled *20 Years* was written by members of the Centre for Contemporary Cultural Studies, and published by the Paul, Jimmy and Mustafa Support Committee. See also Hall and Jefferson (1976: 167–73).

4   Statistics in theory and in practice

1   To speak of '1,000 robberies' or '500 muggings' is practically meaningless. Only if we can say something like 'there were 500 muggings in 19――, as compared to 400 in 19――' do we begin to get some idea of the true situation. Furthermore, robbery and mugging must be compared with other categories of crime. Comparisons with, say, fraud or theft of motor vehicles may appear irrelevant, but it is important to quantify as far as possible precisely where, in the overall scheme of things, we should try to fit the types of crime with which we are here mainly concerned.

2   There is simply no way of describing certain phenomena other than in numerical terms.

3   In the case of some commentators, offences not recorded by police are *not* included in the calculation of the dark figure.

4   Indeed, *by definition*, it cannot be known.

5   To take an extreme case, no one, it is imagined, would dispute that most murders eventually come to light.

6   The most obvious example here is motoring offences.

7   This idea of crime being socially defined is stressed by many later writers, such as by McClintock (1974) when he tells us that 'Levels of acceptability and therefore of legitimacy are often a matter of social and cultural tradition. What would be regarded as a normal angry response among children in school or at play, or among menfolk in certain working-class environments, could amount to a criminal assault in a middle-class community. Rough treatment

of one spouse by another might pass unnoticed in one area, serve as a ground for separation and divorce in another, and be dealt with by the criminal courts in yet a third. What is being argued here is that in reality 'crime' is socially as well as legally defined, and it is suggested that on a meaningful criminological or penological level it is highly dubious logic to deal with one without considering the other.' This is precisely the main theme of Part 2 of this study.

8   The Spanish Inquisition is perhaps an even better example of crime being socially defined.

9   Many people have argued that this has had a crucial bearing on the apparent level of crime. Certainly the change from the 'old-style' approach of a clip round the ear must have had some effect. Police corruption would also come under this heading.

10 Clearly, if the Commissioner happens to be particularly concerned about, let us say, theft from telephone boxes, then this will soon be brought to the notice of those much further down the line.

11 The Metropolitan and City Police Company Fraud Department — more commonly known as the Fraud Squad — provides a good example here. Despite recent considerable augmentation there is little doubt that a further doubling, or even re-doubling, of manpower would still not clear the backlog of offences. There is, in fact, a 'bottomless pit' just waiting to be discovered.

12 A classic case of a change in procedure producing a 'crime wave' is afforded by Lord Trenchard's intervention while Commissioner of Police in the 1930s. Finding that local police stations kept two separate books called 'Crimes Reported' and 'Suspected Stolen', he ordered an amalgamation, and in the following twelve-month period larceny offences rose from 9,500 in 1931 to 34,780 in 1932!

13 As we have seen, these relate only to those persons who have transgressed the legal code of the prevailing social order.

14 Described in Ennis (1967).

15 Admittedly this is a subjective view based mainly on the fact that a random and entirely unprovoked attack is involved. For a further discussion of this point see chapter 8.

16 Not only would no one even expect a 100 per cent report rate, the difference between 65 per cent and, say, 85 per cent is very much less than the huge increases in the number of robberies quoted throughout this study.

17 For a critique of the phenomenological approach to official statistics see Hindess (1973).

18 Chosen for no other reason than because 100 years seemed an appropriate period for the sort of historical comparison here envisaged.

19 It is felt that twenty years strikes a reasonable balance between the need to include a worthwhile period for comparison purposes, and the elimination of those many changes which would have to be taken into account if a longer period were studied.

20   Official census figures for the Greater London area are as follows: 1871 − 3,840,595; 1971 − 7,452,346. This represents an increase of 94 per cent.

21   Daniel Bell's argument concerning 'youth at war' and the consequent increase in crime on their return seems to be refuted by the reduction in robbery in London immediately following the First and, even more so, the Second World War. (Though it could perhaps be argued that the really substantial increases have taken place since the end of National Service in the early 1960s.)

22   See chapter 2.

23   Even in the statistical appendix which analyses the mid-nineteenth-century statistics for Leeds, the sort of errors being talked about are in the range 40–50 per cent, not the many hundreds of per cent which would be required to bring the nineteenth-century level up to that of the present day.

24   The 1977 figure was actually 6,826.

25   In the preface to McClintock and Gibson (1961).

26   For a further discussion of this point see chapters 6 and 8.

5   A study of mugging in London during the 1970s

1   As pointed out in the previous chapter, and also elsewhere in this study, it is not really possible to offer reasoned comment on a particular phenomenon unless the nature of that phenomenon is precisely known. Thus knowledge of the facts is an essential preliminary to explanation.

2   Augmented where necessary by reference back to source material.

3   In other words, a continuous period of six months could easily just miss (or, indeed, just include) a particular peak or trough of mugging activity. By looking at six separate months spread over a longer period of time it was hoped to take a broader, and therefore a more balanced, view.

4   February and August were chosen because they are typical winter and summer months which also − by virtue of being six months apart − break up the total period into equal parts.

5   One might expect that this could well prove to be largely a matter of 'swings and roundabouts', and is therefore a factor which could safely be ignored. As is about to be shown, this is not really the case.

6   As will be explained later, it was arbitrarily decided that crime sheets for the following *three* months would be studied.

7   The data being required mainly as a guide to discussion and policy (*vide* Part 2).

8   It is not easy to describe a gang. The *Oxford Dictionary* defines it as 'a band of persons acting or going about together, esp. for criminal purposes'. It is felt, however, that the group would have to be of at least four persons to constitute a gang in the normally accepted sense of the word.

9   This is to say, the law defines 'Children' as those under 14, and 'Young Persons' as those under 17 years of age, while, even though a person now officially comes of age on reaching his or her 18th birthday, there is no doubt that most people still regard 21 as the more significant age of entry into adulthood. In any case, it is the cut-off point always used in police records, and also by most other researchers.

10 If a group of, say, ten youths are involved in an attack and just one is eventually arrested then a clear-up is recorded. This is not necessarily unreasonable, but does point to some of the many complications hidden behind the bare statistics. To extend the point, for any given number of offences there can be more arrests than clear-ups (since, as in the above example, all ten attackers might be apprehended) or more clear-ups than arrests (since a prisoner may ask for a number of other offences to be 'taken into consideration' – a procedure which can easily produce clear-ups of cases of which police had not previously been aware!).

11 Fifty was chosen simply to give a better impression of the overall age structure.

12 Here, heed has to be taken of statements made by the person attacked. Although one imagines that many people are likely to exaggerate the worth of any loss, there is really nothing that can be done about this.

13 Clearly, it would be possible for a crime sheet to be submitted to the central statistical department four, six, twelve, or even more months after the crime had actually been committed. However, a sample survey indicated that this possibility was most unlikely to have any measurable effect on the final results.

14 See explanation at the beginning of this chapter.

15 That is to say in a chi-square test the .95 level of significance was not exceeded.

16 The assumed greater 'vulnerability' of females mentioned more than once in this chapter is not so much chauvinistic as realistic in the sense that, if a potential attacker was simply after easy money, he would surely be more likely to attack a young girl, with the obvious target of a handbag, rather than a male of the same age who is not only likely to be that much stronger, but will also be carrying his money in a less accessible place.

17 The overall clear-up figures for robbery as a whole (the figures for mugging not readily available) in recent years have been as follows: 1974 – 21%, 1975 – 20%, 1976 – 16%, 1977 – 13%. Thus the trend is confirmed.

18 One of the principal advantages of this study as compared to the published statistics is that it includes details of attackers, even where no arrest was made. These were gleaned from the statements of victims, but obviously there must be occasions when the attack is so sudden, or the light so bad, that even an intelligent guess is not possible. Thus, in the graphs related to attackers, totals do not always amount to 1,010. It should also be mentioned that the

graph dealing with 'Day of week' has been 'standardised', that is to say allowance has been made for the fact that each of the eight months in question did not contain the same number of Mondays, of Tuesdays, of Wednesdays, etc.

19   For an indication of the geographical location of police Districts see diagram 1.1.

20   It is only in relatively recent times that *any* reference to race has been included on the crime sheet.

21   If one is attempting to analyse a sample of, say, 100 muggings, of which it is known that 30 were carried out by 'whites', 30 by 'blacks' and 40 by 'whites and blacks together', then misleading statements such as 'blacks are involved in 70 per cent of muggings' are, strictly speaking, correct. Devices of this kind are, of course, frequently employed by members of such organisations as the National Front.

22   See chapter 7 for a further discussion of this point.

23   This is no doubt due to the fact that, prior to about 1960, not only did police not record race, but racial involvement in crime was simply not a significant factor.

24   Touchiness regarding the question of race is well illustrated by the fact that this typology was originally expressed in terms of 'Race Code'.

25   The figures in table 5.3 certainly tend to dispel the myth that a high coloured involvement in mugging is merely a reflection of a high coloured representation in the population. If this were the case, then one might reasonably expect the identity code breakdown of victims to reflect the position with regard to assailants. It can be seen that this by no means applies.

26   See note 18 above.

27   McClintock and Gibson (1961).

28   For the 'Age of attackers' comparisons, McClintock's totals refer to *all* robbery.

6   Theories of deviance

1   Morris (1957: 1).

2   Or of offenders' homes. For a discussion of the distinction, see later in this chapter.

3   Though it may be of interest to note that correlation coefficients were not known at the time.

4   See Mayhew (1862); also Lindesmith and Levin, 'English ecology of the past century', in Carson and Wiles (1971), and Morris (1957).

5   Nowadays, of course, over-used in a somewhat different sense.

6   As has already been hinted, there were a number of different perspectives among the Chicagoans themselves – Harvey Zorbaugh, for example, conceived of natural areas as the immediate product of land utilisation, while for R. D. McKenzie the natural

area was the result of the recent mixing of population, race, income and population. Of necessity the discussion here, as throughout this chapter, has had to be 'generalised'.

7 As it stands this categorisation obviously applies only to Chicago: however, as will later be shown, it can easily be adapted to other cities.

8 This has a particular relevance to race, and racial discrimination. See chapter 7.

9 As a development of Rex and Moore's approach, much thought has recently been given to the concept of 'social space'. Indeed, Taylor, Walton and Young (1975: 121) tell us that 'the "struggle for space" is at the base of contemporary sociological investigations of city life and the relationships of the struggle for space in the city to the struggle for existence in general'. This notion has been most usefully developed by R. E. Pahl who, acknowledging his debt to Rex, believes that the idea of a housing class should be expanded into a 'socio-ecological' system embracing competition for space in general and the constraints of spatial structure on social structure. Such a development has been welcomed by Rex, and has been expanded by writers such as Baldwin and Bottoms: it will not, however, be pursued further here.

10 Sometimes, of course, the two types of area may be geographically indistinguishable.

11 See later in this chapter for a further discussion of this point.

12 Despite the reservation that this might be considered a classic case of putting a square peg in a round hole!

13 That is to say, if the total zone of transition has a rate of 8.0 muggings per square mile, and 'C' and 'L' Districts a rate of over 100, then clearly the remainder of the zone must have a relatively low rate. (This in itself questions the whole 'zone of transition' concept.)

14 As indicated by police records.

15 cf. All daffodils grow in fields, but all fields do not contain daffodils.

16 Mays (1963: 81).

17 See Sutherland and Cressey (1960), particularly pp. 72–80. The basis of the theory is that 'criminal behaviour is learned in interaction with other persons in a process of communication' (p. 77): that is to say, criminality begets criminality.

18 Mayhew (1862). One of Mayhew's greatest contributions was his recognition of the part played by social factors in the etiology of crime.

19 Booth (1892–97). For example, 'The children are rarely brought up to any kind of work, but loaf about, and no doubt form a nucleus for future generations of thieves and other bad characters' (revised edn, vol. i, p. 33). As Tobias (1972: 288) tells us: 'Charles Booth's survey of the London of the 1890s is there to remind us of the appalling poverty which existed at the end of the century.'

20 'Specifically, Marxism had viewed deviants and criminals as

peripheral relative to its own central concern with power and contention-for-power. Viewing criminals and the deviants as a *Lumpen-proletariat* that would play no decisive role in the class struggle, and indeed, as susceptible to use by reactionary forces, Marxists were not usually motivated to develop a systematic theory of crime and deviance. In short, being neither proletarian nor bourgeois, and standing off to the periphery of the central *political* struggle, criminals and deviants were at best the butlers and maids, the spear carriers, colourful actors perhaps but nameless, and worst of all, lacking in a historical "mission". They could be, indeed, *had* to be, ignored by those devoted to the study of more "important" issues – power, political struggle, and class conflict.' Foreword by Alvin Gouldner to Taylor, Walton and Young (1973).

21   This is true of much of the material contained in this chapter, viz. 'crime' is a function not of an individual's personal characteristics but of the role assigned to him by society. See also chapter 8.

22   Wedderburn (1974: 3). See also Coates (1973), Coates and Silburn (1973), especially part 1.

23   Townsend (1974: 28).

24   Or, as Townsend (1974: 21) puts it: 'Who would dare to lay down a scale of necessities for the 1970s for young women in Britain, consisting of one pair of boots, two aprons, one second-hand dress, one skirt made from an old dress, a third of the cost of a new hat, a third of the cost of a shawl and a jacket, two pairs of stockings, a few unspecified underclothes, one pair of stays and one pair of old boots worn as slippers, as Rowntree did in 1899?'

25   See chapter 4 for statistical confirmation of this fact.

26   'Year-to-year increases in crime rates may be more indicative of social progress than social decay' (Biderman, 1970).

27   Veblen (1912). It is interesting to note the date of this work: clearly the notion of relative deprivation is nothing new.

28   See chapter 4.

29   For whom 'delinquency' = the failure to obey rules.

30   For a further discussion of this point see chapter 8.

31   Matza (1964; also 1969).

32   Rather less so the American. Speaking of early commentators such as Henry Mayhew, Carson (1971: 9) expresses this in terms of 'Then as now British criminology's impact upon social policy far surpassed its contribution to social theory'.

33   For a further discussion of this point see chapter 8.

34   Of course the delinquent subculture – or as Matza prefers to call it, the subculture of delinquency – has occupied a cherished place in the recent history of criminology. Many writers (mainly American), including Albert Cohen, Cloward and Ohlin, Miller, Thrasher, Matza, and Mays – though perhaps differing in their opinions concerning the existence of a distinctive culture or whether there has been a revolt against middle-class values – have nevertheless agreed that the delinquent subculture most certainly exists. This approach has been touched upon on a number of occasions during

the course of this chapter, but will not be examined in any great depth. Apart from obvious restrictions of time and space, it is felt that in the final analysis the concept can be subsumed under the general heading of deprivation. As Howard Jones (1971: 141) puts it: 'It is not difficult to see why, if gangs are created thus out of deprivation, they should be hostile and destructive in their behaviour. Which of us would not be resentful, if robbed of something as important to us as love and acceptance?'

35 See previous chapter.
36 Office of Population Censuses and Surveys (1971). It should be noted that throughout this section all population figures refer to 1971 — even when the present tense is used.
37 See, for example, Wirth (1938: 1–24), and also Clinard (1964).
38 See Pahl (1970). There is also a close link here with the ecological approach discussed at length in the previous section.
39 That is to say 55.1 per cent of 298,615.
40 Here only a *very* abridged version will be considered. For a full deposition see Merton (1962).

7 Race

1 'Immigration is the touchiest subject in Britain today. It can suddenly inflame civilised conversation, create myths and generate friction' (*Daily Mirror*, 17.1.78).
2 For instance the Home Secretary, Mr Merlyn Rees, was widely reported as being 'firmly against direct questions such as "Are you coloured" being included'.
3 Though it is true that there could be a problem of categorisation, as, for example, in the South African situation.
4 'The use of arrest figures as a yardstick is of course a two-edged weapon, for it opens the door to the charge that police discriminate against black people when enforcing the law. The implication is that if police did not discriminate, black people would not be disproportionately involved in the arrest figures' ('Metropolitan Police Memorandum to the Select Committee on Race Relations and Immigration', March 1976, para. 15). However, 'Evaluation of the extent of the involvement of black people in street crime from crime reports relies upon the evidence of the victim. It therefore avoids the charge of discrimination by police which could be raised in the use of the arrest figures. It also provides a yardstick for testing the validity of the discrimination charge' (ibid., para. 21). Hence, while there is simply no alternative to using the arrest figures when studying crime as a whole, the Lambeth sample includes all crimes occurring during the period in question, not just those for which an arrest was made.
5 For the 10–16 age-group the Identity Code 3 involvement was even higher as the following figures show:

	IC1	IC2	IC3	IC4	IC5	IC6
All crimes of violence	61	2	35	1	0	0
Robbery only	52	2	45	1	0	0
Burglary	78	2	18	2	0	0
Autocrime	84	2	11	2	0	0
Shoplifting	68	3	22	5	1	1
All indictable crime	75	2	20	3	0	0

6 Clearly, an Identity Code 3 involvement in robbery of say 80 per cent would appear worthy of study — but might prove to be quite unexceptional if, for example, the proportion of black residents was found to be 83 per cent.

7 Figures issued by the GLC in October 1973 indicate that 7.3 per cent of the population of Greater London had parents both of whom were born in the New Commonwealth, the total of 572,000 being distributed as follows: African 112,000; West Indian 248,000; Indian 156,000; Pakistani 44,000; Sinhalese 12,000.

8 A proportion exceeded by:
   a) City of Westminster   — 83,600 out of 239,750 (34.9%)
   b) LB Ken. and Chelsea — 65,290 out of 188,225 (34.7%)
   c) LB Brent   — 80,315 out of 280,655 (28.6%)
   d) LB Camden   — 58,695 out of 206,735 (28.4%)
   e) LB Hammersmith   — 44,250 out of 187,195 (23.6%)
   f) LB Haringey   — 56,705 out of 240,080 (23.6%)
   g) LB Islington   — 47,025 out of 201,875 (23.3%)
   h) LB Ealing   — 64,605 out of 301,110 (21.5%)

9 A proportion exceeded by:
   a) LB Haringey   — 34,595 out of 240,080 (14.4%)
   b) LB Brent   — 39,180 out of 280,655 (14.0%)
   c) LB Hackney   — 25,455 out of 220,280 (11.6%)
   d) LB Islington — 22,550 out of 201,875 (11.2%)
   e) LB Ealing   — 33,440 out of 301,110 (11.1%)

10 A proportion equalled only by LB Brent with 15,270 out of 280,655 (5.4%). Indeed only one other London Borough has as high a proportion as 4.0% — namely LB Hackney with 9,020 out of 220,280 (4.1%).

11 Of the 'Lambeth West Indians' 13,365 were born in Jamaica. Lambeth's Jamaican population is, in fact, the largest of all the London Boroughs both in proportion and in actual numbers.

12 In the same publication GLC researchers analyse Greater London's New Commonwealth ethnic groups by electoral wards. This analysis shows that two of the central Lambeth wards, Ferndale and Tulse Hill, contain 31.8 per cent and 31.0 per cent respectively black residents.

13 See, for example, Banton (1972).

14 The exact totals tend to vary from source to source. Abbott (1971), page 56, quotes the following 'Net immigration from the West Indies': 1948 — 600; 1949 — 600; 1950 — 700; 1951 — 1,800; 1952 — 2,200; 1953 — 2,300.

15 One hundred to Jamaica, one hundred to Trinidad, etc.

16 'Until 1962 Commonwealth immigration was not controlled and
    in this respect was fundamentally different from the immigration
    of aliens. The right of free entry arose as a corollary of British
    citizenship which, in the days of the Empire, had been granted to
    all those who, willingly or unwillingly, owed allegiance to the
    Crown. Once large numbers had begun to make use of the tradi-
    tional right of free entry it was withdrawn' (Lawrence, 1974: 12).

17 'The first nettle we had to grasp, and so must every one else who
    seeks to do anything about the problem, is the question of inte-
    gration . . . . Britain is a highly organised and still relatively stable
    society, with its own history and culture. It is not easy for peoples
    from countries with equally distinct histories and cultures to gain
    entry to, or win acceptance in, Britain' (Committee of the Youth
    Service Development Council, 1967, p. 9). See also Hiro (1971).

18 Precise explanations of the causes of discrimination need not con-
    cern us here, but see, for example, Jephcott (1964), Hiro (1971),
    and Hall and Jefferson (1976). Certainly any discussion on whether
    or not 'discrimination' exists is irrelevant. It is perfectly clear that
    a certain amount of distrust/jealous guarding of rights/apprehen-
    sion does exist. For convenience this may be called 'discrimination'
    — and it is certainly more marked in the case of those with a black
    skin simply because the 'enemy' (or, perhaps better, the 'outsider')
    is thus more easily distinguishable.

19 The PEP report *Racial Discrimination in Britain*, on which Daniel
    (1968) is based, concluded that discrimination in employment
    is the biggest single criticism in immigrants' spontaneous criticisms
    of life in Britain and is the area in which the greatest number of
    individual claims of discrimination are made.

20 Or at least that version of the English language used in this country.

21 The 1977 Project Report of the Unit of Manpower Studies, en-
    titled *The Role of Immigrants in the Labour Market* (DOE) stated
    that immigrants were found to be more likely than other workers
    to be employed in low-paid industrial jobs, such as those in found-
    ries, where the work was usually hot, heavy and dirty, and in some
    sections of the rubber and plastics industry where conditions
    were often hot, smelly and generally unpleasant. This finding has
    also been confirmed by a number of other studies.

22 See 'Social Ecology' section in the previous chapter.

23 Banton (1972: 81). As Rex and Moore (1967) put it, landlord–
    tenant relationships are what Talcott Parsons would call affective-
    ly neutral, particularistic, self-orientated and specific; in other
    words, confined to paying the rent.

24 Under such conditions, little wonder that migrants are frequently
    accused of being sluttish housekeepers. In this connection the
    comment of Gunnar Myrdal, in his classic study of race relations
    in the United States, assumes considerable significance — 'White
    prejudice and discrimination keep the Negro in low standards of
    living, health, education, manners and morals. This, in turn, gives

support to white prejudice. White prejudice and Negro standards thus mutually "cause" each other' (Myrdal, 1944: 75).

25 See Daniel (1968).

26 By ignoring advertisements which stipulated 'no coloureds' and the like.

27 Though Lawrence (1974: 122) correctly adds that 'when one also takes into account that at the same time as they were beginning school in this country, they were often having to establish personal relationships with a parent (or parents) with whom they had had little contact; that their own culture and pattern of education was usually very different from that encountered in our schools; and that they were settling in those areas least well endowed with educational facilities and services, it is obvious that very great help was needed to ensure that they had anything like the same opportunity to do as well as English children of comparable ability'.

28 Moreover, in September 1965 the National Committee for Commonwealth Immigrants had been appointed by the Prime Minister to advise the government on matters relating to the integration of Commonwealth immigrants. The first Chairman was the Archbishop of Canterbury.

29 Indeed, individuals had no redress *except* through the auspices of the Race Relations Board.

30 The relevant provision, Section 1(1)(a), is clear in itself and states: 'A person discriminates against another in any circumstances relevant for the purposes of any provision of this Act if on racial grounds he treats that other less favourably than he treats or would treat other persons'.

31 For the purposes of this Act the term 'racial group' means a group of persons defined by reference to colour, race, nationality or ethnic or national origin.

32 As stated above, the precise reasons for this need not concern us here, though it might be noted in passing that, quite apart from psychological and historical considerations; the economic concept of competition for scarce resources would certainly appear to have a considerable relevance.

33 Clearly, all coloured immigrants are not West Indian. However, it is with this group we are mainly concerned.

34 Adapted from an approach employed by Jefferson and Clarke (1973, unpublished).

35 See also Jephcott (1964).

36 'I am filled with foreboding. Like the Roman I seem to see "The River Tiber foaming with much blood".'

37 As recently shown to good effect by the disturbances at Lewisham following National Front marches, and the necessity for Sir David McNee, Commissioner of Police of the Metropolis, to ban *all* marches for a period of three months in order to inhibit the activities of the Front, and thereby defuse racial tensions at the Ilford by-election in February 1978.

38 It must be said that this concern is not wholly without foundation.

In the 1977 publication of *Social Trends* it was estimated by the
Central Statistical Office that the coloured population is likely
to rise to about 2,600,000 by the mid 1980s. Although the 'official' interpretation of this figure was that fears of cities being
'overrun' by coloured immigrants by the end of the century 'may
be exaggerated', the total is, in itself, a substantial one.

39   Moller (1977). This had the telling subtitle 'It claims to want a
proud united Britain. Its activities tell another tale'.

40   The proportion of immigrants answering 'yes' when questioned as
to their intentions of settling permanently in Britain have been as
follows: in Slough, 11.5% (Israel, 1964); in a study of coloured
workers employed by London Transport, 4% (Brooks, 1969);
in Bristol, 17% (Rose, 1969); in Nottingham, 4% (Lawrence,
1974).

41   In America, calculations have been made as to what it costs to be
a Negro, by comparing average incomes of blacks and whites with
similar qualifications, etc. For middle-income groups the cost is
over $1,000 a year. In Britain a coloured man often has to pay
an informal 'colour tax' – an extra amount to secure housing,
insurance, and the like – as compared to a white man.

42   In the West Indies ' "lightness" and high social status are approxi-
mately associated' (Patterson, 1963: 224), and as a corollary of
this, marrying 'lighter' is a traditional aspiration.

43   Jefferson and Clarke (1973: 16).

44   A theme which will be expanded upon shortly.

45   And given considerable coverage by the media, as, for example,
in the case of the winning black American athletes' 'clenched fist'
salutes at the Olympic Games medal ceremonies.

46   Much more could be added on the question of family structure.
For example, in the traditional West Indian family the old folk
are treated with respect but, following migration, they find it
very difficult to adapt, and it is the more receptive younger
members who far more readily become attuned to the native
culture. One result of this phenomenon is that the parents can no
longer command the deference which they previously enjoyed
and which they think they are entitled to. This in turn can only
lead to disputes. Or again, 'most black teenagers do not share
either their parents' awe of the whites, or their obsequious depen-
dence on them. The differences go beyond the normal generation
gap. For, unlike their parents, born in the Caribbean and brought
up on stories of Britain as the land of hope and glory and of
"Queen Victoria the Good" by their ancestors and the education
system, the youngsters born and brought up here have no such
illusions' (Hiro, 1971: 94).

47   'Those coloured immigrants who have arrived in this country in
the past fifteen years may unwillingly resign themselves to second-
rate treatment in their search for jobs and houses and their
attempts to gain access to public places and public services. But it
is unlikely that their children, born and educated here, will be

equally docile when faced with frustrations and humiliations of discrimination; anger and violence, rather than self-effacement, may seem to them to be the more realistic response' (Daniel, 1968: 14).

48 See chapters 5 and 8.

49 In January 1974, under the heading 'The Violent Truth of Life in London', the *Evening News* came up with the statement that 'Lambeth has become the borough where many men and women are afraid to go out at night and where shopkeepers keep truncheons under the counter'. In January 1975 *The Times* stated that 'Anyone who walks down Railton Road (which runs through the heart of Brixton's black district) is a fool'. Throughout 1975 and 1976 there were frequent articles carrying such headlines as 'Danger Signals from the Streets of Lambeth'.

8 Conclusions and recommendations

1 Taken to be 'Robbery in the open following sudden attack (of private property only, and *not* following even a brief association)'. See chapter 2.

2 Quoting Turk (1969: vii).

3 A theme expanded upon at length in chapter 3.

4 See chapter 2 for an explanation of how mugging came to be recorded in the Metropolitan Police District.

5 For recorded indictable crime in general, London accounts for about 22% of the total for England and Wales as a whole.

6 For example, C. H. Rolph in the *New Statesman* of 15.7.77, and Louis Blom-Cooper in the *Observer* of 3.7.77. However, as pointed out in chapter 4, not *everyone* agrees that the 'dark figure' represents an increasingly large proportion of the whole. Crick (1974: 25), for example, argues that the man gashed with a bottle in a Friday or Saturday night street fight is now more likely to go to hospital than to stagger home, and other people are more likely to report 'such old if terrible commonplaces', while McClintock (*Crimes of Violence*, Appendix XI, 'A Note on Young Offenders and Hooliganism') contends that a substantial amount of the increase (in indictable crime committed by young offenders) – perhaps as much as half of the total – can be attributed to a greater readiness on the part of the public to report aggressive behaviour by teenagers, 'even in those areas where there has always been a fairly high tolerance of violence' (p. 242).

7 In his article in the *New Statesman* of 15.7.77, mentioned above.

8 As far as the age structure of assailants is concerned McClintock's findings refer to robbery as a whole. Direct comparisons with this study are therefore not possible: however, such comparisons as have been made are the best that can be attempted and, if nothing else, give a good indication of the 'general drift'.

9 66% in 1950, 81% in the 1970s.

10 This figure includes estimates by victims in cases where no arrest
    was made.
11 Figures are available, of course, in respect of much earlier years,
    and these have also been analysed to some extent. It is of interest
    to note, for example, that in 1840 there would appear to have been
    only 35 arrests for robbery in London, of which just 7 (20%) were
    of persons under the age of twenty. However, 'compulsory regis-
    tration of births was not introduced until 1836, and thus it was
    not until the 1850s that birth certificates would have been avail-
    able for the purpose of determining whether someone qualified
    as a juvenile. Registration was not complete until the second half
    of the century, and even then it must often have been difficult to
    prove the identity of a person appearing before the courts and to
    trace his birth certificate' (Tobias, 1972: 15).
12 To tie in with the previous emphasis on LB Lambeth, the age
    structure of the population again offers no adequate explanation
    of the disproportionate amount of juvenile crime: in 1971, 10–19-
    year-olds represented 13% of the population in Greater London,
    just 13.5% in LB Lambeth.
13 For example, the clear-up rate for all known indictable crime in
    the Metropolitan Police District has in recent years been as follows:
    1973 – 28.4%, 1974 – 26.3%, 1975 – 24.4%, 1976 – 22.5%,
    1977 – 21.1%. (It should be noted that these figures refer to all
    age-groups. The position specifically with regard to juvenile crime
    could possibly be affected by the contention that juveniles are
    more likely to be overrepresented in the arrest totals, and therefore
    in cases cleared up – for which much evidence could be produced
    both for and against.)
14 This is something of a 'chicken and egg' argument, but there are
    certainly some people who feel that any apparent increase in
    juvenile (or, for that matter, racial) involvement in crime is simply
    a reflection of the latest police 'purge'. This may possibly be the
    case, but, if taken to extremes, the futility of such a standpoint
    is well illustrated by the remark made to police by a London social
    worker – 'these kids wouldn't have such a bad record if you Police
    wouldn't keep arresting them' (!) (see Marshall, 1974, unpublished).
15 See, also, other examples listed in chapter 1.
16 In 1974 police in London carried out a study of more than 100
    (actually 106) of the most persistent recidivists. Although the
    average age at last referral was only 14¼, between them they had
    amassed a total of 2,151 referrals and had been accused of a total
    of 3,735 offences. 22 of them had actually been *convicted* of
    robbery, 89 of burglary, 101 of theft, and 74 of autocrime. 40 had
    been to detention centre, 10 had been to borstal and 3 had been
    to both. 88 boys who had been made the subject of care orders
    as a result of criminal proceedings amassed a further 510 court
    appearances after the initial care order had been made. Little
    wonder then that Peter Marshall concluded that 'We have a
    situation in London, echoed in Birmingham and Liverpool, not

dissimilar I believe from New York, Chicago and Tokyo, of a major social problem unresponsive to the efforts of Police, Social Workers, Courts and Penal Institutions', or that Scotland Yard made the (much criticised) claim that, of the 32,000 10–16-year olds charged in 1974, 4,500 were already 'hardened young criminals'.

17 See 'Are We More Criminal?', *New Society*, 24.3.77.
18 Though, as has been shown, the change has been marginal in those recent years during which mugging has escalated.
19 A particularly contentious point. However, it must surely be true that when (for example) a child returns home from school to find an empty house, he is that much more likely to be at a loose end and, without guidance, to 'get himself into mischief'.
20 This, of course, is one of the main principles of sociology.
21 Many of these have been expanded upon in previous chapters.
22 'Many people seem convinced . . . that there is a linear progression from disorder in the streets, from mugging and rape to riot and revolution, (Crick, 1974: 21).
23 See particularly Hall and Jefferson (1976).
24 For an extension of this argument see, for example, Jefferson and Clarke (1973). Certainly the Grunwick dispute would appear to provide an excellent case in point.
25 See chapter 7. It is possible that the Front genuinely sees itself as protecting a beleaguered population, more sinned against than sinning, but it is perhaps better described, as it was recently by Lord Hailsham, as 'a thoroughly detestable organisation. Their policies could not be carried out without dictatorship and blood-shed.'
26 As pointed out in chapter 4, Tobias's arguments are themselves open to question, since the available statistics do not support his contentions. However, at least one relevant point is beyond dispute: the reaction of society *to* violence is itself *less* violent. Such measures as capital punishment, flogging, and transportation are, for good or ill, things of the past.
27 A formal definition would be something like 'choice between available styles of living and group identities, taken against a background of the existing social and economic opportunity-structure'.
28 Though it is, of course, no consolation to the victim of a mugging that his attacker was 'deprived' or 'socially disturbed'.
29 Jefferson (1973, unpublished).
30 Hebdige (1974, unpublished).
31 See chapter 3.
32 'nearly all known societies . . . define the male and female roles in markedly different terms. While men are the breadwinners and the protectors of the family they must always be encouraged to adopt a more aggressive attitude to the world' (Mays, 1963: 34).
33 As shown earlier in this chapter.
34 Though it is important to remember that black immigrants have by no means a monopoly on social problems. During the 1960s, as Chibnall (1977: 83) tells us: 'there was a widespread feeling that

social life was moving and changing faster than people could com-
prehend, a feeling which engendered both excitement and anxiety.
It was a time of mild anomie when the "attack on traditional values
and life styles" became a media cliché.' Or as put, in rather more
practical terms, in a *Sunday Telegraph* article written in late 1977:
'High rise living (in Lewisham) like everywhere else inflicts its own
familiar nightmare on black and white families striving to maintain decent standards in the face of remorseless vandalism.'

35 Hence, one of the main conclusions of the study reviewed in chapter 5 was that 'the concentration on male victims, the considerable
reduction in real terms of the average stolen value, and perhaps
even the move away from relatively "out-of-the-way" venues such
as parks and country lanes, all seem to give at least some indication that planned muggings based on the expectation of pecuniary
reward have now largely given way to *ad hoc* opportunist attacks'.

36 Similarly, today's 'Punks' — which provides a suitable opportunity
to mention the importance of music to youth cultures throughout
the ages. In the case of 'Punks', of course, the attendant Rock
music is central (a typical sentiment being expressed by the Tom
Robinson Band's 'Up Against the Wall'): while, for West Indians,
Reggae music plays an important identifying role and provides
what might almost be called a 'rallying call'. See also Hall and
Jefferson (1976).

37 Or, as Hunt (1975: 74) expresses it, 'many muggers undoubtedly
derive special satisfaction from "making a hit" upon a representative
of the hated oppressors'.

38 Teaching English to slaves was strictly forbidden — though ultimately this led to the emergence of a new, and supposedly 'inferior',
creole language.

39 That is to say, Patterson's observation still has considerable relevance in many areas. However, of the district she specifically
mentions, Somerleyton Road now contains only new flats while
Geneva Road no longer exists.

40 The low West Indian attendance at any professional football match
in this country is always very noticeable.

41 See chapter 3.

42 There is, of course, always the possibility that a 'frustrated mugger'
may turn to other forms of crime such as vehicle theft, burglary
or shoplifting. Unfortunately, there is no way in which this could
ever be tested — and in any event a transfer of attention from
persons to property must surely be a good thing for all concerned.

43 Although, *in extremis*, there is no denying the logic of this argument, it must be pointed out that a reduction of, say, 50 per cent
in the number of potential victims would not necessarily lead to
a halving of the number of muggings. In this connection, too,
Mays' (1963: 20) comment on Wilkins' finding that larceny from
motor vehicles is closely correlated with the number of vehicles
registered is highly relevant: 'Following the strictly moralistic
view, it is difficult to explain why more cars should mean more

stealing from cars, unless it is postulated that our moral standards deteriorate proportionately to the number of motor vehicles.'

44 The nearest thing to a definite 'no-go' area came into being in February 1977. Around a maze of dimly-lit pathways criss-crossing a 14-acre building site under Westway, North Kensington, the Greater London Council erected red-letter signboards warning: 'Several robberies – some violent – have taken place here and you are strongly advised to consider using an alternative route.'

45 The dividing line between what should and should not be carried is a thin one. A great deal of criticism was directed against magistrates in London who, in December 1977, dismissed charges of possessing an offensive weapon brought by police against a 24-year-old man whom they had found in possession of a knife. The man had claimed that he was carrying the weapon because he lived in an area in which there had been many muggings.

46 Of the 1,010 muggings studied herein, there were only 47 instances (4.6%) where the victim was *not* alone at the time of the attack.

47 Though, as far as mugging is concerned, it must be said that this does not coincide with this study's findings with regard to time of day.

48 See Marshall (1974).

49 In 1970 the figure was just over 10 per cent.

50 In November 1975 police carried out a 'truancy sweep' in Lambeth and picked up 734 children in twelve days.

51 The Eisenhower Commission.

52 For instance, the battle cry taken up by the press and appearing on car stickers and the like during the 1976 pay dispute: 'Up Police Pay – Down Crime'.

53 For the purposes of comparison it might be noted that New York has about 30,000 officers. London has roughly the same number of police now as it had forty years ago when there was only one-fifth the amount of crime.

54 Recently heeded.

55 Towards the end of 1977 a special squad was set up by police to combat outbreaks of late-night street attacks in Lewisham. One of its methods was to travel on late night buses posing as passengers, which tactic is used with considerable success in America. During 1977 it was reported that a decoy team in Los Angeles made 1,260 arrests in eight months: the Lewisham squad, consisting only of five men and a WPC, made 55 arrests in its first four weeks of operation.

56 In the *Observer* of 3.7.77.

57 'We are determined that after the next election the Conservative Government will be ready to meet the challenge of rising crime, lawlessness and violence which threatens our democratic society.'

58 Or, as Peter Berger has put it, the non-recognition and counter-definitions of social norms are always potentially revolutionary.

59 No one is suggesting that a grant of £2 million was ever likely to make all that much of an impression. To date, however, no

evidence has come to light to suggest that it has done any good at all. Moreover, since any multiple times nought equals nought, larger grants would not be the answer.

60   For a detailed discussion of this group see chapter 7.

61   Members of the Birmingham University Centre for Contemporary Cultural Studies frequently refer to disillusioned youths resigned to an insignificant and servile role during the day who are all the more determined to make up for it at night. As a result, every Mod, for example, 'was existing in a ghost world of gangsterism, luxurious clubs, and beautiful women even if reality only amounted to a draughty Parka anorak, a beaten up Vespa and fish and chips out of a greasy bag' (Hebdige, 1974: 7).

62   The arrival and quick departure of the ten-pin bowling halls provide one example appropriate to the type of teenage youths we are here discussing. In more general terms some importance attaches to the rapid decline of the neighbourhood as the focus of leisure activities and the concentration of facilities in the city centres.

63   Compare, too, Merton's 'goals and means' arguments (1960), and also Matza's contention (1964) that delinquents merely have a bad sense of timing — that is to say that activities engaged in by, for example, university students during Rag Week, or even by rugby players on the field, are little different from what, in other contexts, might well be described as 'delinquent'. 'A number of supposedly delinquent values are closely akin to those embodied in the leisure activities of the dominant society': it is simply that for members of the latter group society provides 'institutional periods' for traits of violence to emerge and to take precedence.

64   In January 1978.

Bibliography

(a) Published sources

Abbott, Simon, ed. (1971), *The Prevention of Racial Discrimination*, London: Oxford University Press.
Alderson, J. C., and Stead, Philip John (eds) (1973), *The Police We Deserve*, London: Wolfe.
Baldwin, John, and Bottoms, A. E. (1976), *The Urban Criminal: A Study in Sheffield*, London: Tavistock Publications.
Banton, Michael (1955), *The Coloured Quarter*, London: Cape.
Banton, Michael (1972), *Racial Minorities*, London: Fontana/Collins.
Banton, Michael (1973), *Police-Community Relations*, London: Collins.
Barrère and Leland (1889–90), *A Dictionary of Slang, Jargon and Cant*, London.
Becker, Howard S. (1963), *Outsiders: Studies in the Sociology of Deviance*, New York: Free Press.
Bell, Daniel (1961), *End of Ideology*, New York: Collier Books.
Belson, William A. (1975), *Juvenile Theft: The Causal Factors*, London: Harper & Row.
Berger, P., and Luckmann, T. (1967), *The Social Construction of Reality*, London: Allen Lane.
Biderman, A. D. (1970), 'Social indicators and goals', in *Social Indicators*.
Bonger, William A. (1916), *Criminality and Economic Conditions*, Boston: Little Brown.
Booth, Charles (1892–97), *Life and Labour of the People in London*, 9 vols, London: Macmillan.
Burt, Sir Cyril (1925), *The Young Delinquent*, London: University of London Press.
Butler, T. R. F., and Mitchell, S. (eds) (1972), *Archbold: Criminal Pleadings, Evidence and Practice*, 38th edn, London: Sweet and Maxwell.
Carson, W. G., and Wiles, Paul (eds) (1971), *Crime and Delinquency in Britain*, London: Martin Robertson.
Chapman, Dennis (1968), *Sociology and the Stereotype of the Criminal*, London: Tavistock Publications.
Chibnall, Steve (1977), *Law-and-Order News: An analysis of crime*

reporting in the British Press, London: Tavistock Publications.

Cicourel, A. V. (1964), *Method and Measurement in Sociology*, New York: Free Press.

Clinard, Marshall B. (1964), 'The Relation of Urbanization and Urbanism to Criminal Behaviour', in Burgess, E. W., and Bogue, D. J. (eds.), *Contributions to Urban Sociology*, Chicago: University of Chicago Press.

Cloward, Richard, and Ohlin, Lloyd (1960), *Delinquency and Opportunity: A Theory of Delinquent Gangs*, New York: Free Press.

Coates, Ken, and Silburn, Richard (1973), *Poverty: The Forgotten Englishmen*, Harmondsworth: Penguin.

Cohen, Albert K. (1955), *Delinquent Boys: The Culture of The Gang*, Chicago: Free Press.

Cohen, Albert K. (1966), *Deviance and Control*, Englewood Cliffs: Prentice Hall.

Cohen, Stanley (ed.) (1971), *Images of Deviance*, Harmondsworth: Penguin.

Cohen, Stanley (1973), *Folk Devils and Moral Panics: The Creation of the Mods and Rockers*, London: Paladin.

Cohen, Stanley, and Young, Jock (1973), *Mass Media and Social Problems*, London: McGibbon & Kee.

Conklin, John (1972), *Robbery and the Criminal Justice System*, Philadelphia: Lippincott.

Corrigan, P. (1977), *The Smash Street Kids*, London: Paladin.

Cotgrove, Stephen (1967), *The Science of Society*, London: Allen & Unwin.

Cox, Barry, *et al.* (1977), *The Fall of Scotland Yard*, Harmondsworth: Penguin.

Crick, Bernard (1974), *Crime, Rape and Gin: Reflections on contemporary attitudes to violence, pornography and addiction,* London: Elek/Pemberton.

Cross, R., and Jones, P. A. (1972), *An Introduction to Criminal Law,* 7th edn, London: Butterworth.

Daniel, W. W. (1968), *Racial Discrimination in Britain*, Harmondsworth, Penguin.

Downes, David (1966), *The Delinquent Solution*, London: Routledge & Kegan Paul.

Durkheim, E. (1951), *Suicide*, Glencoe: Free Press.

Durkheim, E. (1958), *The Rules of Sociological Method,* trans. Solway, S., and Simpson, G., Chicago: Free Press.

Engels, Frederick (1892), *The Condition of the Working Class in England*, London: Allen & Unwin.

Ennis, P. H. (1967), *Criminal Victimisation in the United States: A Report of a National Survey*, Washington: US Government Printing Office.

Fielding, Henry (1751), *An Enquiry into the Causes of the Late Increase of Robbers,* London.

Fox, L. W. (1960), *The Modern English Prison*, Harmondsworth: Penguin.

Galbraith, J. K. (1972), *The Affluent Society*, Harmondsworth: Penguin.

George, Mrs M. D. (1930), *London Life in the XVIIIth Century*, 2nd edn, London.

Glaser, B. G., and Strauss, A. L. (1968), *Discovery of Grounded Theory: Strategies for Qualitative Research*, London: Weidenfeld & Nicolson.

Glass, D. (1954), *Social Mobility in Britain*, London: Routledge & Kegan Paul.

Glueck, Sheldon, and Glueck, Eleanor (1950), *Unraveling Juvenile Delinquency*, New York: Harper & Row.

Goffman, Erving (1963), *Behaviour in Public Places,* New York: Free Press.

Gunn, John (1973), *Violence in Human Society*, Newton Abbot: David & Charles.

Hall, Stuart, and Jefferson, Tony (eds) (1976), *Resistance through Rituals: Youth Subcultures in Post-war Britain*, London: Hutchinson.

Hanway, Jonas (1775), *The Defects of Police, the Cause of Immorality, and the Continual Robberies committed, particularly in and about the Metropolis*, London.

Harloe, Michael, *et al.* (1973), *London: Urban Patterns, Problems and Policies,* London: Heinemann.

Himmelweit, H. T., *et al.* (1958), *Television and the Child*, London: Oxford University Press.

Hindess, Barry (1973), *Use of Official Statistics in Sociology*, London: Macmillan.

Hiro, Dilip (1971), *Black British White British*, London: Eyre & Spottiswoode.

Hobsbawm, Eric J. (1959), *Primitive Rebels*, Manchester: University of Manchester Press.

Holland, G. C. (1843), *Vital Statistics of Sheffield.*

Hood, Roger, and Sparks, Richard (1970), *Key Issues in Criminology*, London: Weidenfeld & Nicolson.

Howitt, Dennis, and Cumberbatch, Guy (1975), *Mass Media, Violence and Society*, London: Elek.

Humphrey, Derek (1972), *Police Power and Black People*, Panther.

Hunt, Morton M. (1975), *The Mugging*, Harmondsworth: Penguin.

Israel, W. H. (1964), *Colour and Community*, Slough, Council of Social Services.

Janowitz, M. (1968), 'The Study of Mass Communication' in *International Encyclopedia of the Social Sciences,* vol. 3, New York: Macmillan and Free Press.

Jephcott, Pearl (1964), *A Troubled Area: Notes on Notting Hill*, London: Faber & Faber.

John, G., and Humphrey, D. (1971), *Because They're Black,* Harmondsworth; Penguin.

Jones, Howard (1971), *Crime in a Changing Society*, Harmondsworth: Penguin.

Klapper, J. T. (1960), *The Effects of Mass Communication*, New York: Free Press.

Lambert, J. (1970), *Crime, Police and Race Relations: A Study in Birmingham*, London: Oxford University Press.

Lawrence, Daniel (1974), *Black migrants: white natives. A study of race relations in Nottingham*, London: Cambridge University Press.

Lemert, E. (1967), *Human Deviance, Social Problems and Social Control*, New Jersey: Prentice Hall.

Lenke, L. (1974), 'Criminal Policy and Public Opinion Towards Crimes of Violence', in *Collected Studies in Criminological Research*, vol. xi, Council of Europe, Strasbourg.

Little, Kenneth (1947), *Negroes in Britain: A Study of Racial Relations in English Society*, London: Kegan Paul *et al.*

McClintock, F. H. (1974), 'Phenomenological and Contextual Analysis', in *Collected Studies in Criminological Research*, vol. xi, Council of Europe, Strasbourg.

McClintock, F. H., and Avison, N. H. (1968), *Crime in England and Wales*, London, Heinemann.

McClintock, F. H., and Gibson, Mrs E. (1961), *Robbery in London*, London, Macmillan.

McClintock, F. H. *et al.* (1963), *Crimes of Violence*, London, Macmillan.

McQuail, Denis (1969), *Towards a Sociology of Mass Communications*, London: Collier-Macmillan.

Marcuse, H. (1964), *One-Dimensional Man*, London: Routledge & Kegan Paul.

Mark, Sir Robert (1977), *Policing a Perplexed Society*, London: George Allen & Unwin.

Marris, Peter, and Rein, Martin (1974), *Dilemmas of Social Reform: Poverty and Community Action in the United States*, Harmondsworth: Penguin.

Marx, Karl (1964), 'The state and the law', in Bottomore, T. B., and Rubel, M. (eds), *Karl Marx: Selected Writings in Sociology and Philosophy*, New York: McGraw-Hill.

Marx, Karl, and Engels, Frederick (1848), *Manifesto of the Communist Party*, in *Marx–Engels Selected Works*, vol. 1, London: Lawrence & Wishart, 1950.

Matza, David (1964), *Delinquency and Drift*, New York: John Wiley.

Matza, David (1969), *Becoming Deviant*, Englewood Cliffs: Prentice Hall.

Mayhew, Henry (1862), *London Labour and the London Poor*, London, 1851. Fourth volume added in 1862, of which a selection included in Quennell, P. (ed.) (1950), *London's Underworld*, London: Hamlyn.

Mays, John Barron (1963), *Crime and the Social Structure*, London: Routledge & Kegan Paul.

Merton, R. K. (1962), 'Social Structure and Anomie', in Wolfgang, Marvin E., *et al.* (eds), *The Sociology of Crime and Delinquency*, New York: Wiley.

Mills, C. W. (1956), *The Power Elite*, New York: Oxford University Press.

Morgan, Patricia (1978), *Delinquent Fantasies*, London: Temple Smith.

Morris, Terence (1957), *The Criminal Area: A Study in Social Ecology*, London: Routledge & Kegan Paul.

Moser, C. A. (1958), *Survey Methods in Social Investigation*, London: Heinemann.

Myrdal, Gunnar (1944), *An American Dilemma: the Negro Problem in Modern Democracy*, New York: Harper.

Pahl, R. E. (1970), *Whose City?*, London: Longman.

Pakenham, Lord (1958), *Causes of Crime*, London: Weidenfeld & Nicolson.

Partridge, Eric (1950), *A Dictionary of the Underworld*, London: Routledge & Kegan Paul.

Partridge, Eric (1970), *A Dictionary of Slang and Unconventional English*, 2 vols, 5th edn, London: Routledge & Kegan Paul.

Patterson, Sheila (1963), *Dark Strangers: A Sociological Study of the Absorption of a Recent West Indian Migrant Group in Brixton, South London*, London: Tavistock.

Priestland, Gerald (1974), *The Future of Violence*, London: Hamish Hamilton.

Prins, H. (1973), *Criminal Behaviour: An Introduction to its study and treatment*, London: Pitman.

Purcell, William (1974), *British Police in a Changing Society*, London: Mowbray.

Radzinowicz, Leon (1977), *The Growth of Crime: The International Experience*, London: Hamish Hamilton.

Reiss, Albert J., Jr (1971), *The Police and the Public*, New Haven: Yale University Press.

Rex, John (1973), 'The Sociology of a Zone of Transition', in Raynor, John, and Harden, Jane (eds), *Cities, Communities and the Young*, London: Routledge & Kegan Paul.

Rex, John, and Moore, Robert (1967), *Race, Community and Conflict*, London: Oxford University Press.

Rolph, C. H. (1961), *Common Sense About Crime and Punishment*, London: Gollancz.

Rose, E. J. B., *et al.* (1969), *Colour and Citizenship*, London, Oxford University Press.

Rowntree, B. S. (1901), *Poverty: A Study of Town Life*, London: Macmillan.

Runciman, W. G. (1966), *Relative Deprivation and Social Justice*, London: Routledge & Kegan Paul.

Sellin, Thorstein (1938), *Culture Conflict and Crime*, New York: Social Science Research Council Bulletin No. 41.

Sellin, T., and Wolfgang, M. E. (1964), *The Measurement of Delinquency*, New York: Wiley & Sons.

Sparks, Richard, Genn, Hazel and Dodd, David (1978), *Surveying Victims: A Study of the Measurement of Criminal Victimisation*, London: John Wiley.

Sutherland, Edwin H. (1949), *White Collar Crime*, New York: Dryden Press.

Sutherland, Edwin H., and Cressey, Donald R. (1960), *Principles of Criminology*, 6th edn, Chicago: Lippincott.

Taylor, Ian (1971), 'Soccer Consciousness and Soccer Hooliganism', in Cohen, Stanley (ed.), *Images of Deviance*, Harmondsworth: Penguin.

Taylor, Ian, Walton, Paul, and Young, Jock (1973), *The New Criminology: For a Social Theory of Deviance,* London: Routledge & Kegan Paul.

Taylor, Ian, Walton, Paul, and Young, Jock (eds), (1975), *Critical Criminology,* London: Routledge & Kegan Paul.

Thrasher, F. M. (1927), *The Gang,* Chicago: University of Chicago Press.

Tobias, J. J. (1972), *Crime and Industrial Society in the Nineteenth Century,* Harmondsworth: Penguin.

Townsend, Peter (1974), 'Poverty as relative deprivation: resources and style of living', in Wedderburn, Dorothy (ed.), *Poverty, Inequality and Class Struggle,* Cambridge: Cambridge University Press.

Townsend, P., and Abel-Smith, B. (1965), *The Poor and the Poorest,* London: Bell.

Turk, Austin T. (1969), *Criminality and Legal Order,* Chicago: Rand McNally.

Turner, J. W. C. (ed.) (1964), *Russell on Crime,* 12th edn, London: Stevens.

Turner, J. W. C. (ed.) (1966), *Kenny's Outlines of Criminal Law,* 19th edn, Cambridge: Cambridge University Press.

Veblen, Thorstein (1912), *Theory of the Leisure Class,* New York: Macmillan.

Walker, Nigel (1965), *Crime and Punishment in Britain,* 2nd edn, Edinburgh: Edinburgh University Press.

Walker, Nigel (1971), *Crime, Courts and Figures: an Introduction to Criminal Statistics,* Harmondsworth: Penguin.

Wedderburn, Dorothy (ed.) (1974), *Poverty, Inequality and Class Struggle,* Cambridge: Cambridge University Press.

Wiles, Paul (1971), 'Criminal Statistics and Sociological Explanations of Crime', in Carson, W. G., and Wiles, Paul (eds), *Crime and Delinquency in Britain,* London: Martin Robertson.

Wilkins, Leslie (1964), *Social Deviance, Social Policy, Action and Research,* London: Tavistock.

Wilmott, P., and Young, M. (1957), *Family and Kinship in East London,* Harmondsworth: Penguin.

Wolfgang, Marvin E., and Ferracuti, Franco (1967), *The Subculture of Violence: towards an integrated theory in criminology.* London: Tavistock.

Wootton, Barbara (1959), *Social Science and Social Pathology,* London: Allen & Unwin.

Wright, Peter L. (1968), *The Coloured Worker in British Industry,* London: Oxford University Press.

Young, Jock (1971), 'The Role of the Police as Amplifiers of Deviancy, Negotiators of Reality and Translators of Fantasy: Some consequences of our present system of drug control as seen in Notting Hill', in Cohen, S. (ed.), *Images of Deviance,* Harmondsworth: Penguin.

Zorbaugh, Harvey (1925), 'Natural Areas of the City', in Burgess, R. (ed.), *The City,* Chicago: University of Chicago Press.

(b) Unpublished sources

Brodie, P. (1970), 'The crime situation within the Metropolitan Police District' (MP internal docket 202/70/227).

Clarke, John (1973), 'The Skinheads and the Study of Youth Culture', Centre for Contemporary Cultural Studies, University of Birmingham.

Clarke, J., and Jefferson, T. (1974), 'Working Class Youth Cultures', Centre for Contemporary Cultural Studies, University of Birmingham.

Crump, R. R., and Newing, J. F. (1974), 'Footpad Crime and its Community Effect in Lambeth', Metropolitan Police Commissioner's Library.

Hall, Stuart (1968), 'The Hippies: An American "Moment" ', University of Birmingham.

Hebdige, Dick (1974), 'The Style of the Mods', Centre for Contemporary Cultural Studies, University of Birmingham.

Jefferson, Tony (1973), 'The Teds — A political resurrection', University of Birmingham.

Jefferson, T., and Clarke, J. (1973), 'Down These Mean Streets . . . . The Meaning of Mugging', Centre for Contemporary Cultural Studies, University of Birmingham.

Jones, T. C. (1973), 'Counting Rules', Metropolitan Police Office.

Jones, T. C. (1974), 'Crime and Race', Metropolitan Police Office.

McClintock, F. H. (1974), 'Criminal violence in industrial society', copy in Metropolitan Police Commissioner's Library.

McClintock, F. H. (undated), 'Violent Crime and the Media', xeroxed paper in Metropolitan Police Commissioner's Library.

Marshall, Peter (1974), 'Juvenile Crime (A "Vicious Perplexity")', Metropolitan Police Office.

Metropolitan Police (1976), 'Memorandum to the Select Committee on Race Relations and Immigration', Metropolitan Police Office.

Pratt, M. J. (1972), 'Robbery and Kindred Offences in the Metropolitan Police District, 1968–72', Metropolitan Police Office.

Silcock, H. (1948), 'The Increase in Crimes of Theft, 1938–47', Home Office.

(c) Articles

Bell, Daniel (1953), 'Crime as an American Way of Life', *Antioch Review*, 13.

Biderman, A. D. (1970), 'Social Indicators and Goals', in *Social Indicators*.

Brooks, D. (1969), 'Who Will Go Back?', *Race Today*, vol. 1, no. 5, September.

Hall, Stuart (1975), 'Mugging: a case study in the media', *Listener*, 1 May.

Harrison, Paul (1975), 'The Young Criminals', *New Society*, 24 April.

Kitsuse, J. I., and Cicourel, A. V. (1963), 'A note on the use of official statistics', *Social Problems*, 11.

Moller, David (1977), 'The Ugly Truth Behind the National Front', *Reader's Digest*, November.

Morris, Terence (1977), 'Are We More Criminal', *New Society*, 24 March.

Murray, Chris (1977), 'The Soccer Hooligan's Honour System', *New Society*, 7 October.

Rose, G. (1966), 'Concerning the Measurement of Delinquency', *British Journal of Criminology*, vol. 6.

Schmid, C. F. (1960), 'Urban Crime Areas', *American Sociological Review*, vol. 25.

Tappan, Paul R. (1947), 'Who is the criminal?', *American Sociological Review*, vol. 12.

Wilkins, Leslie (1963), 'The Measurement of Crime', *British Journal of Criminology*, vol. 3.

Willis, Paul (1976), 'Lads, lobes and labour', *New Society*, 20 May.

Wilson, James Q. (1975), 'The Riddle of the American middle class', *New Society*, 11 September.

Wilson, Robert (1974), 'Crime and Punishment in England', *New Society*, 18 July.

Wirth, L. (1938), 'Urbanism as a way of life', *American Journal of Sociology*, vol. 44.

Wood, Michael (1975), 'Autumn in New York', *New Society*, 6 November.

Zander, Michael (1975), 'What Happens to Young Offenders in Care', *New Society*, 24 July.

(d) Official reports, etc.

Committee of the Youth Service Development Council (1967), *Report: Immigrants and the Youth Service*, HMSO.

Department of the Environment (1977), *The Role of Immigrants in the Labour Market*, Project report by the Unit of Manpower Studies.

Departmental Committee on Criminal Statistics (1967), *Final Report*, HMSO, Cmnd. 3448.

Departmental Committee on Detective Work and Procedure (1938), *Final Report*, HMSO.

Greater London Council (1973), *Research Memorandum No. 425*, March.

Home Office (1955), *Instructions for the Preparation of Statistics relating to Crime.*

Home Office Criminal Law Revision Committee (1967), *8th Report: Theft and Related Offences.*

Office of Population Censuses and Surveys (1971), *England and Wales County Report. Greater London. Parts I, II and III*, HMSO.

Royal Commission on a Constabulary Force (1839), Report, *Parliamentary Papers*, vol. xix.

US National Commission on the Causes and Prevention of Violence
   (1969), *Final Report.*

(e) **Annual returns**

Criminal Statistics, England and Wales, annually from 1893, Home
   Office, HMSO.
Metropolitan Police District: Crime Statistics Summary, booklet issued
   annually by G. 10 Statistics Branch, New Scotland Yard.
*Number of Persons Taken into Custody by the Metropolitan Police
   and the Result of Charges*, annually from 1829 to 1892, Metropoli-
   tan Police Office.
Report of HM Chief Inspector of Constabulary, annually from 1945,
   HMSO.
Report of the Commissioner of Police of the Metropolis, annually from
   1869, HMSO.
Social Trends, annually from 1970, Central Statistical Office, London:
   HMSO.

Index